Keats's Poetry
and the Politics
of the Imagination

Keats's Poetry and the Politics of the Imagination

Daniel P. Watkins

Rutherford • Madison • Teaneck
Fairleigh Dickinson University Press
London and Toronto: Associated University Presses

© 1989 by Associated University Presses, Inc.

All rights reserved. Authorization to photocopy items for internal or personal use, or the internal or personal use of specific clients, is granted by the copyright owner, provided that a base fee of $10.00, plus eight cents per page, per copy is paid directly to the Copyright Clearance Center, 27 Congress Street, Salem, Massachusetts 01970. [0-8386-3358-7/89 $10.00 + 8¢ pp, pc.]

Associated University Presses
440 Forsgate Drive
Cranbury, NJ 08512

Associated University Presses
25 Sicilian Avenue
London WC1A 2QH, England

Associated University Presses
P.O. Box 488, Port Credit
Mississauga, Ontario
Canada L5G 4M2

The paper used in this publication meets the requirements
of the American National Standard for Permanence of Paper
for Printed Library Materials Z39.48-1984.

Library of Congress Cataloging-in-Publication Data

Watkins, Daniel P., 1952–
    Keats's poetry and the politics of the imagination / Daniel P. Watkins.
      p. cm.
    Bibliography: p.
    ISBN 0-8386-3358-7 (alk. paper)
    1. Keats, John, 1795–1821—Political and social views.
2. Political poetry, English—History and criticism. 3. Social problems in literature. 4. Politics in literature. I. Title.
PR4838.P6W37   1989
821'.7—dc20   88-45872
                                                                                      CIP

PRINTED IN THE UNITED STATES OF AMERICA

For
John A. Thompson
and in memory of
Gayle S. Smith

Yet the very corn which is now so beautiful, as if it had only [taken] to ripening yesterday, is for the market.
—Keats, *Letters*

> Now may we lift our bruised vizors up,
> And take the flattering freshness of the air,
> While the wide din of battle dies away
> Into times past, yet to be echoed sure
> In the silent pages of our chroniclers.
—Keats, *King Stephen*

There is no document of civilization which is not at the same time a document of barbarism.
—Walter Benjamin, *Theses on the Philosophy of History*

Contents

Preface		9
Acknowledgments		15
Note on the Texts		17
1	"Formed by Circumstance": Introduction	21
2	"The Latter End of Some Strange History": *Endymion*	35
3	"Love's Fev'rous Citadel": *Isabella* and *The Eve of St. Agnes*	54
4	"As If Calamity Had But Begun": *Hyperion*	85
5	"Coming to the Sacrifice": *Ode on a Grecian Urn*	104
6	"The Great Basement of All Power": *Otho the Great*	121
7	"This Mighty Cost and Blaze of Wealth": *Lamia*	135
8	"Twing'd with Avarice": *The Fall of Hyperion*	156
9	"All Things Turn'd Topsy-turvy": *Jealousies* and *Gripus*	177
10	"The Truth of the Imagination": Conclusion	188
Notes		193
Works Cited		217
Index		225

Preface

AMONG the six major romantic poets, Keats has always been the most resistant to social and historical criticism. Isolated articles have appeared over the years documenting the way his interest in and knowledge of politics, society, history, and economics find their way occasionally into his work, and a recent issue of *Studies in Romanticism* was devoted to the topic of "Keats and Politics."[1] But these articles—many of them excellent—have never achieved a real stronghold in Keats studies, and the view that the defining characteristic of his poetry is its concern with beauty, or, another way of saying the same thing, with the unhappy relationship between human mortality and transhistorical ideals, continues to prevail. Keats himself, of course, is at least partly responsible for this view of his poetry, because he explicitly and often states his desire in his poetry and in his letters for a world that is free from political and economic turmoil. But we are also responsible, for more often than not we unquestioningly accept the poet's own self-representations and fail to consider that the very intensity of his statements and the degree of his commitment in certain poems to a transhistorical ideal might be a desperate response to the pressures descending on him from the world he inhabited.

What is needed if we are to get past the perspectives and values that have dominated Keats criticism is a more flexible and encompassing historical approach than is customarily brought to bear on his work,[2] one that understands that the social dimension of the poetry is not reducible to Keats's own expressed interest in the connections between poetic practice and social reality (which has always been the topic of most interest to political critics of Keats) but discloses itself as well in highly mediated poetic language, in the formulation and articulation of networks of social relations, and in the ideological commitment of poetry to deep-seated structures of authority and systems of belief. Such an approach would not focus exclusively on the specific events of the romantic period in an attempt to draw direct parallels between those events and Keats's poetic expressions, although it would not ignore or suppress these. Nor would it rely mainly on biographical evidence in establishing the social dimensions of Keats's poetry. Rather it would investigate poetic expressions, with all their subjectivist baggage, as objective historical categories, as constituent ingredients of a historical situation where subjectivity is critically significant, but not determining and self-defining. In this way, questions of individual intention would give way to questions of historical genesis, and questions of poetic themes would give way to questions of historical content. Critical focus would shift from text to subtext, from plot-level events to the conditions (networks of relations) enabling and constraining those events, from poetic consciousness to the political unconscious of poetry.[3]

The kind of historical criticism I am talking about would not only depart from mainstream Keats criticism but also would extend many of the more conventional Marxist accounts of Keats and romanticism, particularly those which tend to see Keats's poems as largely private escapist responses to an oppressive industrial capitalist world. John Fekete, for instance, in his brilliant history of modern criticism, describes romanticism as a movement characterized by the privatization of the artist, the commodification of art, and the general isolation of human value from social reality. Keats, for Fekete (as for E. P. Thompson, on whom Fekete is drawing for his thesis), is the supreme romantic example of this tendency: ". . .[T]he abandonment of the effort to change the structure of reality appears clearly in Keats. Nature, which in Wordsworth had stood as an alternative to the ugliness of urbanization and as a response to the town-country division and the alienation of fragmentation, expresses a new disaffection from society in Keats." What this means in terms of aesthetics is that beauty is redefined by Keats, coming to be seen "as something not found in reality but having its source in the separate world of the imagination, the subjectivity of the artist." This subjective world of beauty is always threatened by the material world, and this threat is a major feature of Keats's work: "In Keats the two worlds are opposed but he continues to struggle for their reconciliation and his work is defined by the tension."[4]

This commonplace Marxist view of romanticism and of Keats goes a long way toward clarifying the commodification and then marginalization of art in the modern world. But for all its helpfulness, Fekete's argument does not pursue the possibility of a viable, oppositional social perspective from within the historical framework that it describes; that is, it does not examine the ways that Keats's poetry, even in its most subjective and idealistic moments, registers and critiques the conditions under which it was produced, and thus it leaves unexplained many specifically historical issues and interests at the very center of Keats's poetry. Fekete does, however, provide the basis for such an examination when he describes the tension between the subjective and material worlds that is prominent in Keats's poetry. This tension allows us a point of entry into the network of relations that helped to produce the romantic dilemma and shape romantic aesthetics. The desire expressed in Keats's poems for a subjective world of beauty is not a simple denial of material reality, but a struggle with and against it; thus the poems carry within them the markings, colorings, and shapes of that reality. As M. I. Finley remarks, speaking generally of utopian impulses (and Keats's desire for beauty is finally a utopian gesture): "Utopian ideas and fantasies, like all ideas and fantasies, grow out of the society to which they are a response."[5] In this view, the desire and longing that motivate so much of Keats's poetry provide us with a way of knowing and discussing his world.

What I am proposing, then, is a broader historical account of Keats than most Marxists from Caudwell down to the present have offered,[6] one that would not deny the materialist explanations of the large social, economic, and political changes which produced romanticism, and that would not evade the very real escapist and subjectivist tendencies in Keats, but which nonetheless would redefine the critical-historical significance of his poetry. One dimension of the sort of approach I am describing can be understood best in terms of Robert Sayre and Michael Lowy's broad and compelling recent study of romanticism, which investigates and theorizes the material-historical bases of the subjectivity, mysteriousness, and often sheer mysticism that are so characteristic of art during the romantic period. While Sayre and Lowy discuss continental romanticism, their thesis is directly applicable to British writers: "Many Romantic and neo-Romantic productions are deliberately *non-realistic:* fantastic, fairy-like, magical, oneiric, and more recently, surrealist. Yet this does not at all reduce their relevance and importance, both as critiques of capitalism and as dreams of *another world,* quintessentially opposed to bourgeois society. It would perhaps be useful to introduce a new concept—'critical unrealism'—to designate the creation of an imaginary, ideal, utopian or fantasy universe radically opposed to the grey, prosaic and inhuman reality of industrial capitalist society."[7] This statement offers a critical position that enables us to redeem much romantic writing for Marxist criticism, for it understands that the social and historical dimensions of poetry are not to be determined solely by an author's expressed interest in the connections between poetry and social reality.[8] Poetry is inescapably a symbolic formulation of the network of relations in society, and a historical materialist criticism must learn this symbolism and strive to explain the significance of poetry as both a reflection of and a commentary on the world in which it was produced. To accept the Sayre-Lowy thesis would not mean presenting Keats's poems as transparent documents of human liberty, but rather recognizing the complex ways they are caught up in—and struggle with—the dialectics of history.

It is appropriate here to raise the issues of critical perspective and overall expository unity in this study, especially since not all of Keats's works are handled in exactly the same way. While some of Keats's poems, for instance, are viewed as highly critical of prevailing power structures, others—even some of those written during his maturity—are presented negatively as examples of how art often remains deeply implicated (despite its author's intentions) in oppressive ideological frameworks. Such radically divergent evaluations of individual poems should not be seen as critical wavering. The grounding critical assumptions of this study are that historical reality is the most significant determining force behind Keats's poetry, that that reality is conflicted, torn, and extremely anxiety-ridden, and that Keats's poems emerge from and touch upon that reality in different ways at different moments. My aim is to examine this complex interrelationship between poetry and history in an attempt to elucidate the many dimensions of Keats's response to an emerging industrial capitalism. This response at times appears as a powerful negative critique of bourgeois society, while at other times it reveals extreme ideological blindspots. Thus, while Keats himself was most certainly on the side of the opposition both intellectually and politically, and while his poetry might be said to develop toward a fairly sophisticated vision of history and society, his oppositional voice and poetic development are neither absolutely consistent nor easy. To follow the twisted thread of his poetic labors is not to search for political or intellectual shortcomings that would encourage us to condemn or dismiss his poetry as politically reactionary or retrogressive; rather, it is to begin to understand the complexity of the contradictory historical situation within which he lived and wrote, and thus to understand the wider fields of experience within which his opposition to bourgeois society and his desire for a different and better world developed. In short, it is to assert the absolute historical importance of Keats's poetry.

The need for a historical and political study along the lines I am advocating is suggested by even the briefest survey of Keats's work. *On First Looking into Chapman's Homer, The Eve of St. Agnes, Isabella, Otho the Great, Lamia, Hyperion,* the minor Robin Hood poems, and many of the letters compellingly illustrate that Keats's imagination was informed in fundamental ways by the power relations that dominated his age. At every turn his poetry is socially mediated, even (or especially) at those moments—as in the great odes—when it appears to be most successful in evading history and society.[9] In elaborating these mediations, I do not wish to claim that Keats's poetry is always politically progressive (at times, indeed, I wish to argue quite the opposite), but rather to detail how the responses to and seeming evasions of history that are evident in so much of his poetry might be explained in terms of historical and ideological considerations. Such an effort is not intended to deny Keats's poetry its "poetic" integrity or beauty by reducing it to dry social commentary, but rather to redeem the poetry for material history by extending the critical principles that most often are brought to bear on it, thereby allowing us to understand anew the richness and depth of Keats's work.

Acknowledgments

I have incurred many debts while writing this book and wish to give special thanks to David Sebberson and Tony Rosso, both of whom read portions of the work in typescript, made helpful suggestions for revision, and offered much encouragement and friendship at every stage of the project. I owe a special debt of gratitude to Terry Hoagwood, whose painstaking critical evaluation of the entire manuscript makes this work much stronger than it otherwise would have been. I also wish to thank Donald Reiman, who read the section on *Isabella* and offered much helpful advice when it was submitted in essay form to *Nineteenth-Century Contexts;* Meg Lewis, for her extremely helpful discussions on matters of economic theory during the romantic period; and Jerome McGann, whose practical and theoretical work over the past several years has pointed the way toward a historical and political reassessment of romanticism.

Colleagues, graduate students, and staff in the English Department at Duquesne University have also been supportive. Some of my colleagues read and criticized parts of the book in typescript, and others listened patiently while I attempted to formulate and elaborate my ideas in many lengthy conversations; I am particularly grateful to my chairman, Jay Keenan, and to Sam Tindall, Al Labriola, and Connie Ramirez for these favors. Some of the ideas in this book were first developed in two romanticism courses I taught in 1985 and 1987, and I am deeply indebted to the graduate students in these courses for their energy and intelligence. The English Department staff have also been helpful and supportive, especially Mary Lydon and Steve Fatla, and I wish to thank them as well.

The staffs at Associated University Presses and Fairleigh Dickinson University Press have provided invaluable assistance at every stage in the production of the manuscript. I wish especially to thank Lauren Lepow, managing editor at Associated University Presses; John Drexel, my copy editor; and Dr. Harry Keyishian, editor of Fairleigh Dickinson University Press, for encouragement and much practical advice.

Finally, this project would not have been possible without the encouragement, friendship, and practical assistance of Joanna Foster; she knows how much I owe to her.

Several important studies of Keats appeared too late to be incorporated here. The publication of articles by Kurt Heinzelman and Thomas A. Reed in *ELH,* and especially the publication of Marjorie Levinson's major new book on Keats, attest to the growing interest in reinvestigating Keats's work along historical and political lines. The present study, I hope, will be viewed as a contribution to the general reassessment of Keats signalled by these recent publications.

* * *

Portions of this book were published previously (in very different form) in *Nineteenth-Century Contexts, Clio,* and *English Language Notes,* and I thank the editors of these journals for allowing me to reprint those portions here.

I also want to express my grateful appreciation to Harvard University Press, publisher of Jack Stillinger, ed., *The Poems of John Keats;* Hyder Rollins, ed., *The Letters of John Keats;* and Hyder Rollins, ed., *The Keats Circle.* Quotations from these works are reprinted by permission.

Note on the Texts

UNLESS otherwise noted, quotations from Keats's poems are taken from Jack Stillinger, ed., *The Poems of John Keats,* and line numbers are cited in the text. Quotations from Keats's letters are taken from Hyder Rollins, ed., *The Letters of John Keats,* and appear in the text as *LJK*. Quotations from Byron's letters and journals are taken from Leslie Marchand, ed., *Byron's Letters and Journals,* and appear in the text as *BLJ*. Unless otherwise noted, the correspondence of Keats's friends, acquaintances, and publishers is taken from Hyder Rollins, ed., *The Keats Circle,* and is cited in the text as *KC*.

Keats's Poetry
and the Politics
of the Imagination

1
"Formed by Circumstance"
INTRODUCTION

In his early verse epistle "To My Brother George" (1816), Keats remarks in passing that one of the enduring values of poetry is that, long after the death of the poet, it continues to inspire "the patriot" (73) to "unsheath his steel" (74) and to be read "in the senate" (75), where it may "startle princes from their easy slumbers" (76). While this remark is obscured by the more frequent references in the poem to "wonders strange" (53) that the poet observes and records, to lays of "dear delight" (81) written by the poet to be enjoyed by maids "on their bridal night" (82), and to "soft verse" (108) spun to please "daughters fair" (108), it nonetheless expresses a political view from which Keats never wavered, even after he began to distance himself from his friend and mentor, the radical Leigh Hunt, who had encouraged him and helped to shape both his political and poetic life.[1]

The consistency of Keats's politics is readily apparent in comments made throughout his correspondence. In a letter to Reynolds in April 1818, for instance, he remarked that "I would jump down Aetna for any great Public good" (*LJK* 1:267). To Taylor, only fifteen days later, he repeated the same point: "I find there is no worthy pursuit but the idea of doing some good for the world" (*LJK* 1:271). And while he was nursing his dying brother, Tom, in late 1818 he wrote to Woodhouse, "I am ambitious of doing the world some good" (*LJK* 1:387). Even in the letter written to inform George and Georgiana of Tom's death, Keats speaks of Hazlitt's lectures, Hunt's *Examiner*, the Westminster elections of 1818, and Cobbett (*LJK* 2:24, 28). Finally, a little over a year later, in a letter to Dilke, he voiced his political position in specific terms: "Notwithstand[ing] my aristocratic temper I cannot help being verry [*sic*] much pleas'd with the present public proceedings [i.e., those involving Henry Hunt and the Reform movement]. I hope sincerely I shall be able to put a Mite of help to the Liberal side of the Question before I die" (*LJK* 2:180).[2] Such comments continue to appear in Keats's letters until the end of his life, and they come to be supported by ever more serious efforts to understand and articulate the political life of his own age, efforts encouraged especially by his reading of Hazlitt, who was probably the most important intellectual influence on his life, and whose political position Keats most likely came to share.

But if it is fairly easy to document Keats's political and social views in his correspondence, showing that they are consistent with the remarks made in the verse epistle to his brother George, it is much more difficult to argue that Keats's poems illustrate the political role of poetry expressed in that same verse epistle. In fact, much of his poetry—including the larger portions of the verse epistle to George—seems committed to avoiding the conflicted dimensions of political reality and to celebrating instead the poet "pillow'd on a bed of flowers" (123) apart from the sordid world of politics. The stories of Endymion, of Hyperion, of Lamia, of Psyche, and so on are not stories likely to inspire the patriot to "unsheath his steel" and fight for liberty, and twentieth-century scholars beginning with H. W. Garrod have recognized and approved this fact, arguing that Keats's best poetry is that which is not concerned with politics but with beauty transcending politics.[3] The poetry that endures and inspires, most readers of Keats have argued, is that which is free of the turmoil and struggles of the political and historical moment.

I do not wish to argue, against conventional wisdom, that Keats's best poetry is in fact represented by those few poems which are directly politically engaged (*Otho the Great,* for instance), and indeed I am little concerned with the issue of which poems are superior in a narrow and purely aesthetic sense. Nor do I wish to argue that the great Keats poems are in fact simple allegories of events of the age, and that by reading these poems allegorically we can understand Keats's political views more fully. Rather, I want to insist that the passing remark in the verse epistle to George about the connections between poetry and politics should be taken seriously as an important key to the political and historical depth of Keats's entire corpus; for, while Keats does not explore the matter fully in this poem nor develop it explicitly in later work, this remark is a sure sign that his poetry, from the beginning, is haunted by politics: to raise the issue of how poetry might serve the cause of liberty is to acknowledge the extent to which public life places pressure on poetic activity. Although Keats did not develop an explicit political poetry, the poems themselves, even in their most private articulations, never escaped the turbulence of political and social reality. That his poetry is haunted by mutually exclusive desires to be "dearer to society" (112) and at the same time to be removed from society, caught in a "trance" (25) of "wonders strange," points toward a conflict that is pervasive, running deep beneath the expressive intention of the poems.

To approach Keats's poetic and intellectual life from this direction is to recognize that the self-representations of social and political interest found in the letters (which have been the key starting point for most scholars wishing to examine Keats's politics),[4] as well as the passing direct comments about politics found in his poetry, are at best partial commentaries which do little to illuminate the extent to which his work is situated within and determined by political, social, and historical processes. To put the matter somewhat differently, his explicit comments on politics, history, and society do not constitute the final explanation of their relevance to his life's work, but rather the barest starting point. Behind these comments are the intense struggles and conflicts of history. The story of Keats's intellectual and poetic life is the story of his relation to the times in which he lived. His complex and turbulent poetic articulation and reworking of traditional poetic topics, of myths and legends, and of contemporary and past history and politics are signs of intense anxiety—not simply the psychological anxiety that came of Keats's frequent questioning of his own capabilities, but also the historical anxiety of an age threatened by economic collapse, by the militarization of culture, bad harvests, staggeringly high unemployment, and by a fear both of bourgeois, industrial triumph and of a return to feudalism. Keats was, as he put it in a letter to his brother and sister-in-law, "formed by circumstances" (*LJK* 2:103), and these circumstances (though he does not elaborate them) were political and historical. Caught within the nets of a severe and crisis-ridden historical situation, Keats's poetry discloses (beyond what the poet consciously intended to express) the multiple dimensions of that situation, both its hopes and its fears, its accomplishments and its atrocities.

Without tracing in detail here the many particular developments during the romantic period that might help to account for the particular historical dimension of Keats's poetry (these have been discussed in the excellent work of Thorpe, Muir, Woodring, and others), I want to suggest two matters that help to establish the framework within which the historical investigation of the sort I have in mind might be situated. First is the war with France, and particularly the defeat of Napoleon at Waterloo in 1815, one year before Keats wrote *On First Looking into Chapman's Homer,* which John Barnard calls Keats's "first real poem."[5] Napoleon's defeat is historically significant not only in practical political terms but also symbolically, because many artists and intellectuals of the period had come to associate the French general with the cause of freedom. Even those who disliked him saw him as the last best hope in the struggle against tyranny.[6] His defeat, many believed, meant a halt to progressive historical development and the return of Europe to rule by divine right. Byron is most explicit in voicing this fear. Commenting in his journal after Napoleon's abdication in 1814, he remarks: "[A]nd here we are, retrograding to the dull, stupid old system,—balance of Europe—poising straws upon king's noses, instead of wringing them off!" (*BLJ* 3:218). The *Examiner* ran many articles in the post-Waterloo years reflecting these same concerns and fears. In an essay of 12 January 1817, for instance, devoted to "some of the causes which impede the natural progress of liberty and human happiness," it is observed that

> The ancients sometimes worshipped the sun or stars, or deified heroes and great men: the moderns have found out the image of the divinity in Louis XVIII! They have set up an object for their idolatry, which they themselves must laugh at, if hypocrisy were not with them the most serious thing in the world. . . . This mock-doctrine, this little Hunchback, which our resurrection-men, the Humane Society of Divine Right, have foisted on the altar of Liberty, is not only a phantom of the imagination but a contradiction in terms; it is a prejudice, but an exploded prejudice; it is an imposture, that imposes on nobody. . . . [I]ts two chief supporters are the sword of the Duke of Wellington and the pen of the Editor of the *Times*. (27–28)

Many similar essays appear in this newspaper about the threat of the return of divine right, including essays on the restoration of Ferdinand VII to the throne of Spain and the atrocities that followed. Keats himself remarks in a letter of October 1818 that although Napoleon had done much (particularly in militarizing governments) to impede the cause of liberty, "the divine right Gentlemen have [not] done or intend to do any good" (*LJK* 1:397).

This fear of a return to an older, more oppressive form of government is accompanied by the historical fact that this was the moment of triumph for the bourgeoisie in Europe. That is, the Napoleonic Wars themselves, despite their specific outcome (the defeat of France), mark the final defeat of feudalism and its structures of social authority, systems of social belief, and, generally, its entire network of social relations. As one historian puts it, the wars cracked "the structure of the old social order and laid the foundations of the modern bourgeois state."[7] This fact may help to explain the general ambivalence of many intellectuals in the face of the "Napoleon problem." Byron, Hazlitt, and even Keats were extremely mixed in their assessments of and attitudes toward the French general, who, for most intellectuals and artists of the period, represented the extreme possibilities of the age: its hopes and fears, its achievements and dangers, its humanity and atrocity. Napoleon stood for liberty, but he also stood for the militarization of government; he stood for the resistance to tyranny, but he also stood for a new kind of tyranny; his exploits marked the demise of feudalism, but they also inaugurated the age of the bourgeois state. As Byron described him in *Childe Harold's Pilgrimage,* he was "antithetically mixt," "extreme in all things!" (3:36).

Keats emerged on the intellectual and poetic scene in 1816, at precisely that moment when the historical crisis of the romantic period was reaching its highest pitch: war had effectively industrialized the economy, and the defeat of Napoleon produced a fear of the probable retrogression of society to an older form of government. Not surprisingly, then, the period from 1815 to 1820 (the period of Keats's mature poetry) is one of extreme historical anxiety; this anxiety saturates the cultural artifacts of the period, including the works of Byron, Shelley, and Keats. The many dimensions of this deep-seated anxiety (or of what Frederic Jameson calls the political unconscious) are the focus of this study. But my aim is not simply to read the poetry against the background of these immediate years. Rather, I assume that the developments of the post-Waterloo period were shaped and determined by the much larger and slower historical processes that produced industrial capitalism, and that romanticism was one product of, and response to, that larger development. Put differently, the historical anxiety that can be situated in terms of post-Waterloo political developments must also be situated in terms of the privatization and fragmentation of social life that resulted not simply from the defeat of Napoleon, but rather from the triumph of industrial capitalism, which was controlled and directed by a new ruling class, the bourgeoisie.[8] This point must be stressed, for it locates historical investigation of Keats not only among the empirical details surrounding his life and times, nor only among the poet's expressed intentions and commitments, but, more importantly, within a social context and historical worldview that are fundamentally different, say, from those that define the preindustrial and precapitalist world.

Keats's expressions of political liberalism or radicalism, his expressions of infidelity in religious matters, and his desires to do mankind some good cannot be understood at the level of individual intention alone, but must be placed among the shifts and struggles of this changing and conflicted social world. Similarly, the retreat from politics evident in many of his poems, as well as the poetic expression of an alternative model of hope in a sordid, money-driven society, are not transparent; they generate meanings in relation to the social history they represent. Seen in this light, Keats's achievement cannot be accepted as simply heralding a new model of human liberty: the extreme individualism and subjectivity of much of his poetry, in fact, is a sign of the bourgeois fragmentation of human life. Nor can it be simply rejected as the sterile product of bourgeois culture (or as a splendid example of bourgeois false consciousness), for it powerfully articulates the contradictions within a new world order, the difficulty of making one's way within that world order, and the hope that human life can in some way be transformed so as to be more rewarding and meaningful. In other words, Keats's poetry is both expressive and revealing, a product of a narrowing world and a sign of human integrity—a dialectical fact that any materialist historical investigation must acknowledge and explain.

I want to illustrate some of these anxieties and tensions in Keats by considering here two of his early poems, sketching in one Keats's poetic involvement with history and historical texts, and in the other his views on the historical context of poetic activity. My purpose is not to provide sustained critical analyses of the various thematic layerings of these poems, but rather to highlight the historical significance of several conventional matters that, on the one hand, appear on the textual surface of the poems, and that, on the other, are involved with authorial intention. By sketching such readily accessible issues as Keats's source materials and his poetic questioning of the role of poetry in these early poems, I hope to provide a point of entry into the larger ideological concerns that shape the later works; that is, I want to suggest that many of the issues that normally concern critics of Keats, such as the poet's sources and intentions, are important not simply for what they tell us about the poet and his craft, but also for what they can tell us about the conditions under which Keats's poetry was produced.

* * *

In discussing *On First Looking into Chapman's Homer,* critics often note that while Keats achieves an admirable consistency in tone and metaphor he gets his history wrong when he describes Cortez, rather than Balboa, staring "at the Pacific . . . Silent, upon a peak in Darien" (12–14). This perhaps would be a minor matter, except that it contributes to the common misperception that Keats was not a serious student of history, encouraging us to disregard or to de-emphasize the way issues of historical importance shape and define his poetry, and thus eliding the historical anxiety permeating his work. The fact is, of course, that he was from his earliest school days an avid reader of history books,[9] and the greater portion of his verse shows quite clearly the impact that these works had on his thinking and imagination. This is nowhere more evident than in his sonnet on Chapman's Homer, which is a concerted effort to bring poetry and history together into a single enterprise. Keats's attempt here to master historical texts for the cause of poetry demonstrates not only the importance of historical subject matter to his poetic imagination but also his inability to textualize history entirely. This desire and failure open up rich and critically significant dimensions in his poetry.

Introduction

One work that Keats read at the Clarke residence at the same time he was reading Chapman's Homer, and that probably is the most important historical source for the sonnet, is William D. Robertson's *History of America,* a highly readable, even exciting, three-volume account of adventures and discoveries in the New World. The information and ideas in this book remained important to Keats throughout his life, finding their way into his letters and into many of the mature poems concerned with history and historical processes. The connection between Robertson's book and Keats's sonnet has been noted before, but in a way that is is not completely satisfactory. Many years ago B. Ifor Evans, for instance, successfully used the scholarly methodology of John Livingston Lowes to establish a literary, intellectual, and biographical context for the poem, noting the descriptions of Balboa in Robertson's book as the source for Keats's reference to Cortez.[10] The problem with Evans's account, despite its general excellence, is twofold. First, it does not consider at all Robertson's description of Cortez, which (as I shall show) is strikingly similar to the Balboa description, a fact which may account for Keats's confusion, if confusion it was. Second, and more importantly, it emphasizes Robertson only as a source for Keats, failing to consider the way Keats's reading of history provided a *critical* focus for the sonnet.[11] It is thus appropriate to reconsider the importance of Robertson's *History* to Keats's sonnet, and specifically to consider some additional passages in Robertson that Keats certainly had read and may have been drawing on. My purpose here is not to argue that Keats's reference to Cortez is unequivocally correct or is even what he intended, but to suggest that his knowledge of history and his use of it in his verse are not as intellectually insignificant as we often think, and that in fact they shape his poetic practice in important ways. Indeed, the incorporation of Robertson into the sonnet vividly illustrates Keats's early belief in the consuming importance of history to works of the imagination, and suggests the extent to which he will rely on historical texts in many of his later poems.

Before addressing the problem of the Cortez reference, it might be helpful to point out that the controlling metaphor of the sonnet—travel and discovery—draws at least as much on Robertson as on Chapman. The description of the "realms of gold" in which Keats imagines himself having "travell'd" echoes Robertson's account of many adventures, but particularly of Pizarro's ranking officer, Orellana, who explored the Maragnon River (in South America) in search of treasures. As Robertson describes these exploits:

> The vanity natural to travellers who visit regions unknown to the rest of mankind, and the art of an adventurer, solicitous to magnify his own merit, concurred in prompting him [Orellana] to mingle an extraordinary proportion of the marvellous in the narrative of his

voyage. He pretended to have discovered nations so rich, that the roofs of their temples were covered with plates of gold; and described a republic of women so warlike and powerful, as to have extended their dominion over a considerable tract of the fertile plains which he had visited. Extravagant as those tales were, they gave rise to an opinion, that a region abounding with gold, distinguished by the name of *El Dorado,* and a community of Amazons, were to be found in this part of the New World, and such is the propensity of mankind to believe what is wonderful that it has been slowly and with difficulty that reason and observation have exploded those fables. The voyage, however, even when stripped of every romantic embellishment, deserves to be recorded, not only as one of the most memorable occurrences in that adventurous age, but as the first event which led to any certain knowledge of the immense regions that stretch eastward from the Andes to the Ocean.[12]

I do not mean to suggest that Keats was drawing directly on this passage, but rather that the "goodly states and kingdoms" explored by Orellana and by others in Robertson's work—the active and self-conscious involvement of individuals in history—provide one framework of ideas for Keats's understanding and assessment of Homer, with history as the measure of human greatness. Indeed, according to Keats, Homer's greatness is not simply the result of genius or of the pure imagination; it does not transcend the greatness of such historical episodes as the one described by Robertson. Rather, Chapman's translation enables Keats to see the historical dimension of Homer's work, to see that the events described by Homer are as powerful as those described in the histories Keats had read with such admiration at the Clarke residence. For the first time, Keats says in his poem, he realizes that imaginative literature can offer descriptions of history as compelling as those found in textbook histories.

In the Cortez passage that concludes the sonnet, Keats comes back around to his reading in Robertson, effectively enclosing Chapman's Homer within a framework of specific historical-textual reference. But because he refers to Cortez rather than to Balboa, whom critics since Tennyson's day believe he must have meant, he seems to show himself to be a sloppy historian, giving the impression that for him history itself is secondary to the products of the imagination. If one reads the lengthy accounts in Robertson of Balboa and Cortez, however, the problem of historical reference becomes more complicated than it at first seems: the descriptions of the two explorers are virtually identical, suggesting that Keats was not entirely careless about historical reference. I want here to present both accounts in some detail to illustrate the actual historical material that Keats was probably recalling and thereby to show that his attention to detail and his imaginative handling of history recognize the

Introduction

power and importance of historical fact. The account of Balboa will be presented first, because, according to most critics, he is the explorer Keats actually had in mind.

> The Isthmus of Darien is not above sixty miles in breadth; but this neck of land, which binds together the continents of north and South America, is strengthened by a chain of lofty mountains stretching through its whole extent, which render it a barrier of solidity sufficient to resist the impulse of two opposite oceans. . . . To march across this unexplored country, with no other guides but Indians, whose fidelity can be little trusted, was, on all those accounts, the boldest enterprise on which the Spaniards had hitherto ventured in the New World. But the intrepidity of Balboa was such as distinguished him among his countrymen, at a period when every adventurer was conspicuous for daring courage. . . .
> Balboa set out upon this important expedition on the first of September, about the time that the periodical rains began to abate. . . . When they had penetrated a good way into the mountains, a powerful cazique appeared in a narrow pass, with a numerous body of his subjects to obstruct their progress. But men who had surmounted so many obstacles, despised the opposition of such feeble enemies. They attacked with impetuosity, and having dispersed them with much ease and great slaughter, continued their march. . . . When, with infinite toil, they had climbed up the greater part of that steep ascent, Balboa commanded his men to halt, and advanced alone to the summit, that he might be the first who should enjoy a spectacle which he had so long desired. As soon as he beheld the South Sea stretching in endless prospect below him, he fell on his knees, and lifting up his hands to Heaven, returned thanks to God, who had conducted him to a discovery so beneficial to his country, and so honourable to himself. His followers, observing his transports of joy, rushed forward to join in his wonder, exultation and gratitude. They held on their course to the shore with great alacrity, when Balboa advancing up to the middle in the waves with his buckler and sword, took possession of that ocean in the name of the king his master, and vowed to defend it, with these arms, against all his enemies.
> That part of the great Pacific or Southern ocean, which Balboa first discovered, still retains the name of the Gulf of St. Michael, which he gave to it, and is situated to the east of Panama. From several of the petty princes, who governed in the districts adjacent to that gulf, he extorted provisions and gold by force of arms. Others sent them to him voluntarily.[13]

Robertson's account of Cortez in the New World is punctuated by Cortez's cruelty toward the Indians and by the various mutinous activities of his soldiers against him, all of which eventually led Charles V to reduce his authority in the New World. Near the end of the narrative of Cortez's exploits, Robertson notes one of the explorer's greatest discoveries, using much the same language that had characterized the account of Balboa:

> This division of power in New Spain proved, as was unavoidable, the source of perpetual dissention, which embittered the life of Cortes [sic], and thwarted all his schemes. As he had now no opportunity to display his active talents but in attempting new discoveries, he formed various schemes for that purpose, all of which bear impressions of a genius that delighted in what was bold and splendid. He early entertained an idea, that, either by steering through the gulf of Florida along the east coast of North America, some strait would be found that communicated with the western ocean; or that, by examining the isthmus of Darien, some passage would be discovered between the North and South Seas. But having been disappointed in his expectations with respect to both, he now confined his views to such voyages of discovery as he could make from the ports of New Spain in the South Sea. There he fitted out successively several small squadrons, which either perished in the attempt, or returned without making any discovery of moment. Cortes, weary of entrusting the conduct of his operations to others, took the command of a new armament in person, and, after enduring incredible hardships, and encountering dangers of every species, he discovered the large peninsula of California, and surveyed the greater part of the gulf which separates it from New Spain. The discovery of a country of such extent would have reflected credit on a common adventurer; but it could add little new honour to the name of Cortes, and was far from satisfying the sanguine expectations which he had formed. Disgusted with ill success, to which he had not been accustomed, and weary of contesting with adversaries to whom he considered it as a disgrace to be opposed, he once more sought for redress in his native country.[14]

These descriptions are similar not only in their emphasis on the bravery and leadership of the explorers and on the difficulties they faced during their expeditions but, more importantly, in their discussion of the actual discoveries that were made. Both men, for instance, recognized the importance of the Isthmus of Darien, looking to it as a field of potential discovery, although it was Balboa of course whose expedition proved more successful in this area. Both men struggled successfully against virtually insurmountable obstacles. Most importantly, both men, at the moment of discovery, are described as surveying a gulf that is part of the Pacific (Balboa surveyed the Gulf of St. Michael; Cortez surveyed the Gulf of California). Given the closeness of these descriptions, it is easy to see that Keats, relying on memory, could have confused them, or that he may have combined them imaginatively, compressing them into a single, powerful image of one individual's awareness of a particular and tremendously significant moment in history, once again presenting his view of the primary importance of historical struggle and accomplishment.[15]

When Keats sat down to write his sonnet after a night of reading Chapman's Homer, it is likely that his first aim was not simply to capture the excitement of discovery, but to suggest the excitement of historical inquiry and of the way imaginative literature can contribute to and participate in this inquiry. Taking this view, whether he meant actually to describe Balboa discovering the Pacific is less significant than his own discovery that the imagination and the intellect need not be entirely distinct faculties. As his subsequent poetry bears out—*Isabella, Otho the Great,* the *Hyperion* poems, even *Lamia*—this continued to be a primary concern as he worked with ever greater seriousness to find a poetic voice to express his understanding of historical processes.

At the same time, however, the Chapman sonnet is not entirely a moment of triumph for Keats the poet; in fact, the historical details in the poem reveal the extent to which Keats's thought is entrapped in what McGann has called the romantic ideology. The poetic mastery of a historical subject comes at the expense of history itself, creating a tension that Keats's poetry never entirely lays to rest. While the poem displays the poet's interest in historical texts and in the poetic handling of those texts, it establishes at the same time a rigid dichotomy between beauty and history. That is, the inspiration of the poem arises from Keats's sense of imaginative discovery; moreover, the beautifully expressed sense of wonder at this discovery actually elides much historical reality, and even much of what Robertson chronicles: the savage abuse by European explorers of native Americans; the violence and personal viciousness of Cortez; the imperialist drive for wealth and territory by the European invaders. These matters exist in the extreme margins of the poetic text, becoming visible through Keats's major historical source, and they reveal that the poetic triumph of the Chapman sonnet is in the celebration of the energy associated with discoveries of historical significance, rather than in the articulation or representation of history itself. While this fact in itself does not denigrate the young Keats's poem, it does suggest the kinds of vexing historical-poetic problems that will continue to surface in his poetry as he confronts the facts of historical reality and attempts to find a way to write poetically about them in a world where historical facts often offered little cause for celebration.

* * *

Sleep and Poetry expresses more directly the anxiety implicit in Keats's handling of his historical source material in the Chapman sonnet, voicing this anxiety in the very title of the poem and in the epigraph from

Chaucer, which describes an individual blessed with good health and happiness but who nonetheless "ne might / Rest." This anxiety arises at least partly from Keats's realization that the true poet not only lives in "a leafy world" (119) of "luxury" (59), but also in a world filled with "the agonies, the strife / Of human hearts" (124–25), and that the noblest poetry is that which acknowledges and finds cause for hope in the midst of such agony and strife. While the young Keats reveres the true poet and would himself write noble poetry, he is uncertain whether he can do this in the face of the "muddy stream" (158) of life. His pronounced commitment to "strive / Against all doubtings" (159–60) is a confession of that uncertainty.

But there is also a more specific context for the anxiety that permeates the poem: namely, the conflict between Keats's personal hope that he might produce poetry that will endure through the ages and his conviction that the historical moment in which he lives has made it difficult, if not impossible, to produce true poetry. Obsessed with discovering "an eternal book, / Whence I may copy many a lovely saying / About the leaves, and flowers" (64–66), he believes that the prospects of such a discovery are jeopardized because "a schism / Nurtured by foppery and barbarism, [has] / Made great Apollo blush for this his land" (181–83). While the poem never spells out the particular causes for this schism, it does locate the decline of poetry specifically in England—"E'en in this isle" (172)—and attributes this decline to the fact that "the high / Imagination cannot freely fly / As she was wont of old" (163–65). Echoing the arguments of Wordsworth in the preface to the *Lyrical Ballads*, the poem laments the littleness and artificiality of contemporary poetry, which is so controlled and defined by prevailing structures of authority that it loses sight of its true sources:

> . . . .Ah dismal soul'd!
> The winds of heaven blew, the ocean roll'd
> Its gathering waves—ye felt it not. The blue
> Bared its eternal bosom, and the dew
> Of summer nights collected still to make
> The morning precious: beauty was awake!
> Why were ye not awake? But ye were dead
> To things ye knew not of,—were closely wed
> To musty laws lined out with wretched rule
> And compass vile: so that ye taught a school
> Of dolts to smooth, inlay, and clip, and fit,
> Till, like the certain wands of Jacob's wit,
> Their verses tallied.
>
> (187–99)

Moreover, while Keats acknowledges that such obstacles to great poetry have been opposed by some of his generation, still even the best contemporary verse "feeds upon the burrs, / And thorns of life; forgetting the great end, / Of poesy, that it should be a friend / To sooth the cares, and lift the thoughts of man" (244–47). This tension between Keats's sense of the pressures and difficulties of the historical moment, on the one hand, and his personal desires and commitment "to begin that very day / These lines" (402–3), on the other, is never satisfactorily resolved through the poem; it forms in fact its deep subject, running beneath and encompassing the professed theme of the beauty and virtue of poetry and the courage and nobility of the poet.

Another, related dimension of the poem's anxiety is Keats's emphasis on sleep, which is presented from the beginning as "more full of visions than a high romance" (10). While Keats makes much of the fact that poetry is superior to sleep (19–46), he insists that the latter is essential to the former—"For what there may be worthy in these rhymes / I partly owe to him [sleep]" (349–50)—an insistence that reveals the necessary place of leisure in creative activity. This point is significant because the poem itself states that while the poet arises in the morning "refresh'd, and glad, and gay" (401), he has had no sleep through the evening. Sleep provides the necessary context for poetic activity, as well as a specific framework of reference for the poem itself—the opening eighteen lines and concluding sixty-five lines discuss sleep—and thus Keats's confession that he has spent "a sleepless night" (400) is a confession that his own poetry is being produced under less than desirable conditions. To put the matter somewhat differently, the tensions and connections between sleep and poetry that are articulated in the poem betray not only the personal anxiety and weariness facing one individual who wishes to produce work that will "be a friend / To sooth the cares, and lift the thoughts of man," but also—through the many references to British and world traditions of poetry—the much larger anxiety and weariness of the age and the difficulties of imagining and creating in such an age. The anxiety that appears in the Chapman sonnet through an apparent slip of the pen here finds its way to the level of thematic significance. Thus, the references near the end of the poem to Sappho, Great Alfred, Kosciusko, and Petrarch are both a celebration of great literary and political figures of the past and a recognition of the very great distance between the world inhabited by those figures and the world inhabited by Keats.[16]

* * *

On First Looking into Chapman's Homer and *Sleep and Poetry* lay bare many of the central aspirations and conflicts that persist through Keats's poetry. *I stood tip-toe upon a little hill, Specimen of an Induction to a Poem, Calidore, To Hope,* and other early works elaborate (or are enabled by) the poet's sense of joy and beauty or deep-seated conflicts between leisure and creativity, past and present, joy and fear, and so on—issues, in short, that continue to dominate and define the mature poetry. These aspirations and conflicts are not simply themes; they are the very substance of Keats's poetry. They are enlivened both by Keats's personal anxieties and by the anxieties of the age—that is, by Keats's efforts to produce poetry in an age when poetry was becoming increasingly marginalized and when new structures of authority and systems of belief were being legitimized even while social life and social authority seemed to be returning to past forms. The subjects and themes of Keats's poetry, in other words, are signs of the social history of which that poetry is a part. The early poems, which often lack the control, confidence, and power of later works, reveal the contradictions of this history that the more mature poetry seems to reconcile at the level of imagination. The poetic significance of these early works lies in this historical fact.

2
"The Latter End of Some Strange History"
ENDYMION

THE body of criticism relating to *Endymion,* as Stuart Sperry noted fifteen years ago, is concerned almost solely with the question of whether the poem is an allegory of the soul's ascension or an expression of "the sexual fantasies of a maturing young man."[1] It is not necessary here to trace the history of this critical debate (Sperry has covered this ground in some detail),[2] but it should be stressed that the critical formulations of the poem as spiritual allegory or as erotic fantasy begin from a common set of limiting assumptions: first is the assumption that the poem's meaning is inextricably bound to Keats's authorial intention, and second, more broadly but relatedly, is the assumption that the romantic assertion of the individual subject provides the necessary context for critical investigation. Even Sperry, probably the best critic of the poem, grounds his argument in these assumptions, placing at the center of his discussion the way Keats's original intention (i.e., of articulating "an ascending order of imaginative values") gradually gives way to a recognition of "disappointment and unhappiness as an integral part of human experience."[3] Such an approach ultimately fails to explain how central issues in the poem come to be central, and, more significantly, what these issues may mean outside Keats's own definitions of them. In other words, criticism of the poem is controlled by Keats's, and romanticism's, own ideological commitments.[4]

I do not here wish to deny the substantial contributions of those critics who have attempted systematic analyses and explanations of Keats's poetic intentions, failures, and accomplishments, but rather to shift the critical ground away from this conventional line of inquiry in an attempt to open the poem up to a very different kind of analysis. Specifically, I want to historicize Keats's expressed poetic concern with beauty, truth, love, happiness, and friendship—the major thematic issues of the poem's surface structure—in an attempt to show that these are not constitutive but rather emerge as issues of importance within a specific set of sociohistorical relations. From this perspective, the most important question about the poem is not whether Keats offers a successful poetic formulation of, say, beauty and truth. Nor is the primary critical task an explanation of what Keats means by beauty and truth. The more important issues in the poem, rather, involve the conditions that make beauty and truth paramount concerns for Keats, and the question of what beauty and truth mean in the context of those conditions. To begin inquiry into the poem from this position is not to deny the significance of issues that are important to Keats, but to see their value as historically determined and thus to create the possibility of revealing deeper and much more far-reaching political matters than a purely individualist approach is able to do.[5]

Several commonplace historical facts relevant to the impulse behind *Endymion* and its political situation bear mentioning by way of preface if the poem is to be understood in the way I am suggesting. Christopher Caudwell, Raymond Williams, John Fekete, E. P. Thompson, and others have written at length from a materialist perspective about the specific historical shifts that gave rise to romantic literature in general, and about the specific meaning of Keats's poetry within the context of these shifts. (Thompson, for instance, argues that "Keats was one of the first poets to feel in his own everyday experience the full shock of bourgeoisdom and philistinism,[6] and Caudwell claims that Keats's response to this shock was poetic escapism.)[7] Without sketching these shifts in detail, it can be noted, as Eric Hobsbawm puts it, that one of the distinguishing facts of the age that gave rise to romanticism is that "for the first time in human history, the shackles were taken off the productive power of human societies, which henceforth became capable of the constant, rapid and up to the present limitless multiplication of men, goods and services."[8] One key ingredient in this historical development, according to Hobsbawm, was "the creation of a mechanized 'factory system' which in turn produces in such vast quantities and at such rapidly diminishing cost, as to be no longer dependent on existing demand, but to create its own market."[9] These changes in the forces and relations of production contributed to the tremendous surge of poetic activity during the romantic period, and to the surge of intellectual activity generally. (Note the work during this period of Godwin, Bentham, Ricardo, and Owen, among others, who attempted to explain, direct, and give shape to the events of the age.)

One necessary accompaniment of changing social structures was the dismantling of preindustrial forces and relations of production and of a feudal hierarchy of values. It is precisely this demise of the agrarian world that helps to explain the nostalgic view of the past and of nature which characterizes so much romantic writing, and which helps as well to explain romantic poetry as a poetry of consolation[10]—matters that are given forceful expression in *Endymion*. But more immediately important to an understanding of Keats than this commonplace view of industrial triumph and pastoral loss is the fact that, after 1815, capitalism faced a severe crisis created by postwar unemployment, bad harvests, and rearguard political actions (e.g., the Corn Laws) which were given renewed energy by the defeat of Napoleon. The severity of the postwar situation is indicated in an article which appeared 11 August 1816 in *The Examiner:* "The war has cost the country eight or nine hundred millions of money. This has not been a nominal expence, a playing at ducks and drakes with the king's picture on the water, or a manufacturing of banknotes, and then lighting our pipes with them, but a real *bona fide* waste of the means, wealth, labour, produce, or resources of the country, in the carrying on of the war. . . . [T]he expences of the war might as well have been sunk in the sea; and so they might, for they are sunk in unproductive labour, that is, in maintaining large establishments and employing great numbers of men in doing nothing or mischief; for example, in making ships to destroy other ships."[11] Such articles appear frequently in the *Examiner* and in other papers in the postwar years, suggesting the degree of anxiety and distress pervading British society at the time.[12] That such anxiety found its way directly into the popular imagination of the period is clear from the briefest glimpse at some of the major literary productions after Waterloo; these works are characterized by horror *(Frankenstein),*[13] solitude *(The Excursion, Alastor),* defiant individualism *(Childe Harold* 3), flight from received notions of value and truth *(Manfred),* and the desire for a transcendental redemptive power *(Hymn to Intellectual Beauty)*—they do not, for the most part, articulate visionary bliss or celebrate social, political, and moral hope.[14] While the literature of the second generation writers should not be reduced to a literature of despair, it must be seen as a literature of historical anxiety, characterized both by the energy and power of British bourgeois thought and by the fear that these could not be sustained indefinitely.

It is within this broad context of industrial triumph and within the specific context of postwar economic and political tension that *Endymion* can be most fully understood. The poem is one site where the various political and ideological struggles of the period are formulated and articulated, and where a resolution of social and historical contradictions is attempted. It is a poem that displays the disintegration of public hope and social possibility and at the same time seeks an alternative possibility of value in the mind and in transcendental redemptive powers. While this view of the poem draws to some degree on Caudwell's argument that in *Lamia, Endymion, Ode on a Grecian Urn* and elsewhere Keats constructs "a world of romance, beauty and sensuous life separate from the poor, harsh, real world of everyday life,"[15] I do not wish finally to leave the poem as an example of poetic escapism, or as a simple reflection of, and response to, bourgeois reality. Rather, I want to argue that in its very escapist longings it articulates remarkably clearly the social relations and social contradictions with which Keats's imagination contended. This is not to suggest that the poem should be regarded as an analytical document or even as a pure allegory of postwar British politics. Rather, it is to say that Keats's ideological commitments are predicated upon certain political realities inscribed in the poem. They are not announced, but are expressed figuratively and symbolically, and thus must be decoded using the terms of beauty and truth, love and friendship, imagination and subjectivity set down within the narrative itself.[16]

The political and ideological currents running through the poem cut across the landscape of at least three important and encompassing social matters. The first is the terrible sense of social decay that drives a wedge between Endymion and his community, leaving him isolated and without hope for the world; the second is the construction—out of desire and in the face of social decay—of a realm of subjective meaning that is apparently untouched by social exchange and social hardship, and which is projected as a transocial alternative to everyday human struggle; and the third is the sociopolitical reality that is elided by the narrative but which nonetheless stands behind this newly created subjectivity. These issues constitute the necessary groundwork for all others in the narrative, providing a point of entry into many related concerns that are presented uncritically, such as gender relations, political hierarchy, imperialist ideology, and so on.

Keats's attachment here and elsewhere in his poetry to the mythic past, peopled with characters of extraordinary beauty, sensitivity, and integrity, is not only a sign of nostalgia for a fuller life which may have existed at some prebourgeois moment in time; nor is it only a sign of the poet's innocent love for things spun out of the creative imagination. It is also a sign of the situation of discourse at the time Keats wrote his poem. To relate and embellish the story of Endymion is not to escape from history into myth, nor is it to use myth self-consciously as a means of presenting allegorically the social and political issues of the historical moment. Rather, it is to construct a relatively ordered and relatively stable (though surely mystified) discursive site within a destablized world of economic and political hardship that is capable of reconciling that world with individual desire.[17]

This point can be illustrated briefly by reference to the famous opening lines on beauty. One of the narrative's controlling themes, beauty is here presented in universal terms as a permanent pleasure that is available to humanity. But even as it is described, its universal qualities and its pleasure potential are defined against certain natural and historical realities that are the dialectical pole giving it particular transhistorical significance. That is, the concepts of beauty and joy described by the poet are dependent upon—emerge within and are shaped by—certain processes and pressures that isolate the individual from meaningful experience in the world. Just as in Shelley's *Hymn to Intellectual Beauty* beauty "floats tho' unseen amongs us," providing relief from "this dim vast vale of tears, vacant and desolate," in *Endymion* Keats's beauty that "moves away the pall / From our dark spirits" (1 : 12–13) is a formulation of desire within a larger context of disappointment, and represents an attempt to situate and master this disappointment. It can never do this, however, because it is fundamentally imbricated in historical movement; the "joy" that would last "forever" achieves its status from the historical realities that it would transcend. The extent to which this is true is suggested by the way the introduction describes the defeats of great individuals within history. Faced with the fact of historical loss and fearing that there is no redemption from it, the poet converts grim reality into triumph—"And such too is the grandeur of the dooms / We have imagined for the mighty dead" (1 : 20–21)—resolving at the level of imagination that which is experientially threatening. While the things of beauty may appear to pour "unto us from the heaven's brink" (1 : 24), in a very real sense—as becomes apparent through the narrative—they are produced within history by an imaginative process of conversion which attempts to find meaning in loss. In this sense, beauty is not a universal given, though the poet would have it such, but the product of utopain longing for a sphere where all contradictions are resolved.

Just as the subject matter of the poem itself—the mythic past—takes form under given historical conditions, so the issues within the poem, including beauty, achieve form and definition historically: they are not independently given. This point is important not simply because it insists upon the relevance of sociological matters to the interpretation of poetry, but more critically because it insists that history is the ontological ground for poetic production, thus obliging us to see the narrative in terms of social formation, of which beauty, happiness, friendship, and love are products: they occupy positions within the social totality, constituting spaces of freedom or hope wherein poetic and hence human identity presumably can be fully established.[18] However diffuse or incoherent the presentation of the narrative action may be, it offers itself within a unified context of social reality, a context in which social contradiction is everywhere. To understand this is to create the possibility not only of systematically explaining individual episodes and issues within the narrative, but also of systematically explaining the narrative confusion itself.

The impulse behind the narrative action is the disintegration of a received form of social life, and specifically of a hierarchy of social values. Keats goes to great lengths to establish the pastoral setting of the story, removing the narrative perspective from "the city's din" (1:40), and locating the initial action within a context of natural plenitude. But the preindustrial world of plenitude that he describes is not primitive and egalitarian; it looks very much like the feudal world which the forces of capital in Keats's day had effectively disempowered, leaving only traces of its former grandeur. While many of the characters themselves in this world are "young damsels" (1:135) and "shepherds" (1:139), appropriate to the pastoral and idyllic landscape that the narrative wants to establish, the larger context itself is punctuated by "a multitude" (1:164), "a venerable priest" (1:149), and "a chieftain king" (1:172)—by a "goodly company" (1:129), that is, of "old piety" (1:130)—all of which bespeak a definite order and purpose in social life. In this world, social hierarchy is as yet unviolated, the chieftain king rules the kingdom, the multitude follow in full support, and the priest pronounces the fullness and beauty of a world so ordered. Nature itself reflects the purposiveness of this world: "The earth is glad: the merry lark has pour'd / His early song against yon breezy sky" (1:220–21).

This opening scene of social coherence is defined most explicitly not by the king or by the people, but by the priest. The people who have gathered surround the shrine, make offerings, and listen as the priest celebrates the wealth of the community. The significance of this description is that it demonstrates the primary social role of religion in preindustrial society; religion is the master discourse in this world, the controlling ideology that gives coherence and meaning to every other facet of society. Writing in a different context, Fredric Jameson explains the social significance of religion in preindustrial society, arguing that it was not "a private language or a unique incommunicable form of consciousness [as it was to become, say, in the writings of Blake], but rather ... the sign of group praxis and group membership, ... a badge of collective adherence."[19] This is precisely the role here of the priest, the shrine, and the multitude at worship. The scene is not a celebration of religion per se; it is a celebration of society through the language of religion. Through the narrative, as this specific set of social relations disintegrates, so will this specific religious language.

Even while Keats describes and celebrates the preindustrial world as a world of plenty, seen most explicitly and movingly in the hymn to Pan (1:232–306), he acknowledges that its fate is set.[20] The problem is not simply Endymion's apparent unhappiness ("But there were some who feelingly could scan / A lurking trouble in his nether lip" [1:178–79]), but rather a general sense of death and decay permeating the entire community, even while the institutional rhetoric (in the form of the priest's encomium) celebrates community well-being.[21] Immediately following the hymn to Pan, for instance, the scene comes to be characterized in terms of death, decay, loss of memory, idealization of the past, and so on:

> Young companies nimbly began dancing
> To the swift treble pipe, and humming string.
> Aye, those fair living forms swam heavenly
> To tunes forgotten—out of memory:
> Fair creatures! whose young children's children bred
> Thermopylae its heroes—not yet dead,
> But in old marbles ever beautiful.
> High genitors, unconscious did they cull
> Time's sweet first-fruits—they danc'd to weariness,
> And then in quiet circles did they press
> The hillock turf, and caught the latter end
> Of some strange history. . . .
> (1:313–24)

Across the hillside the people lament "the sad death / Of Hyacinthus" (1:327–28) and the loneliness of Niobe "when her lovely young / Were dead and gone" (1:339–40), while the priest and Endymion contemplate "the silvery setting of their mortal star" (1:359). The point is not that the scene is one of total despair—indeed it is not this at all—but rather that it is highly sensitive to loss and that in the face of this loss it seems to find fulfillment not in the present but in the future—after death: "Each one [has] his own anticipated bliss" (1:373). In fact the anticipation of future bliss is characterized interestingly by a collective desire to resurrect and bestow new meaning on things of the past that have died:

> One felt heart-certain that he could not miss
> His quick gone love. . . .
> . . . .
> Another wish'd, mid that eternal spring,
> To meet his rosy child. . . .
> . . . .
> Some were athirst in soul to see again
> The fellow huntsmen o'er the wide champaign
> In times long past; to sit with them, and talk
> Of all the chances in their earthly walk.
> (1:374–75, 378–79, 385–88)

While this is a picture of spiritual hope, it is also a picture of collective social emptiness, much as the expression of hope at the end of Blake's *Chimney Sweeper* points to exploitation and human sacrifice, and much as

Keats's own description of beauty at the beginning of *Endymion* is predicated upon social collapse ("the dooms" of "the mighty dead") and human difficulty.

This socially pervasive emptiness is distilled in the character of Endymion, who, after sitting through these strange recollections, is described as having "striven / To hide the cankering venom, that had riven / His fainting recollections" (1:395–97). He is "dead-still as a marble man" (1:405) in a contradictory scene of natural wealth and beauty offset by human alienation; it is a scene that is dizzying in its extremity. If, as Roger Sales argues, the early tales of Byron achieved their peculiar intensity and popularity from "the restrictions and burdens of a wartime, siege economy,"[22] this scene reflects the poetic anxiety and plain weariness of a poetry written in the difficult, immediate post-Waterloo years, when unemployment skyrocketed in England, bankruptcies proliferated, and, as Byron put it, Europe was "retrograding to that same dull stupid old system" (*BLJ* 3:218). Without rolling looms and steam engines onto the pastoral landscape as a sign of the historical future, and without giving explicit attention to the financial controversies which appeared regularly in Hunt's *Examiner,* Keats effectively and movingly shows that the world that Endymion once presided over—and continues to lead in name only—is irretrievably lost.

The social fragmentation described in these early scenes, even while on the surface social coherence seems to prevail, is the basis for the quest upon which Endymion embarks; moreover, it is the basis for a dominant feature of romantic poetry in general, namely what Harold Bloom has called the internalization of the Quest-Romance. Bloom argues that "the Romantic movement is from nature to the imagination's freedom (sometimes a reluctant freedom), and the imagination's freedom is frequently purgatorial, redemptive in direction but destructive of the social self. . . . The quest is to widen consciousness as well as to intensify it."[23] What Bloom does not adequately emphasize or explore, however, is the extent to which this poetic phenomenon is determined by sociohistorical context, and particularly by the large structural shifts in the cultural and ideological forces of the age. The effort to "widen consciousness" is an attempt to construct a subjective alternative to troubling historical processes. Romantic internalization is not simply a journey through the subterranean regions of the individual self; it is a difficult and often lonely journey through social reality.

With respect to the story of Endymion, as the avenues of social investment narrow to the point where social life itself seems obtrusive, the chieftain is thrown back increasingly onto his own private resources to discover purpose and direction. Under such conditions, the very desire that motivates him with respect to Cynthia, that even paralyzes him in its intensity, is a sign of the loss of freedom rather than the discovery of it.

The private landscape with which he becomes obsessed, with its infinite twists and turns, is not separate from the social landscape, but is structured by it—the social dwells within the private. In other words, what Keats describes in these early scenes is the opening up of a private space that would resist history even while it is historically contingent, which in fact indulges, or claims its strength from, historical and social fragmentation. The attraction and fear of this private space are that it has not yet been mapped out, opened up by the imagination, or adequately reconciled with the social world on which it depends for its very existence. Thus the long books that follow are punctuated not only by moments of extreme beauty and bliss, when the mind seems to be its own place, but also by Gothic sensationalism and fear, when it appears that the mind will be unable to sustain itself in isolation.

On this view, Keats's narrative strategy entails an effort to construct and define a realm of individual subjectivity, to give meaning and form to the desire which in its turn is the product of social disintegration.[24] And the meaning that is produced here, as in much romantic poetry, entails the active denial of the social upon which it is wholly dependent. Put differently, the ascent of subjective truth that is described in the narrative is also one example of the refraction of the social.[25] It is what Russell Jacoby calls, in another context, "the gloss of freedom under the conditions of its denial."[26] It is utopian triumph and celebration of the private self as it is believed to exist apart from society.[27] Endymion voices this attitude explicitly in the famous speech on happiness, which is usually seen as a key to Keats's own visions of the transcendental imagination. Speaking of love, Endymion remarks:

> Aye, so delicious is the unsating food,
> That men, who might have tower'd in the van
> Of all the congregated world, to fan
> And winnow from the coming step of time
> All chaff of custom, wipe away all slime
> Left by men-slugs and human serpentry,
> Have been content to let occasion die,
> Whilst they did sleep in love's elysium.
> And, truly, I would rather be struck dumb,
> Than speak against this ardent listlessness:
> For I have ever thought that it might bless
> The world with benefits unknowingly,
>
> (1:816–27)

Opting for vision over reality, claiming that "listlessness" is potentially more fundamental and more liberating than social interest ("occasion"), Endymion places his "hope" (1:857) in "love immortal" (1:849). The motivating impulse behind this attitude is stated later in the narrative: ". . . but for me, / There is no depth to strike in: I can see / Naught earthly worth my compassing" (2:160–62). From the start, the attachment to love precludes social reality; love is seen as a space apart from social and historical processes, and thus it takes Endymion ever further into his own isolation, which he believes provides the possibility of freedom and fulfillment.

The inductions to the poem's four books also, to varying degrees, dismantle history and society, denying their priority as organizing categories of human experience. To take only one example, the induction to book 2 claims that all "records" (2:2) "of passed years" (2:3) are available for human examination and knowledge; only knowledge of love remains to be discovered and mastered. The history that is accessible, and that stands over against elusive love, is unappealing, fading from memory, and this leads the poet to believe that history is less significant than love. In one of the strongest passages on this matter, the poet states:

> Hence, pageant history! hence, gilded cheat!
> Swart planet in the universe of deeds!
> Wide sea, that one continuous murmur breeds
> Along the pebbled shore of memory!
> Many old rotten-timber'd boats there be
> Upon thy vaporous bosom, magnified
> To goodly vessels; many a sail of pride,
> And golden keel'd, is left unlaunch'd and dry.
> But wherefore this? What care, though owl did fly
> About the great Athenian admiral's mast?
> What care, though striding Alexander past
> The Indus with his Macedonian numbers?
> Though old Ulysses tortured from his slumbers
> The glutted Cyclops, what care?
>
> (2:14–27)

Once again, the point here is not simply that Keats is voicing typical romantic escapism, but rather that he is setting down the parameters of a private world of desire, wherein the language of history is co-opted, imported into the private space of desire to bestow meaning upon it. Love, for instance, is a "Sovereign power" (2:1), and the poetic effort to elevate this power into a governing position in human experience—to make it into a cultural dominant—is seen in distinctly military terms, as the poet strives "to uprear / Love's standard on the battlements of song" (2:40–41), while "days and nights aid me along, / Like legion'd soldiers" (2:42–43).[28] This is an act of displacement and ideological reconciliation, wherein the crosscurrents of historical change are brought under the control of love, which in its turn is a product of individual desire.

The difficulty of constructing and ordering a compensatory subjectivity is one possible explanation for the diffusiveness and frequent confusion of the narrative, and certainly it helps to explain the anxiety that frequently is seen not only in the character of Endymion but also in the many authorial intrusions into the narrative. As Keats leads his hero into "the hollow, / The silent mysteries of earth" (2:213–14) toward "the goal of consciousness" (2:283), the narrative becomes increasingly difficult to execute and the poetic voice becomes increasingly anxious and self-conscious, incapable of articulating the vision that is desired. Near the mid-point of the poem, the 4000-line project itself comes to be seen as "these sorry pages" (2:719), as a weak form of expression devoid of the "old power" (2:731) that once was capable of organizing and articulating human experience. This feature of the narrative is an instance of what Catherine Belsey describes as the individual subject's attempt in romantic literature to achieve and articulate absolute freedom. Throughout the narrative there are two irreconcilable discourses at work, demonstrating a "dialectic of jubilation and loss,"[29] as the poem attempts to master its objects of hope and desire, and in the process plunges ever deeper into the anxious isolation which it is hoped will be redemptive. What Belsey says of *The Prelude* is equally true of *Endymion:* ". . . what returns to threaten the plenitude of the subject is precisely the repressed condition of its own being."[30]

The way in which the anxieties and desires in the story are laid to rest is intimated in the Glaucus episode, which marks the first significant formulation of beauty, love, and private happiness as definable and attainable categories for the individual. This remarkable scene has often been noted (rightly, I believe) for its expression of human sympathy and political acumen. In an excellent short essay devoted entirely to this episode, William Garrett concludes: "Civilization reclaimed by beneficence and knowledge: applied to the whole of Book III, this theme means that an aspect of friendship is the improvement of society; perhaps friendship then obtains in its most influential and creative state."[31] We need not examine the many different literary characterizations of friendship during the period, nor attempt to understand these characterizations within the framework of bourgeois individualism, to see the limitations of such an admittedly appealing explanation as this.[32] What Keats is doing with friendship here, he had done earlier in the poem with the vocabulary of history and society; that is, he is privatizing it, using it as the starting point for a vision of society, eliding the fact—detailed carefully in the opening sections of the narrative—that society itself is the necessary starting point for all human endeavor. The encounter with Glaucus and the ideas which emerge from this encounter must be regarded in the context of isolation and social fragmentation.

Like Byron's Manfred, who scales the heights of the universe in an attempt to map out an uncharted private landscape, Endymion descends "as deep profound" (2:210) for the same purpose. Unlike Manfred, however, Endymion believes that he discovers a new world of beauty and truth. If in the opening book of the poem the followers of Endymion were disturbed by memories of the past and by an acute awareness of death, in the Glaucus episode the dead are revived and lovers joyfully find their beloved:

> Death fell a weeping in his charnel-house.
> The Latmian persever'd along, and thus
> All were re-animated. There arose
> A noise of harmony, pulses and throes
> Of gladness in the air—while many, who
> Had died in mutual arms devout and true,
> Sprang to each other madly.
>
> (3:788–94)

These people, conjured up after close scrutiny of "the book" (3:677) in Glaucus's possession, come to form a new "multitude" (3:818), one which, unlike that earlier in the narrative, has conquered death and now enjoys unleashed passion, joy, happiness, and presumably social coherence built from individual pleasure. In this new world, hierarchy is not destroyed but interiorized, the social and political language which prevailed in book 1 coming now to describe the world built upon sheer desire:

> . . . large Neptune on his throne
> Of emerald deep: yet not exalt alone;
> At his right hand stood winged Love, and on
> His left sat smiling Beauty's paragon.
>
> (3:862–65)

The world that before had driven Endymion to despair is now resurrected, only now it is shorn of all hardship, and Endymion's individual mind shapes and directs it. All that is left is for Endymion himself to escape "from dull mortality's harsh net" (3:907), to be blessed with a transcendental redemptive power that will affirm and instantiate the power and moral integrity of his vision.

The final book, which describes the union of Endymion with Cynthia, and more particularly the triumph which gives him "command, / . . . on our sad fate" (4:975–76)—that is, which establishes the absolute authority of the transcendental individual ego—lays bare some of the key contributory elements which have been implicit through the narrative. Most importantly, this book brings into focus the historical role of gender relations and of imperialist ideology in the construction of the specific beliefs and values set down in the poem. These ingredients deny the possibility of an innocent reading of the narrative as a simple account of a mythic past and emphasize that poetic production is historically specific and politically significant. While the poem throughout voices a desire to escape entirely the historical moment, and while the subject matter itself seems to suggest Keats's readiness to deny historical determination—or at the very least his willingness to remain silent about the major and unsettling questions facing his age—the portrayal of gender relations and the reconstruction of the idea of the East for consumption by the Western mind locate the poem immediately at a particular historical conjuncture where the triumph of the individual masculine ego is made possible by the imperialistic conquest of the East by Western capitalism.

The Indian maid of course provides the key to the specific enabling forces behind the joyous expressions of the final book, and to understand her importance it is necessary to touch upon the connection between Europe and India immediately before and during the romantic period. The single best work on the political and ideological significance of the East to the West during this period is Edward Said's *Orientalism*, and I want to sketch briefly some of the arguments presented in this work that bear directly upon the political interpretation of *Endymion* that I am advancing. India had begun to occupy an important role in British politics and imagination through the eighteenth century, and it was a role somewhat different from that of Egypt and countries from the near East. The reason for this, Said notes, is that "native authority crumbled there [in India] and opened the land to inter-European rivalry and to outright European political control. . . . [Thus] the Indian Orient could be treated by Europe with . . . proprietary hauteur—never with the sense of danger reserved for Islam."[33] The political control of India, however, through much of the eighteenth century was in dispute: "Britain and France fought each other in India between 1744 and 1748 and again between 1756 and 1763, until, in 1769, the British emerged in practical economic and political control of the subcontinent."[34] Political and economic domination was accompanied by an ideological reconstruction of the East that culminated in the nineteenth century. As Said puts it, "the Orient is an idea that has a history and a tradition of thought, imagery, and vocabulary that have given it reality and presence in and for the West."[35] That is, "the relationship between Occident and Orient is a relationship of power, of domination, of varying degrees of a complex hegemony."[36]

It is this power relation at work that is formulated and articulated in *Endymion*. The East, in the form of the Indian maid, while finally sublimated into transcendental beauty, appears initially as a site of distinct helplessness and need. The Indian maid is lost and Endymion is invited to assist her. The result of this attention is that he is deified and placed in a position of "command" (4:975). His is a position of superiority, ultimately, even though narratively it is presented as a position of inferiority. The political dimension of this relation between the two characters is implicit in the relation of the induction to book 4 to the subsequent narrative. Keats begins the book with an invocation of the "muse of my native land" (4:1) and follows with a reference to the "native hopes" (4:17) of the muse, and to her poetic triumph: "O thou hast won / A full accomplishment! The thing is done" (4:17–18). This induction is followed immediately by the Indian maiden's lament for the loss of her native land: "Ah, woe is me! that I should fondly part / From my dear native land! Ah, foolish maid!" (4:30–31). The ideological ploy here is clear. National regions are situated against one another, arranged within a hierarchy of Western value, in preparation for the narrative appropriation of the East by the West. Once this hierarchy is set in place, the civilized western individual (Endymion) intervenes in the East, which is described as beautiful and yet helpless and in disarray, and he is rewarded with immortality for his troubles. The political reality of this situation—i.e., the First World domination and sublimation of the Third World—is completely elided, replaced in the mind by pure intention, value, integrity, and imagination. The colonization of India by England is accompanied by the colonization of the poetic imagination.

The gender dimension of this process of appropriation and domination is evident, as relations of economics and politics are shown to be most often directly connected, ideologically and materially, to relations of sex. Said describes this dimension precisely in a recent essay on Orientalism: "Orientalism is a praxis of the same sort, albeit in different territories, as male gender dominance, or patriarchy, in metropolitan societies: the Orient was routinely described as feminine, its riches as fertile, its main symbols the sensual woman, the harem, and the despotic—but curiously attractive—ruler."[37] With respect to Keats's narrative, this does not mean that the Indian maid scene should be seen as an allegory of British intervention in India (though such an argument, I believe, could be persuasively made), but rather that two primary fields of political reality—gender and the East—are fused in the poetic imagination, which is explicitly masculine, and brought under its absolute control.[38] This is a poetic maneuver which suppresses political reality, resolving social contradictions ideologically (poetically) rather than practically.[39]

The descriptions of the Indian maid are consistent with the portrayal of women in many of Keats's poems, and consistent generally with romantic portrayals of women.[40] From the beginning she is passive, having been placed in distress by her own bad judgment, and her passivity and need fuel masculine desire:

> Is no one near to help me? No fair dawn
> Of life from charitable voice? No sweet saying
> To set my dull and sadden'd spirit playing?
> No hand to toy with mine? No lips so sweet
> That I may worship them?...
> . . . .
> I am sad and lost.
>
> (4:44–51)

This lament displays a rich list of features against which the masculine ego under patriarchy identifies itself, and over which it claims superiority. It combines physical need—the maid is lost—an alluring, inviting, erotic voice, and an expressed desire to find someone (implicitly understood to be a man) to "worship." It describes a character, that is, whose purpose and identity depend wholly upon a shaping and mastering masculine power. Indeed, the Indian maid becomes for Endymion the site for the fulfillment of both physical desire and even of immortality. As the narrative voice describes her—"[I]f thou wilt behold all beauty's store, / Behold her panting in the forest grass" (4:58–59)—she is a treasure to be discovered and taken, which indeed *wants* to be taken: "there she lay, / Sweet as a muskrose upon new-made hay, / With all her limbs on tremble, and her eyes / Shut softly up alive" (4:101–4). She promises both sensual pleasure and spiritual hope; for this reason she is, as Endymion says later in the narrative, "my Indian bliss!" (4:663).[41]

Endymion's representation of himself in his encounter with the Indian maid as a servant ("I've no choice; / I must be thy sad servant evermore: / I cannot choose but kneel here and adore" [4:300–2]) is by no means an indication of his helplessness or secondary status in this love relationship. However he describes himself, his perspective and his ego define the situation and set the terms of the relationship. It is the Indian maid's passivity, transhuman beauty (at least as Endymion sees it), and need that make possible Endymion's description of himself as a servant; as we know from his social position, stated early in the narrative, he is in fact a ruler. In this sense, he claims to serve that over which in fact he has command. His power and his ego are the constitutional basis for the definition of the feminine here, whether the feminine takes the form of the maid or the moon; they are imposed on the feminine and internalized by her, who is shaped by masculine desire. As Simone de Beauvoir succinctly states (writing in a different context), the feminine is "defined and differentiated with reference to man and not he with reference to her; she is the incidental, the inessential as opposed to the essential. He is the Subject, he is the Absolute—she is the Other."[42] Thus, despite the many professions of the beauty and power of Cynthia, Phoebe, and the Indian maid in the narrative, from the beginning the defining ego—the poet's and Endymion's—is emphatically masculine. The quest that Endymion hopes will provide him with self-knowledge and self-fulfillment is one that entails the construction of a (feminine) site whereon the masculine ego can exercise itself freely. Even as Endymion's "kingdom's at its death" (4:940), a new, subjective kingdom is constructed, one that seems to be strong, even immortal, but which clearly exercises a form of domination no less extreme than the former.

Several additional issues and episodes become clearer in light of the argument presented above. First is the matter of sleep, which Keats here and elsewhere dwells upon at length. In *Endymion,* as in much of his early poetry, sleep is often used to describe a state of "spiritual awareness," as Clarence DeWitt Thorpe has argued,[43] or a state of heightened imaginative activity much like that described, for instance, by Coleridge in the preface to *Kubla Khan.* But while it is this, it also designates a private region inhabited by "that completed form of all completeness" (1:606); it is the place of retreat from the world, and Endymion protects it by converting it into a virtue. This becomes clear after Peona warns him away from "the Morphean fount / Of that fine element that visions, dreams, / And fitful whims of sleep are made of" (1:747–49): "Why pierce high-fronted honour to the quick / For nothing but a dream?" (1:759–60). Endymion responds with the long, famous explanation of the gradations of happiness (1:769–842), which amounts finally to a defense of "listlessness" (1:825) against "the stings / Of human neighbourhood" (1:621–22). The "hope beyond the shadow of a dream" (1:857) which Endymion claims as his ultimate motivation is in fact a hope for sleep itself, for the "blissfull swoon" (4:999) that will, he believes, provide an escape from social contradiction. While his "kingdom's at its death" (4:940) along with "this dusk religion" (4:954), sleep is the only imaginable alternative where figures of beauty can be erected. From this perspective, the poem is as much about the crisis of imagination as it is about the power of the imagination.[44]

While Endymion pursues his private quest and insists that sleep is an avenue which leads to happiness, he depends very directly upon his sister, Peona, who is not given to transcendental visions and who thus presumably cannot hope for the bliss reserved for her brother. The role of Peona in the narrative is striking because she offers a necessary and illuminating counterpart to Cynthia. Like Wordsworth's Dorothy in *Tintern Abbey,* Peona is a nourisher whose primary role, as described by the masculine poetic voice, is to assist Endymion in his effort to achieve visionary bliss. In this role, she performs practical labor that is both supportive and protective in nature. In the early scenes, for instance, when Endymion's distress first becomes apparent, it is Peona who comes to his aid:

> She led him, like some midnight spirit nurse
> Of happy changes in emphatic dreams,
> Along a path between two little streams,—
> Guarding his forehead, with her round elbow,
> From low-grown branchs, and his footsteps slow
> From stumbling over stumps and hillocks small.
> (1:413–18)

This nourishing, laboring support is converted in Endymion's dreams into an ideal bliss in the form of Cynthia, who appears to have magical power to fill the shepherd-king's needs without any explict show of labor. That is, Cynthia is an idealization of Peona; she is a feminine presence cleansed and purified of all the human characteristics possessed by Peona, save one—the feminine capacity for providing erotic pleasure, a capacity that, I should stress, depends directly upon Cynthia's status as image or ideal. To see Peona as a practical helper, set narratively against Cynthia's higher role as goddess, is to understand her "sisterliness." To the degree that she engages in material human activity, and to the degree that she comes into direct contact with Endymion to help him meet his material needs, she is shorn of her erotic potential and sexual passion. When Endymion wins the bliss he seeks, a bliss in which his "command" (4:975) enables him to satisfy his desire, Peona is left among the mundane and everyday world to find her own way "home through the gloomy wood in wonderment" (4:1003).

Finally, I want to add another word about the inductions, which were mentioned briefly above, because these have caused some confusion about the poem's relative coherence.[45] While these inductions admittedly appear scattered and unrelated at times (especially the induction to book 4), in fact they provide a structuring mechanism for the entire narrative, at least in terms of the large symbolic interests I have been sketching. Respectively, the inductions offer commentaries on beauty, love, tyranny overthrown, and British poetry. This pattern follows exactly the line of narrative development in the poem in that the story traces the dismantling of history as the primary organizing category of human activity and the replacement of it with ideals that are at first rather vague but that are finally presented joyfully and confidently. In other words, beauty and love, as the goals of private desire, are erected as the highest human virtues, while history is a tyranny to be overthrown; as this tyranny is defeated, beauty and love co-opt the vocabulary of history and politics, until in the induction to book 4 the triumph of this new subjectivity is celebrated for the entire "native land" (4:1). In short, the ideological process of converting subjectivity into a culturally dominant value is described very broadly in the inductions, while the narrative account of Endymion gives this process symbolic and dramatic force.

The line of argument I have pursued here is intended to suggest that even while there is much of real integrity in the narrative respecting friendship and love, and which suggests that any rebuilding of society must include human compassion—on these topics Keats is among the most sympathetic of the romantics—there is at the same time a deep-seated fear of the world coming apart at the seams, and an attempt to prevent this by projecting a world subject to the control of individual desire. Put differently, even while elements of Keats's own disgruntlement with Regency politics can be found throughout the narrative (and most explicitly in book 3), the poem is finally the product of the same historical crosscurrents that had created the post-Waterloo situation, and what we might wish to see as a genuinely progressive thread running through the story is not a thread of collective praxis but of subjective alternative. It demonstrates both the degree of social fragmentation during the period and the power of the kind of individualism that held an ever more important place within the bourgeois social formation.

Endymion is a poem in which ideals and ideology collide and fuse. In insisting upon this, I am not suggesting that Keats's poetic intentions are bad but that the poem's genesis lies within a context that limits human hope to matters of beauty, truth, friendship, and love, and at the same time assigns these values transhistorical and redemptive powers. Although Endymion from the beginning is given absolutely to a quest for love, and finds it, this does not imply that the kind of love described in the narrative will save us all. Rather, these are signs that human fulfillment is unimaginable within a context of actual human experience. Endymion's Cynthia, Manfred's Astarte, Shelley's Intellectual Beauty all represent transcendental impulses, and as such they point forcefully and necessarily to the historical situation of the romantic poetic voice. What McGann says generally of romanticism is particularly apposite to *Endymion:* "The poetry of Romanticism is everywhere marked by extreme forms of displacement and poetic conceptualization whereby the actual human issues with which poetry is concerned are resituated in a variety of idealized localities."[46] On this view, the relevant factors in any critical investigation of poetry are not only authorial expression or intention but also the sociohistorical conditions under which the poem is produced. As Robert Weimann says generally of poetic production: "[A] writer's intention is only part (and not even the most important part) of that complex of historical origins by which the temporal complication of literary images, themes, genres, modes, and functions can be understood. . . . [T]o ignore this is to remain entangled in the assumptions of individualism."[47] Again, such a position does not denigrate Keats or *Endymion*—one must, I believe, approach this poem, as Walter Evert insists, with awe and respect as a tremendous achievement—but, rather, redeems it and assigns it an important place in the critical endeavor to understand and explain the historical development of individuality and subjectivity.

3
"Love's Fev'rous Citadel"
ISABELLA AND THE EVE OF ST. AGNES

IT is a critical commonplace that Keats's *Isabella* is a poem about politics. As Bernard Shaw remarked many years ago, "If Karl Marx can be imagined as writing a poem instead of a treatise on Capital, he would have written Isabella."[1] But the full significance of its politics has yet to be elaborated, as critics have tended to bypass scrutiny of this poem in favor of others, perhaps because the direct political comments in the narrative have always seemed foreign to Keats's temperament.[2] Keats's own observations about the poem have not encouraged serious assessment. Despite the general feeling of his friends that the poem was extremely worthy of publication (see, for instance, the letter from Woodhouse to Taylor, *LJK* 2:162), the poet himself felt that it was "too smokeable": "There is too much inexperience of live [*sic*], and simplicity of knowledge in it" (*LJK* 2:174). While his complaint here is clearly against what he felt to be the inferiority of the poem itself, this is probably not his only concern. He expresses equally strong reservations about—and at times disregard for—virtually everything he ever wrote, including the great odes, presumably because upon completion of every poem his thinking had matured, or he felt that he could produce better poetry.[3]

The likelihood is that he resisted publication of this poem particularly because he feared the reviewers, especially that they would attack its nonpoetic (i.e., its political) content. As he lamented to Woodhouse in the same letter which complains of *Isabella,* "O that I could [write] something agrest rural, pleasant, fountain-vo[i]c'd—not plague you with unconnected nonsense—But things won't leave me *alone*" (*LJK* 2:174). The extent to which things would not leave him alone is evidenced during and just before the time of composing *Isabella*. As early as February 1818 (roughly at the time he began writing the poem), he was reading Voltaire, Gibbon, and Rousseau, was attending "Hazlitt's Lectures regularly" (*LJK* 1:237), and was becoming very interested in politics and its connection to poetry (see, for instance, *LJK* 1:241).[4] Also, it was about this time that he was beginning to understand the importance of intellectual pursuit to aesthetic pursuit, and to speak increasingly of giving himself to "study and thought" (*LJK* 1:271) in hopes of one day doing some "great Public good" (*LJK* 1:267). He even planned, as he said in April 1818, "to ask Hazlitt in about a years time the best metaphysical road I can take" (*LJK* 1:274). After he completed the poem he continued his interest in politics, reading the *Examiner*, following the Westminster elections of 1819, and discussing Cobbett with friends.

All of these interests found their way (at least indirectly) into *Isabella*, which was written precisely at the moment when Keats's thinking was beginning to mature, at least with respect to the complexity of political reality, and it is most likely that he did not yet feel comfortable handling poetically the variety of issues that were beginning to congeal in his mind. That he was apprehensive about publishing the poem, about giving it up, as it were, to reviewers who were a product of a conservative political (and poetic) climate is not surprising, for it is the least symbolic of his poems: that is, its politics are manifested in important ways in the plot itself, whereas in many of his later works that were written after his thinking about both politics and poetry had matured significantly (*Lamia* and *The Fall of Hyperion*, for instance) political matters are interiorized to a greater degree, embedded in old myths and legends in such a way that the poetry is intelligent, powerful, and political without being reductive, didactic, or crude (as *Isabella* sometimes tends to be). But its very explicitness is important, for it provides a direct point of entry into a variety of complex sociopolitical subjects that characterize many of his later works. What the plot says explicitly about labor, for instance, helps to elucidate other hidden sets of social relations in the poem, relations that structure and govern Keats's poetic vision.

The story of *Isabella* is grounded firmly within a specific set of economic relations, and all ideas and events in the narrative action are controlled by them. In stressing that Isabella's brothers are mercantile capitalists, Keats is doing more than complaining against hard-hearted businessmen (as Shaw would have it), and he is also doing more than suggesting that the money of the brothers makes possible the moment of romantic bliss that Isabella enjoys (as Wolfson has argued). He is documenting the fundamental power that shapes every ingredient of the world he is describing. The nature of this power can be explained very briefly in the light of recent work on the subject of capitalism. Robert L. Heilbroner, in *The Nature and Logic of Capitalism*, offers some lucid insights into the general nature of capitalism that go a long way toward explaining its significance to Isabella's story. Heilbroner states that "the business world" (in *Isabella,* what the brothers do for a living) represents only the surface of capitalism: it is "the outward-facing reality of capitalism and is an inextricable part of whatever capitalism is." But business is not capitalism itself: there is a deeper "nether world" beneath whatever goes on in business, and this world casts a "structuring effect . . . over the course of business activity . . . [and] is never precisely revealed in the pattern of economic events." Yet, Heilbroner asserts, it gives rise to and orders the various social forms through which we carry out our daily activities. In other words, capitalism comprises "behavior-shaping institutions and relationships," and thus extends its power into every aspect of personal and public life, which in turn reflects and is shaped by it.[5]

It is in this sense that the descriptions in the poem of the brothers who are "enriched from ancestral merchandize" (106) must be understood. That they physically abuse some people (as they do Lorenzo) and exploit others for the sake of their own personal wealth without regard to a larger social need is clear and of course important. But their presence in the narrative serves more than a didactic purpose, illustrating Keats's views on the exploitation of labor by heartless factory owners; it also gives us a clue about the kind of social relations that govern the world of the poem. The brothers are the most powerful individuals in the story, determining even whether select individuals are to live or die. But social reality does not reduce solely to their personal power. They participate in a social scheme that perhaps begins from the specific relations of production with which they are associated, but that ultimately encompasses even them and extends its attitudes along with its power into every aspect of experience. They carry out the dictates of capital, but they do not constitute its ultimate reality. To contextualize their role in this way—rather than, say, reducing the world of the poem to their personal authority and wealth, so that events appear to be determined solely by conspiracy or self-will—is to begin to see the underlying structure of their world and to understand the extent to which everyone from laborers to Isabella to the brothers themselves is implicated in it.

The key ideological features of this world, as the relations of production attest, are the privatization of reality (which effectively disempowers people) and the control of people within the context of this privatized world, a control that is given ballast by the fact that people are able (allowed) to think about human experience only in the most personal terms. Indeed, personal life (for instance, Isabella's consuming devotion to Lorenzo) in this world is seen as contradictory to social reality; that is, it is seen as a domain of pure value that retains its purity despite the corruption of the public world. This understanding assures that the prevailing structures of social authority will go unchallenged because they are perceived as irrelevant to meaningful social existence. Eli Zaretsky describes the historical dimension of this point very clearly. With the rise of capitalism,

> the conflict between the individual and society took on a new meaning. On one side appeared "society"—the capitalist economy, the state, the fixed social core that has no space in it for the individual: on the other, the personal identity, no longer defined by its place in the social division of labor. On one side the objective social world appeared, perceived at first as "machinery" or "industry," then throughout the nineteenth century as "society" and into the twentieth century as "big business," "city hall," and then as "technology" or "life," as the domination of the proletariat by the capitalist class became more difficult to perceive. In opposition to this harsh world that no individual could hope to affect, the modern world of subjectivity was created.[6]

This explanation helps us to see that the medieval world of romance that constitutes Keats's (surface) subject matter is rewritten in terms of the breakup of that world, and specifically in terms of its defeat at the hands of capitalism. Keats captures vividly and even frighteningly the way this breakup changed society at the bedrock level, restructuring not only its institutions (shifting the predominant means of production from agriculture to mercantilism) but also its value systems and world view, determining fundamentally the kinds of individual responses to the world that are possible.[7]

This view is not meant to suggest that the money issue by itself is unimportant, but to stress that its importance stretches across the social landscape of the poem. And it helps particularly to explain the love relationship between Lorenzo and Isabella. Most obviously, their affair crosses class lines. Much as Byron does in his Eastern Tales, Keats powerfully captures the way social authority moves swiftly and mercilessly without regard to personal need or desire to protect its ranks from intrusion.[8] But a more telling feature here is the nature of the relationship itself, and the way it participates in and reflects the larger world picture of which it is a part. The exploitation described in the poem is evidenced most clearly, as I noted above, in the relations of production, but it is not restricted to these. The two main victims of the structures of authority prevailing in Isabella's world are women and working men: these historically are the powerless under capitalism. Both are denied access to public power and even public life, allowed only those roles in life that support and actively extend the existing system; they are compelled to serve the ruling elite against their own interests, and are denied the freedom to work for their own human betterment. Indeed, every effort to do so is resisted both by physical and ideological forces.

That they turn to one another emphasizes at least two important points about the conditions under which they live. First, their union suggests a kind of solidarity among the oppressed that might be seen as a threat to status quo authority, and this solidarity of course helps to explain why Lorenzo is so violently murdered. This view goes beyond the abstract problem of crossing class lines and focuses the power interests that are bound up with questions of class. But more importantly perhaps is the fact that their union signifies a deep human (and personal) need for contact and exchange despite the rules of a specific culture. From this perspective, their relationship might be regarded as a utopian impulse, a search for bliss that denies the shaping influence of oppressive economic reality. But if it is so, their relationship is not free of social determination; it is a utopian impulse that very graphically points up the brutal nature not only of nasty brothers but, more importantly, of a particular political and cultural system that exercises absolute authority over people, much as the incestuous relationship between Parisina and Hugo in Byron's poem points up the atrocities of a politically repressive world: the very denial of politics is both a political action and a critique of political power.

One way of understanding the fullness of the poem's depiction of life within the grip of capitalism is to look beyond the love relationship at the center of the plot to Isabella's introduction into the world of brutual circumstance. The depiction of her naivete and idealism giving way to an awareness of human tragedy and human evil, while constituting an initiation at the level of personal experience, at the same time throws into relief both the ostensible and real workings of her world. Events early in the story perhaps suggest that the economic relations controlled by Isabella's brothers constitute an enabling power, making possible in some way the bliss enjoyed briefly by Isabella and Lorenzo. But finally, as evidenced in the plot itself, this is a false representation. What appears to be positive and liberating at first, giving people the leisure and opportunity for finding personal fulfillment, is at last seen for what it is: confining, blind to human need, and determined to preserve its own autonomy and coherence at the expense of human life itself.

The extent to which Isabella's tragedy is socially specific is evidenced clearly in her response to the vision of the dead Lorenzo:

> "Ha! ha!" said she, "I knew not this hard life,
> I thought the worst was simple misery;
> I thought some Fate with pleasure or with strife
> Portion'd us—happy days, or else to die;
> But there is crime—a brother's bloody knife!
> Sweet Spirit, thou hast school'd my infancy:

> I'll visit thee for this, and kiss thine eyes,
> And greet thee morn and even in the skies."
>
> (329–36)

This speech gives substance to the powerful but abstract statements about circumstance that Keats makes in some of his letters (see, for instance, the "vale of soul-making" letter, *LJK* 2:100–4) and in the *Epistle to John Hamilton Reynolds,* a poem written roughly at the same time as *Isabella,* which signals the direction Keats's thought was beginning to take. Rather than attributing misery, for example, to "an eternal fierce destruction" that is regrettably yet unavoidably a constituent part of nature (as he had in the *Epistle* [97]), Keats here locates its source specifically within social life. To understand this emphasis in Isabella's statement is also to understand more fully the nature of her initial naivete, and the nature of her initiation. According to her own comments, she never doubted, even prior to Lorenzo's murder, the reality of tragedy or the difficulties inherent in human life; what she did not know was the extent to which tragedy was humanly and socially grounded, caught up in the daily and ongoing struggles for power within society. With Lorenzo's murder she is "school'd" in the harsh realities of human "crime," in the way politics controls even the most private experiences and commitments.

The poem elaborates this social interest by following Isabella's dream of the murdered Lorenzo with a series of rich symbols of social life. Like Byron, Keats does not evade the details of human violence and atrocity, dwelling on them occasionally at great length; but, again like Byron, his penchant for gore is seldom used only for purposes of sensationalism: he invests horror with social meaning. For instance, when Isabella and her old nurse find and begin digging Lorenzo's grave, their actions reveal vividly the gruesomeness of "wormy circumstance" (385):

> That old nurse stood beside her wondering,
> Until her heart felt pity to the core
> At sight of such a dismal labouring,
> And so she kneeled, with her locks all hoar,
> And put her lean hands to the horrid thing:
> Three hours they labour'd at this travail sore;
> At last they felt the kernel of the grave,
> And Isabella did not stamp and rave.
>
> (377–84)

But however grim the details are here, they are not abstractly horrid; there is a direct and very strong emphasis in the lines on manual labor under oppressive conditions, so that the scene becomes virtually a caricature of the relations of production described early in the poem. Emphatically, the labor process here is the result of, and reflects, the conditions created by prevailing structures of authority. These conditions prevent labor from being humanly productive and are surrounded everywhere by death. Indeed, that Isabella pursues her horrid work calmly suggests the extent to which existing circumstances deaden the labor process to human sensibility and destroy the possibilities and expectations of meaningful experience.

Within a world where labor is nonproductive and where human happiness is made impossible, the public contexts of human experience are gradually elided, collapsed into personal commitments, and then projected as abstractions which stand above the injustices and contradictions of social life. The significance of this elision is seen in the charged language and densely packed images used to describe the placement of Lorenzo's head in the pot of basil. This episode carries both social and religious significance, because it shows the absolute spiritual truth that Isabella comes to associate with Lorenzo's death and at the same time the brutal social facts that stand behind his death. In placing Lorenzo's head in the pot, Isabella creates, as it were, a "garden" (414), which she then invests with her very dearest hopes and sincerest spiritual energy; it is a garden that is "ever fed . . . with thin tears" (425), and that grows "thick, and green, and beautiful . . . / So that it smelt more balmy than its peers" (427). She worships the pot devotedly, committing herself entirely to its richness and beauty to such an extent that all else loses significance for her:

> And she forgot the stars, the moon, and sun,
> And she forgot the blue above the trees,
> And she forgot the dells where waters run,
> And she forgot the chilly autumn breeze;
> She had no knowledge when the day was done,
> And the new morn she saw not: but in peace
> Hung over her sweet basil evermore.
>
> (417–23)

This is an explicit and compelling symbolic rendering of the motives and contexts of human spirituality. Isabella's reverence for the pot demonstrates her sense of the purity in love, a purity that entirely (ostensibly) overarches all else, annihilating the value and even the reality of everything (especially the social relations that govern her world) outside the object and act of devotion. But the startling reality here, of course, is that this, no less than the love relationship itself described earlier in the narrative, is a utopian act, an effect of a specific set of human actions and relations. The presence of the head in the pot makes this point emphatically: the sense of spiritual truth present here results directly from (is fed by) the harsh and horrid violence that has been enacted to hold existing class relations in place.

I do not mean to push this argument over society to the point of absurdity by flattening every image into social relevance, but it is important to understand that to see the poem as a symbolic formulation of social processes entails examination of all details that help to establish the social world in which the characters move about: images and actions become charged with meaning in their relation to the context in which they are placed. The images of the garden and of spiritual commitment, combined with the utter annihilation of all sense of historical and natural context, give us a critical clue to this world, showing us yet another step in the process whereby the prevailing structures of social life are collapsed into private contexts, isolating individuals ever further from a world that controls them through both physical and ideological means, assuring that they will remain powerless to change this world. To look at the linear unfolding of the narrative action is to see initially the economic and political powers that control personal action, and then to see how these powers find their way into the most cherished beliefs of people under their control. This is a world that uproots history from its material base and replaces it with nostalgia, that denies meaningful personal exchange and replaces it with an idealization of love, and that prevents any richness or beauty from entering public life. Instead, it replaces these with a personally constructed beauty. In short, this is a world that displays vividly the way a culture (as Raymond Williams puts it) can "discard whole areas of significance, or reinterpret or dilute them, or convert them into forms which support or at least do not contradict the really important elements of the current hegemony."[9]

One important fact about the power relations described in the narrative is that even the construction of a purely private value scheme (exemplified in Isabella's actions) cannot exempt life from the broad, systematic, and controlling forces of culture. This becomes disturbingly clear in the brothers' response to Isabella's withdrawal from the world. The power they represent and exercise does not stop at the door of private life, even though it has been directly responsible for the privatization of life; it blasts the walls that are erected to insulate value and belief from corruption, destroying even the most private relics that have been invested with personal meaning, thus destroying all value and belief. For instance, the deception and exploitation that are associated with the brothers come to the front once more when they steal and destroy the basil pot, denying Isabella's last personal meaningful possession and thus destroying her life. Her response to this episode is telling, for she shows here the extent to which her life has already been drained of substance; that is, when she finds the pot missing, she spends her time lamenting its loss rather than concerning herself with anything to do directly with life. This is not to denigrate the importance of the pot itself, but to stress that it is a relic that signifies truth; it is not a human relationship itself, but a symbol of a human relationship. In her absolute devotion to the pot, Isabella reveals her real, if unstated, belief that life itself holds nothing of meaning for her; to lament its loss as she does shows her utter inability, after Lorenzo's death, even to see life, much as the Giaour, in Byron's first Eastern Tale, cannot envision meaning or purpose in life after he has withdrawn into the monastery. Such a position both results from powerlessness and alienation and further ensures its continuation.

A final point that bears stressing is that Keats does not stop with the description of personal life as both an effect of and a response to a particular set of social relations. He illustrates as well that these relations extend themselves relentlessly through society to the point where even they become subject to disintegration. This is an idea that finds sophisticated expression in Byron's history plays, particularly *Sardanapalus*. It turns questions of social strength and survivability away from the military and defensive capabilities of a nation to the actual makeup of society itself, stressing that a culture's real enemy is most often not another nation but its own internal power relations and system of values. And, like Byron in *Sardanapalus,* Keats suggests that a culture grounded upon the privatization of life inevitably will destroy itself.[10] The theft of the pot of basil, the plundering of relics that are valuable to others (the romantic handling of the Elgin Marbles issue is relevant here), powerfully captures the extent to which the brothers' world depends upon ever-increasing exploitation and human bloodshed and thus presses culture towards the worship of death, to the point where culture itself dies. In the final scenes, with the brothers' crazed departure, the world in which all the characters had moved about virtually explodes, leaving nothing whatsoever that is meaningful, whether personal or public.

The oppressive conditions defining this world, which move human society headlong towards fragmentation and finally to dissolution, shape and influence every aspect of life, including the nature and direction of the human imagination. The hope and beauty that characterized the brief love relationship give way at last to a view of the world that sees only death and oppression. Early in the narrative, before the workings of the world have been exposed, Isabella's "lute-string gave an echo of [Lorenzo's] name" (15), expressing her desire and hope for the "Great bliss" (71) that would come with Lorenzo's love. After the tragedies that crush her, she does not abandon song, but her poetic rendering of life now necessarily lacks any celebratory character whatsoever; it is only a song of death: "O cruelty, / To steal my basil-pot away from me!" (503–04). This shift, while obvious and expected, makes a significant point about Keats's imagination and more generally about the romantic imagination itself, illustrating vividly its social dimension. Even if the songs of the romantics often attribute hardship and suffering to some abstract human nature or even to a cosmic source (a tendency seen clearly in Byron and even in Coleridge's magical poems), the visions are finally human expressions of a world and life that have established their domination of the imagination.

* * *

The months immediately surrounding the composition of *The Eve of St. Agnes* were among the most tumultuous in Keats's life. Two significant personal experiences during this period are sometimes cited as sources of inspiration for the poem. The excitement and intensity of young love articulated in the story of Porphyro and Madeline come from the poet's newly realized love for Fanny Brawne (which had blossomed Christmas day 1818), while the poetic retreat from epic (i.e., from *Hyperion*) into romance is a response to the pressures and despair arising from the death of Keats's younger brother, Tom, whom Keats had nursed devotedly for months. These experiences, it is said, elucidate many of the poem's formal and thematic dimensions as well. As Stuart Sperry notes, they help to explain "the powerful contrasts that dominate the poem, the play of light against darkness, warmth against cold, gratification against denial, life against death."[11]

While these events certainly are important, they are not the only shaping influences on the narrative, and perhaps they are not the most significant. By 1818, political, social, and historical considerations had taken on new importance for Keats, occupying his attention to an unprecedented degree. In the same letter in which he notified George and Georgiana of young Tom's death, he remarked that "the going[s] on of the world make me dizzy" (*LJK* 2:5), a statement that not only reflects his great personal distress at the loss of his brother but also illustrates his amazement at the swirl of political developments in late 1818 and early 1819. Every issue of the *Examiner,* which Keats read faithfully, during these months carried some new account of a major event or controversy: the heated Westminster elections, the declining British financial situation (Keats states directly that he feared "a national Bankruptcy" [*LJK* 2:62]), Cobbett's attack on Morris Birbeck's Albion settlement in Illinois, efforts to reform Parliament, the treatment of Napoleon after Waterloo, the atrocities of Ferdinand VII of Spain, and much more. That Keats was responsive to these national and international post-Waterloo political issues can be seen everywhere in his letters as well as in the company he kept during these years. In a letter to his brother and sister-in-law dated 14 October 1818 (i.e., when Tom's illness had become quite severe and was absorbing much of Keats's time and emotional energy)[12] he expresses forthrightly his critical judgment of the British political situation: "as for Politics they are in my opinion only sleepy because they will soon be too wide awake—Perhaps not—for the long and continued Peace of England itself has given us notions of personal safety which are likely to prevent the reestablishment of our national Honesty—There is of a truth nothing manly or sterling in any part of the Government" (*LJK* 1:396). Such judgments and speculations are frequent in the letters during these months, as Keats offered assessments of public figures ranging from Hunt to Burdett, lamented the absence in the contemporary world of such honest radicals as Algernon Sidney (who had lived two centuries before), complained about Napoleon (and also acknowledged his greatness), cast aspersions on the leaders of the American Revolution (Franklin and Washington), and noted his reading of the *Examiner*. He also talked with John Snook about "Religion and politicts [*sic*]" (*LJK* 2:60) and with David Lewis about Cobbett and about Lewis's "favorite democrat papers" (*LJK* 2:63).

Many of these political issues were incorporated (in ways that I shall discuss in the following chapter) into *Hyperion*, Keats's first serious self-conscious attempt to use poetry as Milton had done to articulate a political and historical vision.[13] When this project collapsed, perhaps due to the despair brought on by the death of Tom but also due to his dissatisfaction with his formulation of the many and complex issues in the poem, he turned to a simpler poetic form and within the span of one month or less composed an initial draft of the *Eve of St. Agnes*. But this should not be construed as a retreat from politics. In devoting his attention to old romance, Keats was following a strategy he had employed earlier in *Isabella*, relying on a relatively flexible and (for him) simple poetic form for the articulation of politically significant ideas. Much like Byron in the Eastern Tales, poems which seem self-consciously to turn away from social reality, Keats displaces into exotic narrative many public (and intellectual) issues, making them poetically more manageable, if poetically less sophisticated.

Written at least partly while he was visiting his radical friend John Snook at Bedhampton in late January 1819,[14] the *Eve* articulates, at least on one level, Keats's vision of social life in the years immediately following Waterloo, when expanding military power worldwide threatened unprecedented slaughter and social change. In a letter of October 1818, he states explicitly his position regarding post-Waterloo politics. Speaking of Napoleon, he remarks to his brother and sister-in-law:

> The worst thing he has done is, that he has taught them how to organize their monstrous armies—The Emperor Alexander it is said intends to divide his Empire as did Diocletian—creating two Czars

beside himself, and continuing the supreme Monarch of the whole—
Should he do this and they for a series of Years keep peaceable among
themselves Russia may spread her conquest even to China—I think a
very likely thing that China itself may fall Turkey certainly will—
Meanwhile european north Russia will hold its horns against the rest
of Europe, intriguing constantly with France. (*LJK* 1:397)

Such a view of international politics, and of the militarization of the modern world, helps to explain why (as the characterizations of Hildebrand, Maurice, and even Porphyro emphatically demonstrate) in the poem diplomacy does not exist and military power and physical violence are the rule rather than the exception.

But the poem is not mainly about history at the conjunctural level; it is not simply an allegory of the political events of the moment surrounding Keats—even if these events are the most immediate influence—as the setting of the story in the premodern world indicates. At a deeper and more interesting level, the *Eve* turns to past history to consider a social system of belief and value at the moment of severe historical crisis, dramatizing both the causes and consequences of that crisis. Moreover, the feudal setting enables Keats to emphasize not only historical crisis, but also, and equally important, historical continuity, because the crisis of feudalism—as Keats knew from his extensive reading in history—was also, inevitably, a crisis of the present, as it was both the forces and relations of production and the system of values of Keats's own world that had invaded and destroyed feudalism. On this view, the portrayal, for instance, of religion, personal relationships, individualism, and political authority under feudalism—all significant concerns in the *Eve*—constitutes not only a description of the past but also a disclosure of the present. Thus, while the poem may be seen as an allegory of the inner workings of feudalism at the moment of its collapse—as a portrait of past history—it must also be seen in terms of the present, in terms of the modern bourgeois poet's vision of that collapse—a point that insists that poetry is implicated in the shifting structures of authority that the poet movingly and vividly presents.

The literary sources and traditions of medieval subject matter in romantic poetry, and specifically in the *Eve*, have often been noted, and I do not here wish to retrace this ground.[15] However, I do believe that it is important, before examining the *Eve*, to mention several historical accounts of feudalism written during the period, not because they are sources for the narrative but because they are presented by writers whom Keats greatly respected. They may thus provide some insight into his own views of the past and of historical change, as well as into his poetic formulation of these.

One of Keats's favorite historians was William Robertson, who wrote lengthy accounts of the discovery of the Americas and of European and

Scottish history. One work by Robertson that Keats read at Enfield was *The History of the Reign of Charles the Fifth,* a sweeping study of how "the powers of Europe were formed into one great political system" during Charles's reign as Holy Roman Emperor during the first half of the sixteenth century. The historical importance of the era of Charles V, according to Robertson, is that "the great events which happened then have not hitherto spent their force. The political principles and maxims then established still continue to operate.... The age of Charles the Fifth may therefore be considered as the period at which the political state of Europe began to assume a new form."[16] In other words, the structures of social life erected in the sixteenth century were the same structures of social life in Keats's day as well. Thus, for Robertson, an investigation of Charles's era provided an important basis for any assessment of the present.

One key to understanding the modern world that Charles V helped to create, Robertson believed, was an adequate understanding of the old world—i.e., feudalism—that had preceded it. To this end he wrote a "preliminary volume" describing feudalism and the "causes and events" that destroyed it.[17] In a wide-ranging collection of short essays presented under the general title *Proofs and Illustrations,* Robertson sketches the dominant features of the feudal world. At its center, he maintains, was the overriding value of "property in land."[18] Echoing certain fundamental assumptions of social contract theorists of the period, he notes that prior to the Middle Ages land was used to reward soldiers who had participated in military conquest. Because these soldiers then "were in some danger . . . of being disturbed by the remainder of the ancient inhabitants, and in still greater danger of being attacked by successive colonies of barbarians as fierce and rapacious as themselves, they saw the necessity of coming under obligations to defend the community more explicit than those to which they had been subject in their original habitations."[19] Slowly, through a variety of developmental stages, a new social system emerged: ". . . after the death of Charlemagne, when there was scarcely any union among the different members of the community, and individuals were exposed, single and undefended by government, to rapine and oppression, it became necessary for every man to have a powerful protector, under whose banner he might range himself and obtain security against enemies whom singly he could not oppose."[20] In addition to the emerging role of landed property under feudalism, Robertson discusses the developing importance of agriculture (the respective roles of slaves, *villani,* and freemen), books and printing, religion (especially the crusades), customs and manners, the extension of feudal political power, commerce, the military, and the social significance of hospitality.[21] His account is meant to be a general and yet comprehensive portrait of a social world that was born out of struggle and hardship only to be destroyed in its turn by the powers and institutions of the modern world.

A more concise description of feudalism appears in Hazlitt's *The Life of Napoleon Buonaparte* (1828), published after Keats's death but nonetheless relevant as a historical document characterizing a period to which romantic poets repeatedly turned and relevant specifically to the vision of the past offered in the *Eve*. According to Hazlitt,

> The feudal system was in full vigour almost up to the period of the discovery of printing. . . . Before the diffusion of knowledge and inquiry, governments were for the most part of the growth of brute force or of barbarous superstition. Power was in the hands of a few, who used it only to gratify their own pride, cruelty, or avarice, and who took every means to extend and cement it by fear and favour. . . . Each petty sovereign shut himself up in his castle or fortress, and scattered havoc and dismay over the unresisting country around him. . . . The lord himself had no other measure of right than his own will: his pride and passions would blind him to every consideration of conscience or humanity. . . . Religion, instead of curbing this state of rapine and licentiousness, became an accomplice and a party in the crime: granting the forgiveness of Heaven in return for a rich jewel or fat abbey-lands, and setting up a regular . . . traffic in violence, cruelty, and lust.[22]

Whether or not this is a totally fair and accurate account of the Middle Ages, it is a description that was commonplace during the romantic period, and is consistent with Keats's view of the past (as evidenced not only in the *Eve* but also in *Isabella* and elsewhere) as volatile and often oppressive.

Many other historical studies—some serious, some popular—that were read in Keats's day offer similar accounts of the Middle Ages.[23] This suggests that the poetic interest in feudalism (as seen in the work of Scott, Coleridge, Moore, Byron, Keats, and others) was not simply the result of nostalgic longing for a supposedly pure and idyllic past when people were noble in mind and deed, even if much of the poetry of the period made it appear this way. Poetic interest in the Middle Ages was, at least on one level, part of the larger historical and intellectual desire (or need) to understand a world that had been destroyed and then replaced by structures of authority that continued to dominate the modern world. This insight is important to a critical investigation of a poetic "romance" such as the *Eve* because it helps to illustrate that the purely formal and literary historical matters, which Keats scholars have most often emphasized, are determined in large measure by sociohistorical considerations. That is, historical context and historical content—i.e., social relations, structures of authority, structures of belief, and so on—are always poetically significant and often are poetically decisive.

The late eighteenth- and early nineteenth-century view that feudalism was characterized very largely by violence, physical power, and politically-interested religion is perfectly consistent with Keats's handling of feudalism in the *Eve*. Hildebrand, Maurice, and Porphyro are all shown to be potentially or actually violent; the former two are described by old Angela as part of a "blood-thirsty race" (99), and Porphyro is presented as being not only deceptive but also willing to engage in combat with his foes. But the fact of physical violence in the narrative is perhaps a less significant feature of Keats's feudal world than religion, which is presented directly in terms of the connections between systems of belief and systems of political power. Under feudalism, a beadsman (Keats's representative of orthodox religion in the narrative) was not motivated entirely by a pure love for or devotion to God. Rather, paid to pray for others, he was bound by economic conditions to a specific social function that directly implicated his religious practices in the prevailing structures of social and political authority. He was a paid servant who assured that religion was visible in the aristocratic ranks, even if religious sincerity, devotion, and practice were absent.

This understanding of the social role of Keats's beadsman, the first and last character described in the poem, not only emphasizes the unfulfilling value scheme that prevails in the world of the narrative; it also helps to explain the characterization of the individual beadsman himself. While his social function exposes a larger and morally bankrupt set of social relations, it does not follow automatically that he is the source of a corrupt world—the world exposed by his social role is not reducible to individual malice or deception. No less than other characters in the poem, his life is determined in quite specific ways by conditions over which he has no control, so that his activities are an instance of the workings of the larger social world rather than the source. As the narrative stresses, the beadsman himself is perhaps as "pious" (7) and "holy" (10) as anyone in his world; but he is not an entirely free agent promoting a cause of his choice (see, for instance, the final line of the poem). His individual beliefs—whatever they may be—are secondary to the political framework and consequences of his activities, which include praying for the salvation of the debauched aristocracy inside the castle who pay his fee. This is not to say that individual practice is without individual significance, but to insist that it is always socially implicated—and often in ways that are obscured by the individual actions themselves. In this case, what we see in the character of the impoverished beadsman is that religion as a social institution has little to do with the sanctity of community life, and much to do with maintaining the ruling elite.

To distinguish in this way the beadsman's individual actions from the larger social context within which those actions take place is to see his character in a more positive light than many critics do, because it makes possible a clearer view of what his literal physical situation involves. His social position obligates him to practice self-denial and to endure the cold hard environment against which aristocracy is insulated. If his is a life defined by hardship and denial, this is not only because spiritual belief demands them; it is also because aristocracy demands them. Indeed, his difficulties must be seen as one measure of aristocratic triumph—he pays with his life (as we see at the end of the narrative) for the complacency of a class that owns him.

This view of the beadsman emphasizes that in the feudal world as Keats presents it, religious practice is significant in socially specific ways. Such labors as the beadsman performs deny meaning and fulfillment for him even as they serve to prop up the prevailing system of social authority. The extent to which this denial and hardship can destroy pleasure and crush the human imagination are seen vividly in his responses early on to art objects of one sort or another. Praying directly to heaven rather than to the Virgin (a detail that may be seen to distinguish personal need from institutional reality), the beadsman's "frosted breath / . . . / Seem'd taking flight for heaven, without a death, / Past the sweet Virgin's picture" (6–9). As he leaves the chapel, too, "he passeth by" (17) "the sculptur'd dead" (14) of the aristocracy, without giving thought to "how they may ache in icy hoods and mails" (18). Finally, once outside the chapel, he hears "music's golden tongue" (20) from within the walls of the castle, but "another way he went" (25). While his refusal to acknowledge the beauty or even presence of these works of art perhaps results most directly from his vows of asceticism, it also points to the divisions that characterize his world, and suggests the extent to which art is socially and politically controlled and made to support interests that compromise the beadsman. Under such circumstances, human pleasure in works of art is impossible. Painting, sculpture, and music decorate the aristocratic world that the beadsman serves; thus, although they are signs of aristocratic accomplishment, they are also signs of the beadsman's degradation, signs that "the joys of all his life were said and sung" (23) and that only poverty, sadness, and death are left to him in this world. No less than religion, art is under the control of a specific ruling class; the control of art is also the control of people, as evidenced in the responses of the beadsman.[24]

The extreme fixity of social boundaries in the beadsman's world (and the repression that is inherent in this) suggests the fundamental instability of this world. Indeed, Keats portrays feudalism at a moment of severe crisis. Even as he establishes the various features of feudalism, calling attention especially to the physical and ideological means of social control, he invests them with a curious anxiety that raises questions about their permanence. In the tense descriptions of the cold natural world in stanza one (that is, of the owl, the hare, and the sheep) as well as in numerous details that create the tone of the story, anxiety is a dominant feature. The statues of the "angels, ever eager-eyed" (34), "the music, yearning like a god in pain" (56), Madeline's sighs "for Agnes' dreams" (63) and her "anxious" lips (65), Angela's fear that Porphyro will be found out in the castle, and Porphyro's own breathless anticipation of Madeline in her chambers—all bespeak a world of uncertainty.

This anxiety is socially pervasive and not understood—and not seen—by any characters, although it shapes their attitudes, actions, and social life in quite specific ways. The debauchery of the aristocracy is a form of denial or resignation that is seen in much romantic literature, as well as in the personal lives of certain romantic writers (notably Byron). But more than this, Keats portrays the members of the aristocracy either looking to a past world that was supposedly superior to, or at least more interesting than, the present—

> At length burst in the argent revelry,
> With plume, tiara, and all rich array,
> Numerous as shadows haunting fairily
> The brain, new stuff'd, in youth, with triumphs gay
> Of old romance. These let us wish away. . . .
> (37–41)[25]

—or to an ideal, transhistorical sphere, which is also believed to be preferable to the present:

> . . . in vain
> Came many a tiptoe, amorous cavalier,
> And back retir'd, not cool'd by high disdain,
> But she [Madeline] saw not: her heart was otherwhere:
> She sigh'd for Agnes' dreams, the sweetest of the year.
> (59–63)

Not a single character in the narrative is presented as socially whole, nor even as seriously committed to meeting human need and desire through productive social action. This emphatically suggests that, under the conditions set down in the poem, productive human investment in the world is impossible. The beadsman is bound to a social role that pushes him headlong toward "unsought for" (378) death; Maurice, Hildebrand, and the other aristocrats are given over to debauchery, while threatening use of the sword against any who may challenge their authority; old Angela abandons her loyalty to Madeline to aid Porphyro, a foe of the family; Madeline finds nothing of value in her life as it is. In short, even as Keats very effectively describes the dominant features of the feudal world—aristocratic position, military power, religion at the service of the estate, and so on—he shows this world ready to come apart at the seams, disrupting every detail in feudal life even as he sets them down as its constituent features. This severe historical anxiety provides one basis for explaining the wish fulfillment in the poem that Sperry and others have noted,[26] and it must be seen as a key to connecting and understanding the various individual actions and attitudes through the narrative.[27]

I want now to offer a set of explanations for the anxiety just described, arguing first that it arises from the encroachment of mercantilism, commercialism, and capitalism into the feudal world. Certain details and episodes inscribed in the narrative itself provide a credible basis for such argument. In addition, I want to argue that this encroachment brings with it the construction of a new system of social values, seen most clearly within the story in the changing social significance of religion and women. While these arguments are of course speculative, nonetheless they offer a useful starting point, I believe, for attempting to understand the poem anew along materialist historical lines. Further, they are necessary to any attempt to situate Keats's poetic vision historically or, put differently, to any attempt to explain how Keats viewed his own position within a developing historical framework.

The most significant historical detail in the poem is presented once Porphyro has hidden himself in Madeline's room. In describing the excited Porphyro bringing from out of Madeline's closet the various items that will be part of his ritual, the narrator mentions "manna and dates, in argosy transferr'd / From Fez; and spicèd dainties, every one, / From silken Samarcand to cedar'd Lebanon" (268–70). These are the only references in the final draft of the poem to specific place names (with the exception of Provence);[28] this alone is enough reason to make them interesting and perhaps significant. The fact that the references are to cities that played a major role in the commercial development of the West gives them central importance to the poem's social dimension.

Keats could have come across these names virtually anyplace. Some or all of them are mentioned in passing or in detail in the writings of Robertson, Voltaire, Mavor, and other historians (not to mention the Bible) he had read, and I do not wish here to speculate on what the precise sources may have been. Rather, I wish to discuss briefly several accounts of these cities and of commercialism generally that appeared in the histories of the period in an attempt to establish Keats's awareness and probable understanding of the historical significance of his references and to establish their role as a source of tension and historical anxiety in the narrative.

In his history of Charles V, Robertson speaks directly and frequently of the development of commercialism. His general position is that with the rise of commerce came the rise of the modern political state, turning political attention away from the more brutal occupations of the Middle Ages, and disposing nations "to peace, by establishing in every state an order of citizens bound by their interests to be the guardians of public tranquillity."[29] While many examples from both past and present history could be adduced to challenge such a generalization, it nonetheless correctly stresses that commerce was a central ingredient in historical change from the Middle Ages to the Modern Age, and that commerce created a new class of people and hence a new kind of state organization.

Of equal interest are Robertson's observations about the original geographical location of commercial development and about the kinds of commodities that were most important to that development. "The Italians," he remarks, "by their connection with Constantinople and other cities of the Greek empire, had preserved in their own country considerable relish for the precious commodities and curious manufactures of the East."[30] And in his discussion of the Middle Ages he sketches the specific commodities and manufactures that developed out of the East. After the Crusades, Italy not only imported various "Indian commodities," but also "established manufactures of curious fabric in their own country." First among these was "the manufacture of silk, which had long been peculiar to the eastern provinces of Asia."[31] In addition to silk, sugar became a prized commodity and "appears to have been a considerable article in the commerce of the Italian states."[32]

With respect to the actual place names themselves, two writers, Voltaire and Samuel Purchas, offer specific accounts of Fez. In his *Ancient and Modern History,* Voltaire includes a brief description of "the Kingdom of Fez and Morocco," which stresses the tumult that this region historically has experienced, ranging from its defeat at the hands of the Portuguese to its presentation by this nation to Charles II of England, who "afterward ceded it to the kings of Morocco."[33] The region is described by Voltaire as being populated by Moors, Arabian Bedouins, and by Jews; as having long been involved in trade; and as being familiar with the sea mainly as a place of piracy and plunder. A more interesting and much more detailed account of Fez is offered in *Purchas His Pilgrimes,* which Keats never mentions in his letters but easily could have known (Coleridge, for instance, cites this work as a source for *Kubla Khan*). Purchas describes the city as a very active center for manufacture and trade where scriveners, fruit sellers, shoe merchants, milk sellers, cotton sellers, rope sellers, salt sellers, potters, sadlers, and more worked busily to make and sell their goods.

A recent study that draws on English archival material helps to explain some of the reasons why many histories and travel books of the period emphasized the details mentioned by Voltaire and Purchas. In a work entitled *Jewish Society in Fez, 1450–1700: Studies in Communal and Economic Life,* Jane S. Gerber offers a fascinating account of the British involvement in this region during the Middle Ages and immediately thereafter. Gerber gives particular attention to the sugar trade between Fez and England, noting that "unlike the grain trade where the Jews [of Fez] dealt directly with European potentates or their agents, the sugar trade was conducted largely with English merchants in an atmosphere of intense competition."[34] Although the English were often at a disadvantage in trading with Fez because "business transactions were not simultaneous"—i.e., "they would be forced to wait many months for payment" (in the form of sugar) for the goods they had brought into Fez, which allowed "the price of the sugar [to] fluctuate to their disadvantage"— nonetheless, through the sixteenth century "sugar accounted for 93% of the English imports from Morocco."[35] This trade did not diminish significantly until after 1603, when English-Moroccan political relations deteriorated as well. From this period, the Moroccan sugar trade was directed primarily to Holland.[36]

These details are especially interesting in light of the emphasis in the *Eve* on the many sweets associated with Porphyro's ritual in Madeline's bedroom:

> . . . he from forth the closet brought a heap
> of candied apple, quince, and plum, and gourd;
> With jellies soother than the creamy curd,
> And lucent syrops, tinct with cinnamon;
> Manna and dates, in argosy transferr'd
> From Fez. . . .
>
> (264–69)[37]

Once these lines are placed in the context of the English sugar trade and more generally in the context of English international economic relations, it becomes clear that the feudal world Keats is describing is not a static entity, even if it appears so, but is in fact constantly changing; it is part of an ongoing chain of historical events that are elided by both physical and ideological means. Although the system of values described in the poem is predominantly feudal, it is dependent upon other values and activities that challenge the prevailing world order even while they support it.

The reference to "silken Samarcand" (270) is similarly charged with historical significance. In his account of feudalism (noted above),

Robertson writes specifically about the Eastern silk industry in a way that is directly relevant to the *Eve*. In his account of the benefits accruing to Italian commerce after the crusades, he notes that "silk stuffs were of such high price in ancient Rome that only a few persons of the first rank were able to purchase them. . . . Roger I, King of Sicily, about the year 1130, carried off a number of artificers in the silk-trade from Athens, and, settling them in Palermo, introduced the culture of silk into his kingdom, from which it was communicated to other parts of Italy. This seems to have rendered silk so common that about the middle of the fourteenth century a thousand citizens of Genoa appeared in one procession in silk robes."[38] While Samarkand is not mentioned in this description, Robertson illustrates clearly the major role that silk played in the Middle Ages as a sign of social position and power; moreover, as Miriam Allott notes in her edition of Keats's poetry, Samarkand was "famous for its wealth and as a market for silks."[39] Like the reference to Fez, the reference to Samarkand calls attention to a source of the goods and material wealth that are enjoyed without question by the characters in the narrative—and by modern readers and critics of Keats's poem. Throughout the poem are descriptions of "golden dishes," "baskets bright / Of wreathed silver," "pearls," "warmed jewels," Madeline's "silken" chamber, a "silver cross," and much more, all of which bespeak luxury without acknowledging a source.[40]

Perhaps the most interesting and significant reference to Eastern trade centers is to "cedar'd Lebanon." Miriam Allott speculates that this is a reference to Psalms 104:16: "The trees of the Lord are full *of sap:* the cedars of Lebanon, which he hath planted."[41] While this may be the most direct source for the reference, it does little to explain its significance within the larger context of the narrative, for it fails to explain the role of either the place name or its association with lumber. Another biblical reference to Lebanon that perhaps throws a bit more light on the matter occurs in the Song of Solomon 3:9–10: "King Solomon made himself a chariot of the wood of Lebanon. / He made the pillars thereof *of* silver, the bottom thereof *of* gold, the covering of it *of* purple, the midst thereof being paved *with* love, for the daughters of Jerusalem." While this passage never mentions cedar by name, it does assign a role or function to Lebanese timber and thus, by implication, explains the practical reason for Lebanon's association with cedar: this region of the East has always been known for its building timber. Samuel Purchas makes this same point, noting especially the use of Lebanese timber in the shipbuilding industry: "Don John di Castro speakes of this Fleet of Salomon, and sayth, the Timber whereof it was made was brought from Libanon and Antilabanon (so little signs saw hee, or heard of any Trees or Wood in these parts) and saith, that from Toro all the Coast is West, and without any Port but Sues, and that therefore Cleopatras Fleet was brought by Land from Nilua, to Sues over the Isthmos."[42] Such historical details suggest that the reference to Lebanon provides a point of contact between Fez, Samarkand, and the Western feudal world occupied by Porphyro and Madeline: Lebanon (arguably) provides the raw materials from which the "argosy" (268) that transports goods is built.[43]

"Fez," "silken Samarcand," and "cedar'd Lebanon," in short, are inscribed in the narrative as the sources for the material goods that constitute the wealth of the feudal world, although these sources are so taken for granted as to be virtually invisible. These locations are not allowed to occupy a central place in the descriptions of feudalism because the coherence and power of feudalism depend upon their marginalization. In addition, these place names provide an important insight into the anxiety that is pervasive in the narrative, because they point to a set of social and economic relations that refuse to remain marginalized. That is, the power of trade, the expansion of the world, the increasing influx of commercial wealth into the structures of feudal life are disruptive of all social stability, and they finally—as Robertson and Hazlitt argue—overturn aristocratic feudal rule.

To historicize the place names in the narrative and to focus on the tension between an old feudal aristocracy and an inchoate commercial culture is to begin to establish a sociohistorical context within which to interpret the specific characters and episodes in the poem. I want to make an attempt in this direction by considering several possible historical-critical explanations for Porphyro. Again I do not insist that these explanations can be verified by authorial intention (though the particular kind of reading Keats was doing during these years in both history and literature suggests that such an argument could be made); rather, I suggest that they can be used to politicize the poem and to situate it historically.

The point of connection between the speculations that follow is the assertion that Porphyro, despite his ostensible aristocratic social position, is most fully understood in terms of the forces that are invading and disrupting feudal order. This is seen first and most clearly of course in his literal secretive venture into the castle, where he seduces and then escapes with Madeline. But to focus only on these plot episodes is to remain entrapped within an individualist or subjectivist critical perspective, which obligates us to interpret narrative action solely in terms of individual choice, eliding the deep social contradictions and struggles that set the terms of that choice. To move beyond such a perspective it is necessary to explore the various ways that characters—in this case, Porphyro—can be positioned within the larger networks of social conflict inscribed in the narrative, so that they are not seen merely as transparent and self-constituted identities but rather as concretizations of a multiplicity of relations. This is not to deny their individuality, but to refuse to regard individuality as an unmediated given.

The name Porphyro itself has particular significance, especially in the context of the commercial forces represented by the Eastern trading centers, discussed above. One meaning of his name is *purple;* moreover, the so-called "purple industry" flourished in Lebanon in antiquity. The history of this industry is discussed concisely by Philip K. Hitti, who traces the various regions where purple first became popular. The Greek interest in purple, for example, is related in an anecdote about Helen of Troy. Helen, "strolling along the beach to while away her captivity, noticed how a shellfish which her dog had chewed turned its mouth into a deep purple colour, which she so admired that she expected any suitor before receiving any favour to produce a dress dyed with *porphyra.* But," Hitti stresses, "the Tyrian purple [that is, the purple from southern Lebanon] was the most famous and most precious of the dyes of antiquity."[44] It "is mentioned among the articles of luxury imported by Venetian merchants in the late eighth Christian century. In the Byzantine period the privilege of making the dye was confined to a small group and after the fall of the empire the knowledge of it was almost completely lost in the East. In England, where it was carried from the East, the industry survived in isolated regions as late as the seventeenth century."[45] The relevance of this information to the historical development of commercial trade, and of both to the *Eve,* is suggested by Hitti's comment, immediately following his discussion of porphyra, about the growth of navigation in the East, which was facilitated in large measure by the Lebanese "cedar logs, unsurpassed in durability."[46]

These historical details about the origin and spread of Eastern commodities manifest themselves in the *Eve* in very interesting ways.[47] From the beginning Porphyro is described in terms true to his name, as when he is struck with the "stratagem" (139) for winning Madeline: "Sudden a thought came like a full-blown rose, / Flushing his brow, and in his pained heart / Made purple riot" (136–38). And the "purple industry" impresses itself on the world of the poem elsewhere as well. When Madeline retires to bed, for example, her linen is described as "smooth, and lavender'd" (263),[48] while the casement in her room is

> All garlanded with carven imag'ries
> Of fruits, and flowers, and bunches of knot-grass,
> And diamonded with panes of quaint device,
> Innumerable of stains and splendid dyes,
> As are the tiger-moth's deep-damask'd wings.
>
> (209–13)

Just as Porphyro himself has quietly and secretively invaded the world presided over by Maurice and Hildebrand, the commodities of the East have found their way into this world to the point where the social and economic relations that make their existence possible threaten to dismantle feudalism altogether. It should be stressed here, however, that it is not the East per se that is disruptive, but rather commerce, which of course is controlled by the West.

If Porphyro's name enables us to see his character as one concretization of a set of economic relations that invade feudalism, it also enables us to consider him as a carrier of certain ideological relations that arise with commerce.[49] Specifically, he can be associated with religion and worship in at least two ways. First, as the *Oxford English Dictionary* notes, a Porphyre is "a kind of serpent" that is "about the bigness of a span or more, which in outward aspect is like to the most beautiful and well coloured Purple." To view Keats's hero in these terms of course is to see him as a subversive in an idyllic or edenic past world, one who seduces the innocent female away from the structures of authority and everyday life that heretofore have constituted reality. In this respect, the narrative action reenacts the biblical Fall, calling our attention to the way systems of value and belief change as material situations change. Secondly, and relatedly, Miriam Allot notes that Porphyro's name is "perhaps suggested by Burton's references to the neo-Platonist Porphyrius in *The Anatomy of Melancholy.*"[50] Porphyry is also mentioned in Gibbon's *Decline,* which Keats had been reading during 1818 (see *LJK* 1:237 and 369) and extensively in *Volney's Ruins,* which he never mentions in his letters but easily could have known through his contacts with the Hunt-Hazlitt-Shelley circle. The significance of the philosopher for the point made above about religion and worship in the *Eve* is that he was a staunch antagonist of Christianity, and thus his name adds historical scope to the denial by Keats's hero of the various Christian rituals and beliefs that he encounters in the castle, from his willingness to provoke violence "upon holy days" (119) to his intrusion into the religious ritual that Madeline is observing.

Porphyro's name, in short, combines both commercial and religious elements that directly challenge the structures of authority controlling Madeline's world. This is not to say that he is the embodiment of an absolute evil, but rather that his character enables us to see certain disruptive historical forces at work, which come to be interpreted—by Maurice and Hildebrand, for instance—as absolute evil. That is, the serpentine dimension of his character must not be read simply allegorically in terms of the myth of the Fall, but must be historicized, combined with the rise of commercialism, which his name also evokes.

To associate Porphyro with the serpent of the biblical Eden and with the anti-Christian Greek philosopher is not to deny him the capacity for sincerity or worship. In fact his entire pilgrimage, characterized most compellingly by his willingness to place his life in danger for what he loves and believes, is motivated by his devotion to Madeline. This fact emphasizes not only his individual capacity for love; more generally, it indicates a secularization of worship—that is, a shift of belief from God to the world that does not abandon the rituals and vocabulary of Christian belief. This point is made early in the narrative when Porphyro arrives at the castle hoping "that he might gaze and worship all unseen; / Perchance speak, kneel, touch, kiss—in sooth such things have been" (80–81).[51] Driven by physical desire, his actions and attitudes take on the vocabulary and the piety of the system of belief that he is disrupting. The point is made explicitly again near the end of the poem after he completes his own personal ritual of devotion. Madeline awakens, only to hear Porphyro say to her: "Ah, silver shrine, here will I take my rest / After so many hours of toil and quest, / A famish'd pilgrim" (337–39). Clearly Porphyro has usurped a system of belief that is grounded in a transcendental or transhistorical notion of power, turning it to his own libidinous advantage.

Although Porphyro's actions are often seen as a necessary corrective to both the beadsman's and Madeline's sterile and cold otherworldliness,[52] in fact they dramatize a very real and specific type of domination that arises alongside the emergence of commercial culture—namely, the domination of women. The humanization of religious belief as Keats presents it is also the privatization of desire and it has direct implications for the role of women in society. The masculine humility, sincerity, and piety displayed toward women is purchased with deception and sheer masculine will, a fact that has been demonstrated convincingly by Jack Stillinger in one of the most famous and most interesting essays on the poem.[53] To historicize the issues that Stillinger raises is to expose the poem's political and patriarchal dimensions.

We can begin to understand the importance of gender relations in the narrative by considering the significance of the poem's title. The subject of the *Eve*, as we know from Woodhouse, was suggested to Keats by Isabella Jones. Keats may have read about St. Agnes in Burton, Jonson, or in John Brand's *Observations on the Popular Antiquities*. The description in the latter work is particularly interesting in terms of the narrative action. According to Brand, "St. Agnes was a Roman virgin and martyr, who suffered in the tenth persecution under the Emperor Dioclesian, A.D. 306. She was condemned to be debauched in the public stews before her execution, but her virginity was miraculously preserved by lightning and thunder from heaven. About eight days after her execution, her parents, going to lament and pray at her tomb, saw a vision of angels, among whom was their daughter, and a lamb standing by her as white as snow, on which account it is that in every graphic representation of her there is a lamb pictured by her side."[54] One irony here is that Keats sets his story of passion during a religious holiday celebrating virginity; but, more than this, he presents a startling difference between Agnes, the young woman of legend, and Madeline, the young woman of his story, for unlike Agnes, Madeline's virginity is not preserved. Madeline, indeed, is debauched, physically subjected to masculine passion—and in public, at least insofar as the reader is witness to the event—so that whatever ideal she is made to represent (and Keats does represent her in idealized terms, as is made clear in Porphyro's outpourings after his passion has been spent) is the product of Porphyro's conquest of her. She is woman as the Other, as the silent and passive object of masculine power that makes the masculine transcendental ego possible; she is the site whereon masculine identity is stamped; she is, in short, without identity except insofar as she receives identity from that which controls her. And, again, this control is not simply ideological—not simply the result of Madeline's being "Hoodwink'd with faery fancy" (70)—but physical as well: sexuality in this instance is not only the expression of a benign energy; it is a form of political power. When Porphyro "melted" "into her dream" (320), the hope (however naive) and innocence represented by the legend of St. Agnes melt also. Madeline awakens to the cold reality of masculine domination that speaks of "trust" (342) only after the feminine has been entirely conquered, that worships woman only when she is under man's control.

The ideological dimension of this process of control and domination is presented quite interestingly in the narrative descriptions of how the legend of St. Agnes is passed down from generation to generation. Madeline learns the "legends old" (135) from "old dames" (45) who spin tales of love and hope, and of dream lands untouched by the sordid activities that define their actual lives:

> They told her how, upon St. Agnes' Eve,
> Young virgins might have visions of delight,
> And soft adorings from their loves receive
> Upon the honey'd middle of the night,
> If ceremonies due they did aright.
>
> (46–50)

Women are instrumental in perpetuating a set of illusions that weaken rather than empower them. Thus, they are implicated directly in the structures of authority governing the feudal world. But this does not turn them into conspirators: their actions are not a deliberate show and exercise of power in the way that Maurice's, Hildebrand's, or the "argent revelry" (37) are; rather, they are the product of a social environment that denies public power and even hope to women. Like the "youth" (40) who are immersed in "old romance" (41), and like Porphyro who sincerely worships Madeline, they do no more than live out their lives in an anxious and crisis-ridden world, looking (again like the knights and like Porphyro) for a domain of human investment that is more meaningful than the one they have inherited. That their efforts in fact take them further away from real control over their lives (as witnessed not only in Madeline's vulnerability, but also in the spiritual status of Agnes and the servile status of Angela) is a sign of the mystification of the social relations and political struggles that entrap them. In such a situation, feminine practice—performing rituals of self denial (as Madeline does) or acting as an accomplice to assure the success of one man's "stratagem" (139) against a woman (as Angela does)—contributes to feminine powerlessness. This is not to say that there are no discriminations to be made as to the relative virtue or evil of the various actions described in the narrative—the actions of men in this story are clearly signs of oppressive power—but rather that none of the characters stands outside the structures of authority and belief which prevail.

An additional matter that helps to locate the role of women in the changing nature of patriarchal relations from feudalism to commercialism can be seen in the descriptions of labor in the story.[55] This is a highly complex issue, and I do not wish to do more here than suggest that the presentation of labor is gender-specific and that this presentation helps to elucidate the nature of social change being described. First, with the exception of Agnes and Madeline, women are presented in terms of labor; thus (following Marx)[56] they must be seen as the source of value within culture, although the ideological structures of authority in the narrative invert this fact. For instance Angela, as the castle servant, exemplifies the actual role of most women under feudalism, a role that underwrites the actions of men; the material significance of her role, however, is obscured not only by the negative characteristics associated with her but also, and more tellingly, by the masculine obsession with Madeline as a virtual spirit (note, for instance, the description of Madeline's "maiden eyes divine" [57])[57] and by the tendency of powerful men to present themselves, not women, as toilers.

This latter point, especially, elucidates the workings of masculine authority in the world of the poem. When Porphyro enters the castle pleading with Angela to tell him where Madeline is, he alludes to the labors of women:

> "Now tell me where is Madeline," said he,
> "O tell me, Angela, by the holy loom

> Which none but secret sisterhood may see,
> When they St. Agnes' wool are weaving piously."
>
> (114–17)

But later, when he is in Madeline's room, worshipping her unseen, he speaks in very different terms, suppressing the material labor practices that produce the beautiful tapestries in celebration of St. Agnes (i.e., suppressing the fact that it is women, not Porphyro, who toil at the looms), and representing himself as one whose labors have rendered him weak: "It seem'd he never, never could redeem / From such a stedfast spell his lady's eyes; / So mus'd awhile, entoil'd in woofed phantasies" (286–88). Similarly, after he has melted into Madeline's dream, he calls her a "silver shrine" where he will "take my rest / After so many hours of toil and quest" (337–38). Just as Porphyro co-opts the language of religious orthodoxy to mystify the secularization of worship and advance his own personal libidinous interests, here he co-opts the language of labor to obscure real labor practices, and thus to secure further his position and power within the patriarchal framework of value.[58]

The material and ideological processes described here promote the domination of women at least in part by silencing them, while at the same time foregrounding the masculine voice. This is seen not only in the literal plot-level fact that Porphyro enters the world of the narrative proclaiming his intentions (105) while Madeline does not speak until very near the end of the story (307), but also in the general descriptions of what is expected of Madeline in the St. Agnes ritual. When she retires to her room to prepare for bed, for instance, she is completely silent:

> No uttered syllable, or, woe betide!
> But to her heart, her heart was voluble,
> Paining with eloquence her balmy side;
> As though a tongueless nightingale should swell
> Her throat in vain.
>
> (203–7)

When she does speak, awakened by Porphyro crawling into her bed, it is to express her desire for the transcendental masculine voice that had been heard in her dream: "Give me that voice again, my Porphyro, / Those looks immortal, those complainings dear!" (312–13). Further, her role requires complete self-denial, complete vulnerability; she retires to bed "supperless" (51), she "couch[es] supine" (52), she cannot "look behind" (53), and she cannot speak: she is absolutely stifled, a "still unravish'd bride of quietness" (*Ode on a Grecian Urn* 1) whose role is to receive her identity and her purpose from Porphyro. He indeed not only enters the castle eager and talkative, but once in Madeline's room takes over her "hollow lute" (289) to play "an ancient ditty, long since mute" (291), while Madeline is able only to "moan forth witless words" (303). His is a position of power, from which he articulates his desires and in so doing bestows her identity, while "she hurried at his words" (352), conforming herself to his expectations. In short, just as the narrative voice is masculine, characterizing the feminine as it sees fit, so within the narrative Porphyro's voice gives meaning and direction to the silent and passive Madeline.

I want to return now briefly to the more general issue discussed earlier of the changing world order from feudalism to commercialism, in the hope that the specific relations between characters just presented will help to clarify and substantiate this as the major issue in the narrative. Passing details throughout the poem emphasize the imminent demise of the world symbolized by the castle and the emerging strength of the world symbolized by the mobile Porphyro. Not only is there in the castle "a shielded scutcheon [which] blush'd with blood of queens and kings" (216), but also virtually every description of the castle itself reeks of death and decay. The mansion is "foul" (89); Maurice, like Angela, is old (90, 104); the rooms of the castle are overrun with "cobwebs" (110); and the gallery is "dusky" (186). Further, when Porphyro and Angela find a place to talk, away from revelers who are his enemies, it is in a "pale, lattic'd, chill [room], silent as a tomb" (113). At the end of the narrative, too, after Porphyro and Madeline have escaped into the storm, heading for a "home" "o'er the southern moors" (351), the "warrior-guests, with shade and form / Of witch, and demon, and large coffin-worm, / Were long be-nightmar'd" (373–75). Against these descriptions of the castle and its inhabitants, Porphyro is presented as a "child" (108, 178), a "puzzled urchin" (129), a youthful and energetic individual who both invades this exhausted world and offers an alternative to it; he promises not a "mansion foul" but a "home." His voice, his song, the exotic details of his ritual that oppose the austerity of Madeline's, his desire, and his individualism all point in the direction of the world that is to come, that will replace the old beadsman and the argent revelry alike. The followers of Hildebrand and Lord Maurice may feel the pressure of this new world, as the anxiety associated with the castle suggests, but they are unable to stop it.

This view of the narrative action and details helps to clarify the poem's conclusion, when Porphyro and Madeline leave the dying castle and "fl[y] away into the storm" (371). This conclusion is not simply a statement of transcendental escape in which, as M. A. Goldberg puts it, Madeline and Porphyro "move out of the world of human time, beyond the mortal realm of sensations."[59] Nor should it be regarded, at the other extreme, as a sign of Keats's pessimism. Rather, the social and historical contexts within which the action is set suggest that the storm into which Madeline and Porphyro move might be viewed as a sign of the ongoing difficulties and struggles of a rapidly changing world. Stated bluntly, the storm is the objective correlative of history itself. Porphyro comes across the moors, invades the castle—not militarily or with the use of physical violence, but subtly and secretively—and destroys it and everything it represents. What is revealed in the course of these developments is the tumult of a commercial and bourgeois system of cultural values and economic relations that sweep stormily across the historical landscape, redefining it in specific and yet unforeseen ways. While the beadsman, the Baron, the "warrior-guests" (373), and old Angela die or are benightmared, and while their world is forever lost, Porphyro and Madeline—and the values that have come to be associated with them—venture mysteriously into the storm, touching the deepest corners of nature itself.

The *Eve* is an astonishing example of how historical pressure shapes poetic practice. Virtually every detail can be located among the crosscurrents that eventually destroyed feudalism, thus providing an excellent point of entry into the processes of sociohistorical change. Moreover, the narrative implicates bourgeois poetic practice itself in the historical process that brought commercialism and eventually industrialism to power. Put simply, this is not an objective narrative description of past history, but a narrative written from within a very specific historical problematic, which means that the portrayal of feudalism is colored by the realities of the bourgeois world. The very issues that come to the surface in the story—the secularization of worship, personal relationships, the privatization of desire, gender relations—are issues that emerge with bourgeois society, not with feudalism; thus even as they allow us to see some of the pressures operating on a dying feudalism, they also provide a glimpse of the anxiety, alienation, and human fragmentation that came with commercial culture. While Keats perceives feudalism, his subject matter, as the raw material used in the production of his narrative, he unavoidably draws upon the assumptions and values of his own sociocultural situation. These values and assumptions ultimately help to structure the poem's meanings.[60]

In *Marxism and Form*, Fredric Jameson discusses some of the differences between preindustrial art and bourgeois art; his comments, while not directly related to the specific arguments of this essay, help to clarify what I am calling the bourgeois dimension of the *Eve*. In preindustrial art, he argues,

> social institutions are not felt as external traditions, as forbidding and incomprehensible edifices: authority is vested in the king or priest, is immanent to them. As human actors they express it fully in a three-dimensional way. The physical objects of such a world are equally

immediate: they are clearly human products, the results of preordained ritual and of an immediately visible hierarchy of village occupations. . . . The works of art characteristic of such societies may be called concrete in that their elements are all meaningful from the outset. The writer uses them, but he does not need to demonstrate their meaning beforehand.[61]

Bourgeois art, on the other hand, is more fragmented, more complex, and more individualized: "Even those most basic components of the story, the characters themselves, become problematical: now they have *personalities,* and the choice of personality traits, the portrayal of the hero as dreamy and idealistic rather than choleric and cynical, demands organic justification within the work itself." Moreover, Jameson continues, "there is . . . a separation between public and private, between work and leisure, and the story must find its elbowroom in a world in which men's lives are divided between routine drudgery and sleep."[62] Thus stories are often set on weekends or on holidays, as the *Eve* is, and the characters use this precious "free" time to discover and express their truest and deepest feelings.

The *Eve* demonstrates Jameson's point very well, for while its expressed subject matter is the preindustrial world, where political and religious hierarchy are certain, it is run through with anxiety, redefinitions of personal practice and social institutions, and presuppositions about individuality, spirituality, and personal relationships that reflect Keats's own world rather than the one that preceded it. This is not to denigrate the poem, or even to question its aesthetic integrity or intention, but to insist that Keats is, as all artists must, using the past as a way of formulating the present; the feudalism he presents is feudalism as both described and formulated from a bourgeois position within the early industrial world. The themes, characterizations, and presuppositions behind the aesthetic choices are bourgeois in nature, and the recovery of their historical specificity enables us to understand more fully the conditions under which Keats produced his work and his inability ever to escape those conditions. To view the poem in this manner is to glimpse its importance for us, for the economic, political, and patriarchal themes at the center of Keats's poetic vision are at the center of our world as well.

4
"As If Calamity Had But Begun"
HYPERION

IN late 1818 and early 1819, during the months of Tom's final illness, Keats spent much time thinking afresh about politics, society, and literature. Tom's untimely death doubtless brought home to Keats the seriousness of the poetic work to which he had devoted himself and helped to move him toward a largeness of vision that is absent in most of his earlier poems, from *Sleep and Poetry* through *Isabella*. His new sense of the power and importance of intellectual life, and his attempt to articulate his commitment to a historically aware poetry, are evident everywhere in his letters during this period. His correspondence is punctuated not only with remarks about the importance of his studies and about conversations with such radical friends as David Lewis, but also with observations on the poor quality of Hunt's poetry, the British obsession with "money-getting" (*LJK* 2:14), the death of literature (Scott and Byron, he believed, were the only "literary kings in our Time" [*LJK* 2:161]), the articles in the *Examiner* about Hobhouse and Cobbett, and more. This was a time, as he put it to Haydon, during which he had been "moulting" (*LJK* 2:32). While in the past he had "been cheated into some fine passages" (*LJK* 2:43), this was not, he now knew, the same as great poetry. Gradually he was beginning to understand the largeness of vision needed for genuine poetic accomplishment: "I see by little and little more of what is to be done, and how it is to be done, should I ever be able to do it" (*LJK* 2:32).

Probably the greatest influence on Keats's thought during these months of self-reappraisal was Hazlitt, whose essays in the *Examiner* and whose *Lectures on the English Poets* encouraged Keats to rethink the nature of the poetic imagination and its connection to politics, history, and society. In the *Lectures,* Hazlitt not only discusses such questions as poetic identity (which had interested Keats at least since 1817, when he wrote his famous "Negative Capability" letter) and the defects of modern poetry; more specifically, he speaks at length of Milton (whom Keats was carefully rereading and studying, as his annotations in his copy of Milton's poems show), attributing that poet's greatness, in part at least, to his intellectual sophistication and patience. Milton, Hazlitt says, "did not write from casual impulse, but after a severe examination of his own strength, and with a resolution to leave nothing undone which it was in his power to do."[1] This comment anticipates Keats's letter, written a few months after the *Lectures* were completed, in which he remarks to Haydon: "I have come to the resolution never to write for the sake of writing, or making a poem, but from running over with any little knowlege [sic] and experience which many years of reflection may perhaps give me—otherwise I will be dumb" (*LJK* 2:43). Until now he had written hurriedly, with the idea of completing the project at hand (note, for instance, his determination in *Endymion* to write 4,000 lines, attending primarily to the length of the poem); such a strategy, he now believed, was inadequate to great poetry, which he hoped someday to be able to write.

Keats was strongly influenced not only by Hazlitt's comments on Milton but also by his stinging attack on the conservative publisher William Gifford on the subject of the poetic imagination. In a letter to George and Georgiana Keats, Keats recounts at great length the central parts of Hazlitt's argument, and in so doing offers what may be regarded as a sort of credo for the kind of poetry he was now trying to write. Because Hazlitt's argument is critical to an understanding of Keats's poetic development, and because Keats himself saw fit to quote it at length, I wish to quote it here as it appeared in Keats's letter:

> I [Hazlitt] affi[r]m, Sir [Gifford], that Poetry, that the imagination, generally speaking, delights in power, in strong excitement, as well as in truth, in good, in right, whereas pure reason and the moral sense approve only of the true and good. I proceed to show that this general love or tendency to immediate excitement or theatrical effect, no matter how produced, gives a Bias to the imagination often consistent with the greatest good, that in Poetry it triumphs over Principle, and bribes the passions to make a sacrifice of common humanity. You say that it does not, that there is no such original Sin in Poetry, that it makes no such sacrifice or unworthy compromise between poetical effect and the still small voice of reason—And how do you prove that there is no such principle giving a bias to the imagination, and a false colouring to poetry? Why by asking in reply to the instances where this principle operates, and where no other can with much modesty and simplicity—"But are these the only topics that afford delight in Poetry &c" No; but these objects do afford delight in poetry, and they afford it in proportion to their strong and often tragical effect. . . , or their desireableness in a moral point of view. "Do we read with more

pleasure of the ravages of a beast of prey than of the Shepherds pipe upon the Mountain?" No but we do read with pleasure of the ravages of a beast of prey, and we do so on the principle I have stated, namely from the sense of power abstracted from the sense of good.... Do you mean to deny that there is any thing imposing to the imagination in power, in grandeur, in outward shew, in the accumulation of individual wealth and luxury, at the expen[s]e of equal justice and the common weal? Do you deny that there is any thing in the "Pride, Pomp and Circumstance of glorious war, that makes ambition virtue"? in the eyes of admiring multitudes? Is this a new theory of the Pleasures of the imagination, which says that the pleasures of the imagination do not rise soly in the calculations of the understanding? Is it a paradox of my creating that "one murder makes a villain millions a Hero!" or is it not true that here, as in other cases, the enormity of the evil overpowers and makes a convert of the imagination by its very magnitude? ... I have admitted that there are tyrants and slaves abroad in the world; and you would hush the matter up, and pretend that there is no such thing in order that there may be nothing else. (*LJK* 2:74–76)

What is interesting here are not only Hazlitt's comments on power and the imagination, which occupied Keats to an ever greater extent after this period, but more significantly the context within which he discusses these. The statements that Keats has chosen to copy for his brother and sister-in-law offer what is essentially a materialist explanation of the imagination; that is, it is an explanation predicated upon the assumption that poetry is historically implicated, taking its form and character from circumstance. Concomitantly the imagination and morals do not exist in a permanent sphere of pure and unchanging value; they exist within, and are determined by, specific contexts that can be known and articulated. To deny that this is so, Hazlitt informs Gifford, is to suppress the real power relations operating within every corner of society and thus to assure that injustice and tyranny will prevail. Such a position focuses upon the internal makeup and essential contradictions within social formations themselves, rather than assuming that a given culture (say, England) can be fully homogeneous and that all threats to this homogeneity come from the outside. This view of the imagination, I believe, helps to explain why Keats returns repeatedly during this period (see for instance the famous vale of soul-making letter [*LJK* 2:102–4]) to the question of circumstance and its shaping influence on human experience, and why, further, he speaks with increasing frequency in his letters during this period of politics, history, and social change. These concerns find their way directly and in important ways into his poetic practice.

Hyperion is Keats's first major effort to combine the intellectual sophistication of Milton's poetic vision with the complex social, historical, and literary insights presented in Hazlitt's writings of 1818–19. While it perhaps fails in many of its objectives (as suggested by Keats's attempt to rewrite the poem, and then by his abandonment of it entirely), the poem attempts to appropriate many of the ideas with which he was self-consciously engaged and effectively presents many of the issues and themes that will inform his poetic practice for much of the remainder of his life; not only are the perennial Keats themes of truth and beauty to be found in the narrative, but also a variety of issues ranging from the problem of power to the questions of circumstance, social hierarchy, creativity, and loss. The broadening of Keats's perspective and the deepening of his intellect that brought him to a poetic exploration of these and other matters must be seen as central to the enormous formal and technical advances that this work marks over, say, *Endymion,* completed only months earlier.

To place *Hyperion* in the context of Keats's age and in the context of Hazlitt's influence is to recognize that it is essentially a political poem with a moral purpose. As such, it should be seen as an attempt to voice republican or libertarian principles consistent with Keats's own expressed political commitments. These dimensions of the poem of course have long been known. Kenneth Muir has remarked that "the revolutionary climate of the time contributed to, if it did not suggest, the subject of the poem." And more recently John Barnard, in discussing Milton's influence on *Hyperion,* has noted that "Milton was exemplary not only as a poet but as a patriot and political hero," and that Keats attempts to emulate him: "Although Keats was not an atheist or a revolutionary, his first version of the *Hyperion* story implicitly supports a liberal view of both politics and religion."[2]

This liberal political vision informing the poem includes a dark side that several historical critics have noticed. Aileen Ward correctly points out that as he moved further into the project, "Not the glory but the cost of the struggle preoccupied" Keats, and Marilyn Butler echoes this idea when she states that "the sensibility, the bewilderment of loss, the essential innocence of Keats's fallen gods capture a modern pity for the helpless individual victims of the historical process."[3] But the actual entanglements, the dimensions of loss, the intellectual debates surrounding political change, the circumstances that energize one group while disempowering another—these have yet to be systematically considered or sketched in the narrative. One reason they have not been considered is that the narrative itself, for all its poetic beauty, is inconsistently handled, subject to ever greater contradictions and difficulties that finally defeat the project. Despite these narrative deficiencies, however, it is possible to develop a fuller political analysis than has yet been attempted, and to formulate a variety of Keats's interests, objectives, and strategies, which are embodied and projected in the narrative and which open up critically significant areas of romantic thought.

One of the key difficulties in addressing *Hyperion* has to do with Keats's source materials. While it is not necessary to turn a discussion of the poem into a study of sources, it should be recognized that this is a particularly important problem in this instance—not because Keats wanted to present a story that had been told in earlier literature, and that scholars have not yet discovered, but because his understanding of the meanings of Greek myth is critical to the specific use to which these myths have been put in the poem. For instance, whether Keats believed that the Olympians were sympathetic or villainous gods determines in very large measure the kinds of interpretations that may be attached to the narrative action. This specific question of how the Olympians should be seen was most important during the period, and Keats would have been aware of the controversy. Both Byron and Shelley wrote poems in 1819 celebrating the Titan Prometheus and condemning the tyrant Jupiter, and the Olympians—especially Jupiter—were often presented in negative terms. But to see them in this way, Keats knew, entailed a questioning of Apollo, the Olympian god of poetry, whom Keats apparently wished to celebrate. Any political interpretation of the poem must attempt to sort through this controversy to determine whether it is manifested in the narrative and, if so, how.

In addition to the allusions he found in Milton and Shakespeare, the descriptions of mythology offered in Lempriere's *Dictionary of Classical Mythology,* and the story of Saturn that is recounted in Hesiod's *Theogony,* Keats in all likelihood drew on two major sources: Andrew Tooke's *The Pantheon* and William Godwin's *The Pantheon* (published under the pseudonym "Edward Baldwin"). The former he had read from early adolescence, when he was introduced to it at the Clarke's, and the latter was published originally in 1806 and had run to four editions by 1814. The importance of these works for Keats's poem is that they offer highly divergent accounts of the same subject matter, and in fact Godwin remarks in his dedication that his purpose is to correct the deficiencies in Tooke. Specifically, he wished to remove what he considered to be the unhealthy Christian biases in Tooke's work. As he remarks in his preface: "The book . . . written in Latin by the Jesuit Pomey, and known among us by the name of Tooke, contains in every page an elaborate calumny upon the Gods of the Greeks, and that in the coarsest thoughts and words that rancour could furnish. The author seems continually haunted by the fear that his pupil might prefer the religion of Jupiter to the religion of Christ."[4] While Keats's experiences with the Elgin Marbles and his extensive poetic use of classical myth make it plain that he was sympathetic to the old gods and their tribulations and greatness, it would be wrong, I believe, to accept uncritically that Keats, upon reading Godwin, rejected Tooke and embraced Godwin (even though Keats often remarked his own unchristian principles, a fact which would seemingly place him closer to Godwin than to Tooke). First of all, Keats had his own problems with Godwinian philosophy (note for instance his remark in a letter that "Dilke will never come at a truth as long as he lives, because he is always trying at it. He is a Godwin-methodist" [*LJK* 2:213]). Thus, if he was aware that "Edward Baldwin" was in fact Godwin, he probably would have been less than an uncritical supporter of the newly compiled *Pantheon.* But of even greater significance is the fact that *Hyperion* and later poems show the continuing influence of Tooke, not so much in the Christian bias that Godwin condemns as in the sociohistorical dimensions of classical myth that Tooke takes pains to develop. These concerns in Tooke allow Keats to embrace myth as a source for poetry and to invest that source with sociohistorical significance. While Keats doubtless relied on Godwin for certain specific details in *Hyperion,* he also integrated materials from a variety of other sources, including Tooke.[5]

The debate over classical mythology current at the time is in one respect insignificant compared to much larger and complex social considerations. These included tremendous economic expansion, made possible by the long war with France; the elimination of virtually all of England's competitors on the international market; a strong push in the post-Waterloo years for a reformed Parliament; a fear, after the wars, that Western Europe would return to the absolute monarchical rule of earlier centuries. At the same time, however, it is an important debate—and it is important to consider what Keats may have read while this debate took place—because it is one center of gravity for the growing interest among British intellectuals and artists in questions of cultural and social power. The importance of the issue is seen most clearly in the fact that the struggle for control of how ancient myths were to be interpreted was inextricably entangled with the effort by Lord Elgin and other antiquarians to bring the Greek marbles to England (Haydon, Keats's friend, and Byron, one of Keats's examples of a great poet, may be seen as representatives of the opposing positions in this controversy), an effort that necessarily and intensely politicized Hellenism. The marbles and myths alike were charged with political relevance, and efforts by artists to use classical allusions and mythology as the basis of vision, or as a means of tapping the imaginative energies that many believed belonged to the ancient past, were saturated in the social, political, economic, and historical developments of the present that had brought things Greek to the forefront of the British imagination.[6]

We can begin to glimpse the political dimension of romantic Hellenism when we consider that poetic interest in Greek mythology enjoyed something of a renaissance most fully during the years when faith in the French Revolution had all but disappeared, and in the period immediately following Waterloo. The historical anxiety of the post-Waterloo years, when the freedoms that had been won during the revolutionary period of the 1790s seemed to be on the verge of defeat by a restored absolutism, led Shelley, Byron, Keats, and other liberal-minded artist-intellectuals to retreat to classical subject materials, perhaps because these provided a means of formulating an idyllic past of human possibility and achievement that could be used as a basis for once more energizing contemporary defenders of liberty who saw loneliness and defeat everywhere about them. In this respect, the gods of ancient times that haunt romantic poetry—whether it is Prometheus in Byron and Shelley, or Hyperion and Apollo in Keats—are political icons, charged with sociohistorical significance.[7] But that significance is highly complex, for one consequence of reformulating classical myths to suit contemporary needs and desires was, for Keats at least, to produce a poetry that was not so much idyllic as it was haunted. Keats's use of Phidian lore produced a poetry that is run through with the anxieties of the present that the poet wanted to overcome—a poetry that portrays, in displaced form, many of the episodes, contradictions, and fears accompanying the severe social and historical changes of the post-Waterloo moment.

Any consideration of Keats's source materials, and any interpretation of his poetry that is based on these source materials, must recognize this larger political and ideological context within which classical mythology achieved importance for Keats, for it provides the necessary means of getting at the hopeful, fearful, often contradictory, and historically important meanings of his poetry. When *Hyperion* is situated within the context of ideas just presented, it becomes apparent that Keats's handling of his subject matter is historically revealing, not only in terms of the issues and themes he attaches to the story of the Titans, but also in his changing attitudes both toward the motives and significance of the narrative action, and toward many of the characters, who are given sometimes sympathetic, sometimes unsympathetic roles. Such matters as these are saturated in the social, political, and ideological concerns of the historical moment, and an investigation of them suggests intellectual and conceptual reasons—beyond the purely technical reasons expressed in his letters—why Keats finally abandoned the poem.

The central question controlling the narrative of *Hyperion* concerns the process by which one social hierarchy gives way to another, despite the efforts and desires of individuals. Like Shelley in *Prometheus Unbound,* Keats presses the issue of originative and controlling power, looking for a causal explanation of social change, and like Shelley he never comes up with an answer. In his first expression of grief over his fallen nature, Saturn asks Thea, wife of Hyperion:

> ". . . Who had power
> To make me desolate? whence came the strength?
> How was it nurtur'd to such bursting forth,
> While Fate seem'd strangled in my nervous grasp?"
>
> (1.102–5)

Just before the narrative breaks off, too, when Apollo is becoming aware of his new power, Keats has the young god ask: "'. . . Where is power?'" (3.103). In both instances the individuals caught up in change believe that they have no authority or control over that change. Saturn is "benign" (1.198) and has a "heart of love" (1.112), and yet he is denied both his power over himself and over his world, a fact that seems to imply that sincerity of purpose and exercise of power are independent of one another; Apollo has been deified despite the fact that he sits idly on the margins of the changing world.

To center in this way on the highly abstract presentation of the power issue is to begin to glimpse the frenzied and uncertain social conditions (both at home and abroad) under which *Hyperion* was written, as well as the seemingly inexplicable nature of social changes then taking place. At home, the *Examiner* (as noted in the previous chapter) had long been running lists of national bankruptcies, articles on reform and political unrest, and unemployment and poverty. On 25 August 1816, for instance, one essay begins with the observation that "on all sides, the symptoms are now fast increasing of the instability of the present state of things. It cannot possibly last." The general tenor of such articles as this one anticipates Keats's comment in October 1818 that "as for Politics they are in my opinion only sleepy because they will soon be too wide awake" (*LJK* 1:396). With respect to the international situation, the prospects held out little hope as well. After the defeat of Napoleon in France, the villainous Ferdinand VII found himself on the throne of Spain, much to the chagrin of Shelley, Hunt, and other liberals and radicals in England. The article in the *Examiner* just quoted also remarks that "the King of Spain, *impotens quidibet sperare,* running from very impotence into the excesses of encroachment, is making haste to bring on the intolerable point, at which human nature must vindicate itself, or be other than what it is." Shelley's comment in his *Philosophical View of Reform* (1819) is equally damning: "The tyrant Ferdinand, he whose name is changed into a proverb of execration, found natural allies in all the priests and a few of the most dishonourable military chiefs of that devoted country [Spain]."[8]

Even many of the more outspoken radicals who decried the Holy Alliance and the increasingly difficult economic conditions in England found themselves being criticized by other liberals and radicals for their opportunism. In a letter to Hobhouse, for instance, Byron says of Cobbett and Orator Hunt, "I am glad to hear you have nothing to do with those scoundrels" (*BLJ* 7:80). Although Keats himself, following Hazlitt, was avowedly on the liberal side in the political debates of the day, the historical situation—as these comments show—was so marked by anxieties, contradictions, and uncertainties, that it virtually paralyzed him, leading him to remark on more than one occasion that he believed he could best serve humanity by writing rich and beautiful poetry. Many others besides Keats, who were also politically liberal or radical, simply lost hope, coming to believe that the reactionary forces in England would inevitably triumph despite energetic and moralistic opposition.

One of the most controversial issues at the level of the historical conjuncture that would have energized and helped to shape Keats's imagination at this time is Bonapartism. Although Napoleon's defeat had come three years earlier, he remained a mighty political icon, and many supporters of revolution (including Keats) had very mixed feelings about the man who, many believed, had hurt rather than helped the cause of liberty. And yet his was such a grand presence that it could not simply be dismissed. An article in the *Examiner* in May 1817 describing the rise and fall of Napoleon suggests the continuing presence of the French general in the popular imagination, and in terms that sound strikingly similar to Keats's descriptions of the fallen Saturn: "There was a time, and all must remember it, when Bonaparte was considered as almost a supernatural being, whose life was so extraordinary, that his death was expected to be miraculous; but this little book [of Napoleon's political life] shews him to have been a man liable to weaknesses and diseases, to the influence of events, and the flatterings of success. One rubs one's eyes to be convinced which is the dream, his present situation or his former glory; and then one begins to doubt if either be true!" While Keats was generally unsympathetic to Napoleon (*LJK* 1:397), and while he usually placed him among the worldly rather than among the godly (*LJK* 1:207, 395), the popular view of the French general included the godlike qualities presented in the above article, and they certainly would have been absorbed by Keats, as they were by Byron,[9] as part of his imaginative vision of social power and social change.

Keats's refusal in *Hyperion* to designate a single originative source of power, leaving his characters in confusion on this question that is most important to them, suggests the influence of his mentor Hazlitt—especially Hazlitt's conception of power presented in the letter to Gifford, which Keats quotes in the letter to George and Georgiana Keats, discussed above. That conception attaches power directly to circumstance, describing a dialectical relationship between any individual act of power and the larger social conditions which make that act possible. The precise point of Hazlitt's argument is that Gifford's desire to cleanse imaginative power of the circumstances surrounding it—that is, of the conditions which determine it—reifies or fetishizes it, and this makes tyranny possible and even inevitable, because it elides the social contradictions and human struggles that energize the imagination.

While Keats has his gods follow what is essentially Gifford's line of concern, at the same time he presses beyond Gifford with a view of power as circumstantially motivated and shaped, thus pointing up the inadequacy of the questions with which these heroes are most concerned. That is, while Saturn and Apollo alike personalize and internalize the events taking place that have severe consequences for their respective situations—i.e., they want to know what power has defeated the one and deified the other—Coelus presents a very different view of events. Speaking to Hyperion, who is afflicted with anxiety about his own imminent personal demise and who is coming to display many of the characteristics of his fallen brothers and sisters, Coelus, the parent of the Titans, remarks:

> ". . . I am but a voice;
> My life is but the life of winds and tides,
> No more than winds and tides can I avail:—
> But thou canst.—Be thou therefore in the van
> Of circumstance; yea, seize the arrow's barb
> Before the tense string murmur."
>
> (1.340–45)

This is not a speech that assures Hyperion's triumph, but rather one that refocuses the god's attention away from himself to the larger situation of which he is a part. Only by recognizing this larger situation, Coelus implies, can personal confusion and anxiety be allayed and action become possible.

When Hyperion is motivated by Coelus to action, his fellow gods also become animated: "Saturn sat near the Mother of the Gods, / In whose face was no joy, though all the Gods / Gave from their hollow throats the name of 'Saturn'" (2.389–91). This is the role that Hyperion is meant to play in the narrative: he is invested with a significance that stands midway between the personalized defeat of Saturn and the personalized triumph of Apollo, representing a difficult but finally more comprehensive vision of the processes by which some social hierarchies collapse and others emerge. The point is not that he provides a means of titanic triumph—Keats never intended to chart Hyperion's victory—but rather that, in resisting the fragmentation which accompanies social change, he provides a means by which the contexts of triumph and defeat can be known. This is a much more ambitious task than simply delineating the demise of one structure of authority and its replacement by another.

The point here is that the story Keats tells is one of a once secure social order, which had been defined by a spirit of collectivity, and which now finds itself entirely divided and fragmented, with individuals personalizing and internalizing the changes taking place around them. The social or institutional dimension of this division and fragmentation is seen in the description of Hyperion's threatened but as yet unfallen palace:

> . . . His palace bright,
> Bastion'd with pyramids of glowing gold,
> And touch'd with shade of bronzed obelisks,
> Glar'd a blood-red through all its thousand courts,
> Arches, and domes, and fiery galleries;
> And all its curtains of Aurorian clouds
> Flush'd angerly. . . .
> . . . .
> . . . and neighing steeds were heard,
> Not heard before by Gods or wondering men.
> Also, when he would taste the spicy wreaths
> Of incense, breath'd aloft from sacred hills,
> Instead of sweets, his ample palate took
> Savour of poisonous brass and metal sick.
>   (1.175–89)

The anxiety described here is shown to be social and institutional in nature; pervading the entire network of social relations, it neither arises solely from individuals nor is specific to them. In fact, only gradually does this anxiety ripple outward, causing Hyperion to shudder (1.170) and "his winged minions in close clusters [to stand], / Amaz'd and full of fear" (1.197–98). As this anxiety intensifies and the world of the gods splinters, the once collective spirit of the Titans shatters, deteriorating to the point where the most natural expression among the fallen gods appears now to be private, and every effort to regain the strength that comes of collectivity appears impossible.

The privatization of what was once titanic energy and expression is seen everywhere in the narrative, beginning with Saturn's recognition that "I have left / My strong identity, my real self" (1.113–14), a vague statement that nonetheless begins to describe not only Saturn but also the other Titans. As a fallen god, Saturn is dominated by "passion" (1.135), "struggle" (1.136), and "fever" (138), and he lacks self-control: ". . . and then again he snatch'd / Utterance thus" (1.140–41). Enceladus is described in similar terms as "Now tiger-passion'd, lion-thoughted, wroth" (2.68). And even Hyperion is characterized in these terms. As he enters his palace, he is "full of wrath" (1.213); when he nears the cupola housing the sun, "there standing fierce beneath, he stamped his foot" (1.222); and when he begins to speak "his voice leapt out, despite of godlike curb" (1.226). That this is one sign (not to be confused with the cause) of defeat is suggested by Coelus, who tells Hyperion:

> "Now I behold in you fear, hope, and wrath;
> Actions of rage and passion; even as
> I see them, on the mortal world beneath,
> In men who die.—This is the grief, O Son!
> Sad sign of ruin, sudden dismay, and fall!"
>
> (1.332–36)

As Coelus knows, Hyperion is beginning to absorb the tensions and anxieties—the growing weakness—running through his palace; these in turn weaken the god by detaching him from the institutional framework of his power, leaving that power to stir recklessly and angrily within himself, and thus creating a situation of potential destruction.

The question of the privatization of experience that accompanies the changing social structures, and of the frustration and wrath which emerge from it, is complicated very interestingly by Oceanus. Without mentioning the social and institutional issues that are set down in other sections of the narrative, Oceanus speaks directly and firmly in universalisitic terms, much as Hazlitt (see Hazlitt's letter quoted by Keats, above) accuses Gifford of doing, in an attempt to explain the utter destruction of an entire hierarchy of values and social order. He recognizes that the fallen gods are consumed by wrath (2.173) and that this is a sign of their fallenness, but he does not examine the material contexts of this wrath; rather, he advances an elaborate and abstract theory of the natural laws of progress, arguing that the present destruction makes possible a change for the better:

> "My voice is not a bellows unto ire.
> Yet listen, ye who will, whilst I bring proof
> How ye, perforce, must be content to stoop:
> . . . .
> We fall by course of Nature's law, not force
> Of thunder, or of Jove. . . .
> . . . .
> . . . our fair boughs
> Have bred forth, not pale solitary doves,
> But eagles golden-feather'd, who do tower
> Above us in their beauty, and must reign

>   In right thereof; for 'tis the eternal law
>   That first in beauty should be first in might."
>   (2.176–78; 181–82; 224–29)

Like Coelus, who had attempted to curb Hyperion's wrath, Oceanus understands the authority of circumstance—"O folly! for to bear all naked truths, / And to envisage circumstance, all calm" (2.203–4)—but, unlike that god (who by virtue of being only a voice stands outside the contexts of action, serving as a sort of chorus for the narrative), he does not acknowledge the role of agency within circumstance, arguing rather that individual or collective intervention be given up in favor of natural and eternal laws that must triumph.

Such a position, which echoes many of the elaborate social and economic theories set forth in Keats's day, leaves unconsidered the networks of relations, the structures of social authority, and the hierarchies of social value that undergird and control the Titan world; it matter-of-factly advances a natural right—rather than, say, a divine right (the other popular theory of social order during this period)—explanation of rulership, effectively rendering public participation of any sort pointless. Within such a context as this, beauty is that which floats uncalled to a position of authority; for this reason, Oceanus is not likely to represent Keats's views on the subject, which are perhaps much more complex than those of any single character in the narrative.[10] To put the matter somewhat differently, Oceanus's comments, while perhaps more appealing than Enceladus's call for revenge or Hyperion's growing anger, are finally another instance of privatized value, an attempt to rationalize a vicious and violent situation and to reconcile at the level of a proclaimed eternal truth the contradictions and horrors that this situation has produced. In short, Oceanus's argument is an ideologically burdened explanation of social change that achieves its authority by eliding the true complexity of the social and historical conflict that threatens the Titans.

The speeches of Clymene and Enceladus effectively discredit Oceanus's argument, and yet they do so in counterproductive ways that show the extent to which the consciousness of the Titans has come to be shaped by circumstance. Clymene, for instance, who, like Oceanus, offers brilliant isolated comments on the situation of the Titans, builds her presentation upon personal sorrow, turning incapacity into a controlling reality. In describing the beauty of Apollo's song, Clymene states that her own singing becomes increasingly pointless, until finally "I threw my shell away from the sand" (2.278): ". . . Grief overcame / And I was stopping up my frantic ears" (2.289–90). She is driven so far back into herself that hope is impossible and she sees and can speak only of "those pains of mine" (2.297). Enceladus intends his own call for revenge as a corrective to this sort of introspection, passivity, and "baby-words" (2.314); yet, his position is finally no more satisfactory than that which he condemns, for it begins from wrath and violence, that is, from the very characteristics that Coelus had earlier described to Hyperion as destructive to true divinity and true power (1.332–35). While characterizing Hyperion as a model, unfallen god, Enceladus clearly celebrates, in his own speech, values and tendencies that destroy godhead. He succeeds in momentarily rousing the fallen Titans by calling upon them "to feed fierce the crooked stings of fire, / And singe away the swollen clouds of Jove" (2.329–30), but this call is not a sign of his ability to lead them to victory and to the restoration of their power; it is, rather, a sign of the pervasive and angry desperation of the shattered world of the Titans. The narrative itself implies as much in its focus upon the imminent demise of Hyperion.

In short, Oceanus, Clymene, and Enceladus compellingly display the effects of the social collapse that has taken place. However, for all their sincerity and desire, they do not point a way out of contradiction and hardship, and perhaps for this reason Keats abandons the fallen gods altogether after book 2 in favor in favor of the triumphant Olympians, who would seem to represent a moment in which power, knowledge, and beauty are harmoniously combined.

The introduction of Apollo in book 3 provides a glimpse of the reconciliation of contradiction and of a wholeness of being that the fallen gods of the earlier books had desired but were denied. Apollo appears to possess a knowledge, innocence, and beauty that would prove Oceanus's speech true, and to represent a set of values that Keats wanted to elaborate in his mature poetry. As Ronald Sharp remarks, "the knowledge that Hyperion lacks is precisely the knowledge that Apollo, like Keats, passionately seeks and eventually discovers."[11] Clymene earlier had remarked the young god's "new blissful golden melody" (2.280), and the general description in book 3 is of a god, yet innocent of his powers, on the brink of greatness. While his deification entails both melancholy and pain, it represents a positive advance beyond the qualities that had been attached to the Titans. As James Jones puts it, "in Apollo's deification, the birth of a new and more expansive mode of consciousness" is presented; it is "a higher god-like consciousness that man can attain."[12] Apollo, in other words, would seem to represent values that Keats himself accepted, and to be a model of what Keats hopes that humanity can accomplish.

But if the newly-deified god is portrayed sympathetically, he nevertheless is a problematic character in the larger context of the narrative. This becomes clear if we consider his exchange with Mnemosyne on the topic of power, the same topic that had occupied Saturn early in the narrative.

Like Saturn, who wished to know "'Who had power / To make me desolate?'" (1.102–03), Apollo desires to know

> ". . . Where is power?
> Whose hand, whose essence, what divinity
> Makes this alarum in the elements,
> While I here idle listen on the shores
> In fearless yet in aching ignorance?"
>
> (3.103–7)

While never answered within the narrative itself, these questions nonetheless have implicit answers that can be derived both from within the narrative and from Keats's letters. They are answers that do not necessarily accord with the specific desires of the characters, for they are not logical and source-oriented but, rather, historical and political. To understand this, it is necessary to consider once more Keats's interest in Hazlitt's letter to William Gifford. In the portion of that letter quoted by Keats, Hazlitt remarks of course upon Gifford's "love of Power" (*LJK* 2:72); but he also speaks more theoretically about "the language of Poetry [which] naturally falls in with the language of power" (*LJK* 2:74); about "the sense of power (in poetry) abstracted from the sense of good" (*LJK* 2:75); and about the way "evil overpowers and makes a convert of the imagination" (*LJK* 2:75). Hazlitt's point is that the imagination is never entirely innocent, that it is connected in fundamental ways to power, and that power is socially, historically, politically, and ideologically charged. As he states the matter explicitly to Gifford: "I have admitted that there are tyrants and slaves abroad in the world; and you would hush the matter up" (*LJK* 2:76).

What this means in terms of Keats's narrative is that while the tremendous power and knowledge to which Apollo is heir come from a source that cannot be immediately seen and that cannot be logically explained, they are clearly entangled in the bedrock changes in social structure and social authority detailed in the story. To put it bluntly, Apollo's power is made possible by Hyperion's demise. The narrator's question, "Where was he [Apollo], when the Giant of the Sun [Hyperion] / Stood bright, amid the sorrow of his peers?" (3.29–30), is answered in the subsequent descriptions of Apollo: he was waiting to be deified by the power that Hyperion was in the process of losing. His greatness, that is, is bought at a price: the humiliation, grief, dread, and fall of those who came before him. Mnemosyne, a Titan who survives by giving her allegiance to the Olympians, escorts the young Apollo to his new position of power; and her actions entail surrendering her loyalties and her birthright—entail, in other words, an absolute commitment to strengthening the Olympians' authority over the Titans. The full social implications of Keats's presentation are reflected perfectly in Walter Benjamin's *Theses on the Philosophy of History:*

> ... all rulers are the heirs of those who conquered before them. Hence, empathy with the victor invariably benefits the rulers.... Whoever has emerged victorious participates ... in the triumphal procession in which the present rulers step over those who are lying prostrate ... the spoils are carried along in the procession. They are called cultural treasures.... [W]ithout exception the cultural treasures ... owe their existence not only to the efforts of the great minds and talents who have created them, but also to the anonymous toil of their contemporaries. There is no document of civilization which is not at the same time a document of barbarism.[13]

To explain Apollo in these terms is not to condemn that god's intentions, but rather to suggest that in the largest sense his intentions are but one ingredient in the social entanglements within which they are caught. While he may indeed be ignorant of the driving forces behind the changes taking place, and while his desires and sympathies may indeed be noble, his power is touched with the blood of others (if gods have blood), a fact that is at least suggested in the imagery that Keats uses to introduce Apollo. The "red wine" (3.18), the "vermilion" (3.20) shells, the maid who "blush[es] keenly" (3.22) make possible the "golden theme" (3.28) and the "golden bow" (3.43) of the young Olympian god.

In the character of Apollo can be seen the extent to which all history pours into the individual, empowering him beyond what he is capable of grasping, pointing him in a direction that he cannot fully control, and giving him even the specific features of his very consciousness. To situate Apollo within this historical context is to recognize that while it is proper to argue that *Hyperion* is a poem about consciousness,[14] it is not a poem about autonomy; quite the reverse, it explores the emergence of the individual subject within a specific moment of social and historical change. To put this matter somewhat differently, as the Titans and the order of which they are a part begin to shatter and fragment, leaving them alienated and in a "slumbrous solitude" (1.69), historical energy gathers behind the individual consciousness. The world of the Titans, which Hesiod and others called the Golden Age, is presented as a collective and shared world of plenty that is being destroyed; the world of the Olympians is a world where individual consciousness is a frontier to be explored, and where individual possibilities seem limitless; it is a world, in other words, of the imperialistic imagination. The Olympians experiment with their new power mercilessly and thoughtlessly, destroying the domains once occupied by the Titans; as Thea tells Saturn:

"'... thy sharp lightning in unpractised hands / Scorches and burns our once serene domain'" (1.62–63). Apollo shares this expansive and acquisitive attitude, claiming beauty and value for his individual capabilities. Looking for "other regions than this isle" (3.96) to touch with his power, he states:

> "... Point me out the way
> To any one particular beauteous star,
> And I will flit into it with my lyre,
> And make its silvery splendour pant with bliss."
>
> (3.99–102)

The demise of one mythology and the emergence of another, for Keats, is not simply a matter of the less beautiful giving way to the more beautiful; it is a matter of the material and the ideological dimensions of experience undergoing radical structural change, so that life and consciousness themselves have to be entirely thought anew.[15]

To approach the story of the Olympians and Titans in this manner—that is, not simply in terms of the characters' (or Keats's) self-representations, but also in terms of the conditions that give shape and meaning to those self-representations—is to recognize the vexed nature of power and consciousness, the major themes of the story. It is to understand, for instance, that Keats's description of Apollo's ascent to power cannot be explained as a solution to the problems of consciousness or to the problems of alienation and loneliness described in the Titans. Rather, that ascent marks an introduction to new kinds of difficulty.

This becomes apparent at the very moment when Apollo becomes aware of his new knowledge. As his eyes are "enkindled" (3.121) with the prospect of his deification, and as he begins to undergo the transformation into godhead, he is shaken with uncertainty and hardship:

> Soon wild commotions shook him, and made flush
> All the immortal fairness of his limbs;
> Most like the struggle at the gate of death;
> Or liker still to one who should take leave
> Of pale immortal death, and with a pang
> As hot as death's is chill, with fierce convulse
> Die into life: so young Apollo anguish'd.
>
> (3.124–30)

While these lines clearly press toward deification, the images and allusions accompanying that deification are anxiety-ridden and death-haunted. In fact, the forces of change that produce a new and unified power generate such intense pain that "Apollo shriek'd" (3.135), and at this point the poem breaks off.¹⁶ The thematic significance of these descriptions is elucidated by a much earlier description of Thea as she approaches the fallen Saturn in book 1; in this scene, the narrator speaks of "a listening fear in her [Thea's] regard, / As if calamity had but begun" (1.37–38). Apollo's deification, for all the greatness that it is intended to signify, marks one fulfillment of that calamity, not only for the Titans but for consciousness in general.

This is not to suggest that Apollo should be viewed as malicious or as the direct cause of the hardship described elsewhere in the narrative, for certainly he should not. However, he is the representative figure of a new hierarchy of values, and as such he necessarily carries with him the historical fact of triumph over those who preceded him. The fallen Titans' pain cannot be entirely annihilated: it remains within the political unconscious of the new order as a necessary and shaping force of that order. For this reason Apollo, despite his beauty, cannot represent a form of consciousness capable of reconciling all conflict, nor can his power transcend the conditions and contexts within which it emerged. This becomes clear when Keats rewrites the poem a few months later, exploring in more specific detail than he does here some of the conflicts and struggles that assure ongoing anxiety, pain, and hardship.

For all its shortcomings, *Hyperion* marks a significant turning point in Keats's poetic practice, because—almost against the poet's will, it sometimes seems—it comes up against the irresistible reality of material life, with all its historical, social, and ideological complexity, and concludes almost despairingly that not even the gods can escape that reality.¹⁷ When he expressed his initial idea for the poem to Haydon in January 1818, he distinguished it from *Endymion* by remarking that "in Endymion I think you may have many bits of the deep and sentimental cast—the nature of *Hyperion* will lead me to treat it in a more naked and grecian Manner—and the march of passion and endeavour will be undeviating—and one great contrast between them will be—that the Hero of the written tale being mortal is led on, like Buonaparte, by circumstance; whereas the Apollo in Hyperion being a fore-seeing God will shape his actions like one" (*LJK* 1:207). This idea, however, could not be carried out, because Keats came to conceive of gods differently over the next ten months or so as he realized that, like Buonaparte, they too are shaped by circumstance. This meant that the pure Miltonic epic, as he had conceived it in 1818, could not be written. What was needed was an imagination capable of articulating the full historical complexity of power, circumstance, and human experience—an imagination, that is, of the sort Hazlitt had described in his letter to Gifford—and it is thus not surprising that after abandoning the first *Hyperion* Keats not only began writing short and highly disturbed odes that were at once escapist and historically charged, but also composed two historical dramas, *Otho the Great* and *King Stephen,* that attempted to address systematically some of the matters he had discovered in *Hyperion.*

5
"Coming to the Sacrifice"
ODE ON A GRECIAN URN

ONE of Keats's characteristic poetic responses to personal, intellectual, and historical anxiety was to create imaginative alternative worlds free of all struggle and conflict, a response that, during April and May 1819 produced his astonishingly beautiful odes. In the earliest of these, the *Ode to Psyche,* while acknowledging the sad demise of Olympian order ("O latest born and loveliest vision far / Of all Olympus' faded hierarchy!" 24–25), he also concentrates poetically on constructing "a fane / In some untrodden region of my mind" (50–51); he desires to retreat into "a rose sanctuary" (59) characterized by "quietness" (58), where love is possible. In an age riddled with pain and violence—characteristics that also marked history and myth alike—he nobly sought to preserve and celebrate the delightful and virtuous dimensions of human life. This intense desire and poetic accomplishment are consistent with his expressed opinions in his letters on the horrors and atrocity of political and religious oppression.

At the same time, however, even as Keats elaborated his progressive and sympathetic position on politics and religion, and even as his poetry is reinterpreted in political and historical ways as expressions of desire for human betterment, the extent to which his thought and writing often remain implicated in and controlled by certain facts of oppression during the romantic period must not be overlooked. Many of the oppressive features of Keats's world that he desperately sought to push out of his poetic vision come back to haunt that vision in different ways. His work is politically and historically significant not only for its utopian dimension, its dream of a better world, but also for the way it is saturated in the loneliness, tensions, contradictions, and struggles that characterize the bourgeois culture of which it is a part, and which, as we have seen, characterize the plot-level episodes of a poem such as *Hyperion.*

The extent to which Keats's poetry remains implicated in—and thus helps us to know—historical and social contradiction can be seen quite clearly in the *Ode on a Grecian Urn,* one of his most beautiful and problematic works. Despite this poem's expressed and laudable desire to find permanence and beauty behind the turmoil and mutability of everyday life, it duplicates ideologically a form of oppression that Keats and his age never escaped, even when they situated themselves knowingly and firmly against political and religious tyranny, as Keats clearly did— namely, the oppression of women. As in the work of many other romantic poets, and as in some of his own earlier poems (for instance, *Endymion*), gender is an ideological blind spot. By investigating and documenting its role in the *Urn,* it is possible to show how even Keats's most sincere utopian impulses against the atrocities he elsewhere describes with abhorrence inevitably are marked by elements of oppression and sometimes even by violence.

The argument I wish to make takes its point of departure from Tilottama Rajan's excellent and important book, *Dark Interpreter: The Discourse of Romanticism,* which sets as its task to demonstrate the anxiety of romantic texts. This anxiety is vividly expressed in the *Urn,* Rajan argues, as "the poem seeks to project on the urn [a vision] that is constantly challenged and disrupted by the vision of art that emerges from the urn itself—in all probability a funeral urn."[1] Emphasizing the conflict between the urn's flat surface, which constitutes a "figured curtain of art," and its depth, which "contains the ashes of the dead, of a civilization that is past," Rajan charts the poetic attempt to contain, enclose, or overcome this conflict by creating "a fictitiousness that excludes the urn's real function."[2] Although Keats recognizes the existence of the "depth and ambiguity" suggested by the urn's interior, he does not give them full expression, because "to search beneath the surface, by seeking the historical Greece underlying the Arcadian fiction, would be to ask what becomes of the abstractions of idealism when they are incarnated in the real world and made the property of real men and lovers. In the fourth stanza Keats almost does this. But at the crucial moment he draws back from excavating too deeply in the archaeology of the idealizing consciousness, fearing a complete dissolution of the surface." Thus, Rajan concludes, "irrespective of who speaks them, the last lines of Keats's poem reaffirm the rhetoric of the surface and reduce questions to the flatness of statement and the urn itself to its merely decorative appearance."[3]

While it is certainly correct and even necessary, as Rajan urges, to see the funeral urn as a reminder—for us, as for Keats—of past civilizations now dead, it is also important to understand that history is not simply that which must die. To imply, as Rajan does, that history is represented only by the ashes in the funeral urn and by the poet's sense of his own mortality, while arguing that the figures and images on the urn and in the poem represent fictions, or qualities that would resist or overcome this history, is to posit a static dualism between the individual imagination and historical reality: history equals mortality, while art (one can hope) equals the enduring power of the individual imagination. Such a formulation limits historical explanation by obscuring the fact that the figures and images on the surface of the urn are no less historical than the ashes contained within the urn. Indeed, the conflicts and tensions in the poem that Rajan considers are not so much a product of the irreconcilable differences between historical (mortal) and fictional (enduring) properties, or of the difficult relations between surfaces and depths, as they are of a single, complex historical reality, which defines both. In other words, the textual anxiety that Rajan describes is also an expression of historical anxiety. On this view, history is not simply depth, or that which is curtained over by the products of the imagination; it is, rather, the ontological ground that encompasses and gives rise to all human activity and that therefore necessarily limits, empowers, and defines poetic practice.

To situate poetic practice within this framework of ideas is to acknowledge that it cannot be explained in purely textual terms. Keats is not simply meditating on and recording the details inscribed on a perfectly cloistered museum piece—he is committing a historical and political act, using the urn to formulate the past. This act also formulates and discloses the historically specific system of values and beliefs of Keats's own historical situation, characterized by social fragmentation, alienation, and loneliness, all of which intensified and became culturally pervasive with the rise of a nonagricultural economy and population, and which helped to produce subjectivity as a culturally dominant ideology.[4] That the *Urn* never escapes these social contradictions, but rather is constituted by them, is seen most impressively in the fact that while truth and beauty are clearly uppermost in the poet's mind and are formulated and articulated in moving poetic language, their integrity is bought at a very dear price. The values underwriting the poetic vision of beauty and truth derive from one of the most powerful supports of capitalism during Keats's day, namely, patriarchy, which takes for granted the masculine nature of creativity, the passive nature of femininity, and the definitional role of the father.[5] Although never stated explicitly, these values are pervasive, and they movingly expose Keats's occasional tendency to flatten certain issues of human oppression and human struggle into a natural conflict between the desire for immortality and the fact of mortality.[6] I want to trace this patriarchal morality through the poem as a necessary, albeit submerged, ingredient in the vision that is offered, illustrating its historical and political role in Keats's poetic imagination during this difficult period of his life.[7]

The intensity with which patriarchal morality is drawn in the poem can be accounted for, partially, in biographical terms.[8] (I should stress, however, that I do not wish to reduce the issues in the *Urn* to Keats's personal eccentricity; I take for granted that the contradictions in Keats's life and in his poetry are also at least partly the contradictions of his age.) In a letter to Benjamin Bailey, written less than a year before the *Urn*, Keats remarked:

> I am certain I have not a right feeling towards Women—at this moment I am striving to be just to them but I cannot—Is it because they fall so far beneath my Boyish imagination? When I was a Schoolboy I though[t] a fair Woman a pure Goddess, my mind was a soft nest in which some one of them slept though she knew it not—I have no right to expect more than their reality. I thought them etherial above Men— I find then [sic] perhaps equal—great by comparison is very small— Insult may be inflicted in more ways than by Word or action—one who is tender of being insulted does not like to think an insult against another—I do not like to think insults in a Lady's Company—I commit a Crime with her which absence would have not known—Is this not extraordinary? When among Men I have no evil thoughts, no malice, no spleen—I feel free to speak or to be silent—I can listen and from every one I can learn—my hands are in my pockets I am free from all suspicion and comfortable. When I am among Women I have evil thoughts, malice spleen—I cannot speak or be silent—I am full of Suspicions and therefore listen to no thing—I am in a hurry to be gone. (*LJK* 1:341)

Five months later (in a letter in which he also discusses his views on beauty and truth)[9] he remarked to his brother about the "inadequacy" of women (*LJK* 2:19). The anxiety evident in these comments attends one of the poetic impulses behind many of Keats's poems. In *La Belle Dame Sans Merci* he depicts woman both as the highest object of masculine desire and at the same time as the victimizer of men; in *The Eve of St. Agnes*, as we have seen, he describes the young Madeline as the object of a Peeping Tom's prurience and as a person who benefits from subjecting herself to the Peeping Tom's will; in *Lamia* he portrays woman as a beautiful yet witch-like creature who attempts to isolate man from the public world, where he supposedly belongs; and in *The Fall of Hyperion* he portrays woman (in the character of Moneta) as a cold, blind goddess, directly connected to money, whose willingness to serve poetic man exacts a very high price. Such examples from his life and poetry suggest that the portrayal of the feminine in the *Urn* is not an exception but a tendency in his poetic practice.

Before sketching the specific way the *Urn* defines and structures femininity in erecting its vision of beauty and truth, it might be helpful to ask what, exactly, is feminized in the poem, and what use is made of those things that are feminized. First, the urn itself is presented as a "still unravish'd bride of quietness" (1). It is worth recalling that the urn is stationary and silent throughout, both in the way it is described and defined by the poet and in the way it serves as the still object of his contemplation, as the receiver of his anxiety, hope, desire, and despair: just as the interior of the urn is said to be the repository of the ashes of the dead, so too the exterior is the repository of and inspiration for the poet's imaginings. Second, the figures on the urn themselves mirror the relation between poet and urn/object. The male figures are likened to "men or gods" (8), while the women, like the urn, are presented as stationary, frozen in time ("she cannot fade" [19]). Moreover, the male figures engage in "mad pursuit" while the female figures "struggle to escape" (9). Without arguing that the poem's description of these figures sounds almost like a description of rape, it should be emphasized that the masculine aggression is presented as a "wild ecstasy" (10), although literally nothing in the descriptions of the female figures (who are described as "loth" [8]) suggests even desire, and certainly not ecstasy. Third, the sacrifice described in the penultimate stanza also appears in masculine and feminine terms. In a religious ritual, a priest leads to death a "heifer lowing at the skies, / And all her silken flanks with garlands drest" (33–34). Again, we need not insist that the description here is of a literal woman—though it is worth noting that in Keats's day, as in our own, "heifer" was a common term used to describe not only cows but women, and also that in most rituals, such as the one described, it was typically a bullock and not a heifer that was sacrificed—to see that the violence being enacted, and religiously sanctioned, is gender-specific.[10]

Put differently, poetics and ideology in the poem are inextricably entwined. Poetic activity involves the structuring of quite real power relations, as well as the defining of these power relations as noble and as the source of virtue, integrity, and morality; it transforms oppression into an acceptable, even laudable, form of social existence. To recognize this active, value-producing function in the poem is to understand, with Michele Barrett, that gender has less to do with biological difference than with political reality; it must be identified in terms of "division, oppression, inequality, internalized inferiority for women,"[11] that is, in terms of specific and controlling forces and relations that emerge from social practice, of which poetry is one form.

The production of this masculine ideology in the *Urn* follows a very clear path, one which Rosemary Radford Ruether's theory of the struggle against the mother, or the feminine, helps to illuminate. According to Ruether, the suppression of women is a historically explicable phenomenon, in which "the female person, possessing a different but strong body and an equal capacity for thought and culture, was subverted and made to appear physiologically and intellectually inferior." Ruether charts the process of this subversion through three diachronic stages, which she labels the Conquest of the Mother, the Negation of the Mother, and the Sublimation of the Mother. "The stages of this history," Ruether says, "are . . . reflected in the changing ideology or symbolization of the 'feminine' in (male-defined) culture."[12]

In her discussion of the Conquest of the Mother, Ruether notes that this first phase originated when the center of economic life shifted out of the family. Two central developments contributed to this shift:

> The first is the transition from tribal or village to urban life. The urban revolution originally affected only a small segment of society, with most of society remaining agrarian and family-centered handicraft economies. But it created a new elite group of males whose power was no longer based on the physical prowess of the hunter or warrior, but on the inherited monopoly of political power and knowledge. Females were equally capable of entering into this kind of power on equal terms, but instead they were excluded from it and consigned to an ornamental role—with occasional exceptions.[13]

This urban revolution was followed by "the development of mass industrialization, which diffuses urbanization over more and more of the world and shifts economic production increasingly from the family to a workplace separated from the home. For the first time women as a group became marginal to production and economically dependent on male work for survival."[14] This account, which focuses primarily on the economic realities underlying the historical development of gender relations, draws heavily on Engels's *Origin and History of the Family*, and entails a critically significant ideological dimension, in which women are seen in purely passive terms. Situated outside the world of public power, women become "restricted to a sheltered sphere": "Dress, confinement, lack of physical development, direct bodily repression through corsets, footbinding, or veils mold women . . . into an unnatural physical weakness and psychological timidity." At the same time, "a male-identified consciousness [is elevated] to transparent apriority."[15]

According to Ruether, the elevation of masculine consciousness leads to the second historical stage, the Negation of the Mother:

> Creation is seen as initiated by a fiat from above, from an immaterial principle beyond visible reality. Nature, which once encompassed all reality, is now subjugated and made into the lower side of a new

> dualism. . . . Consciousness is abstracted into a sphere beyond visible reality, including the visible heavens. This higher realm is the world of divinity. The primal matrix of life . . . is debased as mere "matter" (a word which means "mother"). . . . Maleness is identified with intellectuality and spirituality; femaleness . . . with lower material nature. This also defines the female as ontologically dependent and morally inferior to maleness.[16]

The third phase involves the idealization of women, which arises "as the corollary of the repression of physical sexuality and procreation. The Virgin Mary was the antetype of spiritual femininity over against 'carnal femaleness.' However, it was only in the romantic reaction following the French Revolution that this concept of spiritual femininity became secularized and generalized as a myth about the superior nature of women."[17] The reason for this, Ruether argues, is that

> In the aftermath of the French Revolution, when the very fabric of Western civilization seemed to be undermined, European thinkers went scrambling to recover bits and pieces of a threatened social order. . . . Romanticism sought, simultaneously, to renew human sensibilities through contact with the mystical depths of nature, from which rationalistic man had become alienated, and to compensate for the depersonalized world of industrialism and democracy that threatened the house of patriarchal society.[18]

This development is socially and historically pervasive, incorporating under its power the institutions of marriage, religion, family, sexuality, and aesthetics, and producing, finally, in Ruether's opinion, "the dehumanization of society."[19]

This is a condensed description of Ruether's theory, but it illustrates, I think, her basic points, which are that masculine morality and value, as exercised under patriarchy, depend fully on active oppression and conquest; that the conquered is woman; and that the hierarchy of values resulting from this conquest prevents "reciprocity."[20] The masculine "view of what is over against itself is not that of the conversation of two subjects, but of the conquest of an alien object. The intractibility of the other side of the dualism to its demands does not suggest that the 'other' has a 'nature' of her own that needs to be respected and with which one must enter into conversation. Rather, this intractibility is seen as that of disobedient rebellion."[21] In being conquered, the feminine is not only silenced but also transformed, denied all human complexity and made into the passive repository of masculine desire. The purity and morality that come to be associated with this silenced femininity derive from the masculine ability to use the feminine—just as it uses the world—to its own ends. In effect, the feminine is cherished because its subordination serves the masculine ego's carefully constructed sense of itself.

Ruether's argument may be seen as representing homologically the general pattern of Keats's *Urn*. That is, while the poem does not address thematically the problem and nature of the historical development of patriarchy into its present form under capitalism, its portrayal of the feminine follows symbolically, and with remarkable force, the historical pattern described by Ruether. And though the poem does not of course present an account of the hard economic conditions upon which Ruether grounds her theory, it does reveal the form which gender relations take under those conditions. In its intense struggle to avoid or suppress all matters of historical consequence (note Rajan's argument, above), the *Urn* presents itself finally as a near-perfect articulation of the process by which patriarchy establishes its authority, and of patriarchal morality as it existed in Keats's day.

A more direct concern involves the function of poetic practice as a function of history. In describing above the place of the feminine in the poem, I noted that the urn itself, the presentation of the figures on it in stanzas 1 and 2, and the presentation of the sacrifice in stanza 4 constitute the important gender specific references. It now should be noted that the conflict described in stanza 1 ("What men or gods are these? What maidens loth? / What mad pursuit? What struggle to escape?" [8–9]) is not simple love play. The maidens are described as "loth"—a word that means more than reluctant and certainly more than coquettish[22]—and their struggle is shown to be quite desperate, just as the movement of the male figures is characterized by a sort of Dionysian ecstasy. What is more, the scene is described in terms of the masculine effort to hypostatize the conflict, and in fact the final scene is one of masculine victory, in spirit if not in body, as the maidens are "frozen" into objects of masculine desire:

> Bold lover, never, never canst thou kiss,
> Though winning near the goal—yet, do not grieve;
> She cannot fade, though thou hast not thy bliss,
> For ever wilt thou love, and she be fair.
>
> (17–20)

This hypostasis, which allows the "bold lover" ever to behold women as "fair," generates in the poem a virtual madness of ecstacy (stanza 3): love, happiness, and song weigh the lines down as the poet attempts to articulate the pleasures that he imagines are "still to be enjoy'd" (26), until the prospect of such extreme sensual delight overwhelms him, producing the consideration of religious ritual.

The sacrifice that occupies stanza 4 is traditionally seen as a discovery by the speaker of figures on the urn previously overlooked, a discovery that calls the poet's attention from the beauties that had occupied him to the truth that is expressed in even the most inspiring works of art.[23] This view is essentially correct in terms of the poetic voice controlling the poem, but it is incomplete in terms of the social relations working themselves out through the poem's larger ideological structures. Certainly the tone is somber as the poet describes the "little town" with its silent streets, its emptiness, and its general desolation; but the somberness comes with the religious ritual of sacrificing the heifer—that is, in Ruether's terms, of negating the feminine, not only through physical violence (the sacrifice), but also by "lowering" or "debasing" the feminine (see Ruether's comments, above) by presenting it in animalistic terms (heifer). Further, not only is the event presided over by a priest; the town itself sits under the watchful eye of the "peaceful citadel," a distinctly military image recalling the struggle of the preceding stanzas, which is now completed, having been followed first by celebration and now by ritual. Even as the scene reflects seriousness and sincerity—recalling Ruether's account of the development of a masculine religion—the physical resources of the masculine world stand by as a certain reminder of the specific power behind the ritual.

Conquest and negation are accompanied by a sublimation of the feminine, implicit from the poem's opening lines describing the urn as the "still unravish'd bride of quietness" (1), as a pure resource of the highest imaginable values. While the scenes on the urn tell the story of the triumph of men over women, the urn itself remains quiet and pure, giving the struggles inscribed on its borders the gloss of a "flowery tale" (4). The urn is a "sylvan historian" (3), one that quietly and in appealing tones tells the version of history that patriarchy wants to hear; for this reason, it is spiritualized and revered, seen to carry forth to subsequent ages eternal and uncontestable truths. It is a "cold Pastoral" (45) not because it is deceitful but because it appears to be cleansed of the hot pursuits and struggles of material history. Its coldness, in fact, is directly connected to its perceived embodiment of things eternal and to its claimed friendship to all humanity:

> Thou, silent form, dost tease us out of thought
> As doth eternity: Cold Pastoral!
> When old age shall this generation waste,
> Thou shalt remain, in midst of other woe
> Than ours, a friend to man.
>
> (44–48)

Thought is subordinated to belief, history is transformed into mortality, the urn is presented as a constant that endures, providing humanity with the structures of belief that are not to be questioned: all real human struggles are naturalized and idealized, taken out of the domain of history as conflict, and the feminized object made to carry this message of the imaginative beauties that overarch the truth of mortality is revered no less than the Virgin, of whom we are reminded by the description of the urn as an "unravish'd bride" who bears forth those qualities that (so the poet seems to think) offer a grace to humanity:[24]

> "Beauty is truth, truth beauty,"—that is all
> Ye know on earth, and all ye need to know.
>
> (49–50)[25]

Applying Ruether's theory to the *Urn* reveals a sort of "existential cannibalism,"[26] in which the ethical system of one group (in this case, symbolized in the statement "beauty is truth, truth beauty") is made possible by the violation and domination of another. This domination is exemplified not only in the poem's structure, but also in the act of poetic production itself; the poem appropriates the urn, even as the urn appropriates certain historical phenomena by transforming into art—and thus sanctifying—a specific view of human relations and values. On this view, stanza 4 does not offer an unsettling recognition that disrupts the illusion of beauty, as Rajan argues; rather, it naturalizes and sanctifies sacrificial acts. Sacrificial death and natural death, in fact, become one, equally accepted and revered. The mediations that define death in terms of specific realities—the conflict described in lines 8 and 9, the "other woe" hinted at in line 46, the poetic use made of the feminine—are transformed and frozen, made to serve the final vision of beauty and truth, terms that are discussed in the same letter in which Keats describes his own gynephobia (see the letter to Bailey, quoted above). What de Beauvoir says of the oppression of women generally bears on the process described in the *Urn:* "Now, what peculiarly signalizes the situation of woman is that she—a free and autonomous being like all human creatures—nevertheless finds herself living in a world where men compel her to assume the status of the Other. They propose to stabilize her as object and to doom her to immanence since her transcendence is to be overshadowed and forever transcended by another ego *(conscience)* which is essential and sovereign."[27] The effect of the speaker's comments in the *Urn* is to stabilize the urn, thereby stabilizing the masculine view of history by flattening the urn to single significance (i.e., "beauty is truth," etc.).

One consequence of the poem's unfolding vision is the production of sheer sterility under the title of beauty. The ashes in the funeral urn are not, of course, written into the poem itself, but are present by implication. They do not simply challenge or disrupt the figures drawn on the surface of the urn, but emphasize a reality that is shown repeatedly to constitute the surface itself, as well as the poetic depiction of this surface. The urn is a "cold Pastoral"; the "little town" is "emptied" as "good folk" leave, presumably to participate in a sacrifice; struggle defines the first two stanzas; "other woe," which also implies present woe, is projected for the future, long after the speaker has perished. This is not to deny the spiritual and transcendental impulses that critics have rightly noted as motivations for poetry, but to argue that in this case the impulse both arises from and promotes sterility; it describes beauty under the conditions of its human impossibility, presenting hope (much as Blake does, though ironically, in the *Songs of Innocence*) that is grounded in hardship and sacrifice. This throws an important light on the final lines of the poem. Far from being a statement of a dialectical relationship—which, for instance, might be rendered thus: "beauty leads to truth, and truth leads back once again to beauty"—these lines express a masculine equation, one that identifies domination of the feminine with transcendental beauty and value. The point is not that the truth of our mortality causes us to cherish a hope for something—in this case, art—that will endure,[28] but, rather, that what we hold dearest is covered over with the blood of others; the sacrifice of stanza 4 and the ashes contained within the urn are a constituent part of the value scheme articulated in the poem, and these surely are the sacrifice and ashes of women, a point that is illustrated by the developing and sharpening focus of the poem. In the *Urn*, men and maidens are described in tandem until the final lines, when Keats moves toward the statement about beauty and truth, at which time woman is written out of the poem, present now only in the hypostatized form of the urn, which remains as "a friend to man" (48). The spiritual and the aesthetic are conflated, and their credibility comes at the expense of the feminine.

One important feature of the poem that helps to elucidate its historical dimension is silence, which I have mentioned above and which I now would like to consider in more detail. It is common to interpret the many references to silence in the poem as a sign of purity, as an indication that Keats is concerned with matters of the soul or spirit. The spirit, according to this argument, hears what the flesh cannot, a point symbolized in this poem, as well as elsewhere in Keats, by emphasis on stillness and silence.[29] The difficulty with this perspective is not that it stresses matters of spirit and soul—although these are important concerns in the *Urn*, and certainly bear critical investigation—but rather, that it begins from idealist assumptions that prevent awareness of the fact that silence is always feminized. The conquest, negation, and sublimation of the feminine entail a violation of feminine expressive capacity, much as Tereus (to use a particularly brutal example), after raping Philomela, rips out her tongue in the belief that her enforced silence will assure his continued power and ostensible integrity within the family.[30] The denial of the feminine voice both enables and emboldens the masculine voice, allowing the poet's mind and imagination to run freely over the images on the urn, interpreting and defining them at will.

If silence is meant to suggest spirituality and transcendence in this poem, clearly Keats assumes that spirituality and transcendence are wholly masculine. The silence that is described in such compelling and beautiful language is the silence of the Other, and it is a sign of the denial of power; like the urn itself, it is interpreted as the speaker sees fit. One way the poem deflects attention from this fact is by alluding to its own aesthetic medium and stating that the power of language possessed by the poet is in fact not real power. When the poet asserts that the urn's stillness and "quietness" actually "speak" a purer language than poetry ("Sylvan historian, who canst thus express / A flowery tale more sweetly than our rhyme," 3–4)—a self-effacing statement of reverence that, in terms of Ruether's theory, must be seen as sublimation—he suggests that a major focus in the *Urn* is on the difference between visual and verbal art forms, and that the medium of sculpture is superior to that of poetry because it is quieter and hence purer. This effectively draws attention to aesthetic and, by extension, to spiritual matters, eliding not only the gender issue involved in these distinctions but also the fact that it is masculine poetic language that is able to claim its own inferiority, a claim that is also a subtle and magnificent display of power. The emphasis on voice and silence articulates once again the conflicts in the poem between the passive feminine and the active masculine, pointing to a hierarchy of values that, even as it claims superiority for the silent, feminine urn, reveals superiority for the masculine poetic voice.

Another way of considering the role of silence in the poem is to recognize that the suppression of the feminine is also a suppression (or at least a limiting) of knowledge of historical process. To put it crudely and reductively, history is a noisy, human affair; the poetic act in this case sets about to contain and silence it, to "freeze" it into a "flowery tale,"[31] forgetting not only that even in Arcady death figures prominently *(et in Arcadia ego)* but also that both death and life are historically and socially mediated. On this view, the determinant power of patriarchy transforms art itself into a handmaiden of tyranny. The poet does not want to actually *hear* the death cries of history inscribed everywhere on the urn, as well as contained within it, but prefers instead to celebrate those "unheard" melodies—idealizations of human experience—that allow the illusion of harmony, an illusion that betrays the fact of oppression. To silence the Other, and to celebrate this silence as spiritually and poetically inspirational, severely limits our knowledge of history.

The politics of silence that I am describing can be seen clearly in the opening two lines, which establish the patriarchal voice controlling the remainder of the poem. By portraying the urn first as the "unravish'd bride of quietness" and as the "foster-child of silence and slow time"—that is, in terms of the institutions of marriage and the family—and by identifying the feminine position with respect to these entirely in terms of silence, these lines securely position the urn as an object of masculine desire. More important, however, is the visible manipulation of the images, which suggests the poetic refusal to allow the urn its historical status within a network of market—and gender—relations. Especially in line 2, silence is not necessarily natural; in fact, it has been fostered onto the urn.[32] Again like the silent Philomela in the nightingale myth, the urn seems to be "still unravished" because it is inextricably bound to quietness and silence, controlled and defined by these in the "slow time" of historical process, which has made wives and daughters into so much property to be tended and shaped by masculine desire. Or to put the matter somewhat differently, Keats's description of the urn as a "Sylvan historian" may be a lament for a preindustrial world of agrarian bliss, but even in such an imagined world the patriarchal negation of the feminine remains intact.

I want now to consider briefly the role of desire in the *Urn* in an attempt to show that this is not an innocent category, even when it is understood as a desire for beauty. In her reading of the poem, Rajan argues that "Keats seeks in the urn a closed, Apollonian form. . . . Certain elements in the initial description of the urn appear to correspond to this desire."[33] While this certainly describes Keats's own self-representation of the situation, it is incomplete in historical terms because it assumes that this desire is the product of Keats's own "refusal to consent to incompleteness";[34] it individualizes and subjectivizes the term, and, in so doing, elides the context within which it arises. In a very real sense, the desire upon which the poetic vision is built is both a product and a reflection of unsatisfactory and repressive social relations: the expression of desire is also a sign of the denial of desire. This does not contradict—and in fact, confirms—the above argument about the masculine oppression of the feminine, for that oppression makes social and, therefore, human wholeness impossible. Thus, the desire for completeness of being intensifies in proportion as oppression intensifies.

Poetic desire is neither transcendental nor purely subjective, but social and historical, firmly caught up in the relations that are articulated everywhere in the poem. This desire is both a signature of and a contribution to human inequality, for in its radically individualistic cast it assumes that a superior realm of value will be gained not by changing the world but by transcending it. Taking this view, poetic desire is, to borrow Lukács's phrase, a "negation of history,"[35] or what Caudwell calls, in describing Keats's poetry, "a flight *from* reality."[36] This is not to question the sincerity of Keats's desire, but simply to insist on its historicity. A comment by G. V. Plekhanov (although not about Keats) states explicitly the position I wish to advance:

> The ideal of beauty prevailing at any time in any society or class of society is rooted partly in the biological conditions of mankind's development—which, incidentally, also produce distinctive racial features—and partly in the historical conditions in which the given society or class arose and exists. It therefore always has a very rich content that is not absolute, not unconditional, but quite specific. He who worships "pure beauty" does not thereby become independent of the biological and historical social conditions which determine his esthetic taste; he only more or less consciously closes his eyes to these conditions.[37]

I do not think that Keats is consciously ignoring the material conditions which underlie his poetic practice—I certainly do not believe that he is engaged in malicious deception—but that his poem participates in a system of social values that structurally excludes the feminine from history, just as it removes collective intervention from the realm of possibility.

Finally, several issues at the level of historical conjuncture, discussed briefly in the previous chapter, must be addressed again here because they both elucidate the anxiety in the *Urn* and provide an important context for understanding the patriarchal assumptions in the poem. In March 1817 Keats wrote two sonnets about the Phidian Marbles that Lord Elgin had brought to England, and it is clear that from the beginning he shared the enthusiasm for and admiration of the marbles expressed by many of his friends. As Clarence DeWitt Thorpe says in an editorial note to the two sonnets written to Haydon on the occasion of seeing the marbles,

> After a long and bitter controversy Haydon had convinced the sceptics that the Elgin Marbles were genuine works of the Phidian school, and had been largely instrumental in their purchase by the government (though at a price which netted Lord Elgin £16,000 less than the £51,000 they had cost him). The sonnets show Keats's state of mind after seeing these new wonders: he is stunned, dizzy with swirling ideas, and unable to bring his crowding impressions into order. Later he is to achieve perfect expression of his experience with Greek art in the *Ode on a Grecian Urn*.[38]

Haydon, who introduced Keats to the marbles, was similarly impressed, noting that "in the Elgin Marbles, the Composition, that is the arrangement of objects, to express the end in view as a whole, is perfect. The science of the parts that compose these objects individually [is] profound, and the execution of these parts to express the conceived Idea, of the end of the object, particularly as referring to the said whole [is] easy, vigorous, & powerful. The whole, the result of genius in the conception, arrangement, & industry & perseverance of execution."[39] Hazlitt too said of the marbles that "their forms are ideal, spiritual. Their beauty is power. By their beauty they are raised above the frailties of pain or passion."[40]

The actual beauty of the marbles notwithstanding, there was a great deal of controversy in Keats's day about their presence in England—a controversy in which Keats did not participate, but about which he must have known, especially as Haydon was an avid supporter of Lord Elgin (see, for instance Haydon's *Diary* 2:12–13). Byron was particularly bitter in his condemnation of Elgin's raids on Greek culture and art, attacking the antiquarian both in *Childe Harold* 2 and in *The Curse of Minerva*. In a letter of 1811, Byron remarked to Hobhouse that "Lord Elgin has been teazing to see me these last four days, I wrote to him at his request all I knew about his robberies, & at last have written to say that as it is my intention to publish (in Childe Harold) on that topic, I thought proper since he insisted on seeing me to give him notice, that he might not have an opportunity of accusing me of double dealing afterwards" (*BLJ* 2:65–66).[41]

This controversy is important because it points explicitly to the political context within which Keats wrote poetically about questions of beauty and truth. The ravaging of Greece for artifacts of great beauty to be sold to the British government, which in turn put the artifacts on display as a sign of British culture and power, and the suppression of the political realities of these acts, are material signs of the system of values controlling Keats's world. Not to acknowledge the absolute and determining significance of England's possession of the marbles is to suppress this context and, thus, to distort and redefine aesthetic concerns presented in the *Urn,* diverting attention from the specific historical acts of violence and political power, of which the feminization of the Other is a part.

On this view, the exercise of imperialist power (i.e., Elgin's exploits in Greece, as well as England's involvement in India and the New World) and the debasement of women are equally forms of political oppression, inextricably entwined within a single social situation that helps to explain the anxiety, even neurosis, in the *Urn*. That Keats chose to present as self-evident the power and beauty of the marbles, and to feminize the object of his poetic musings, suggests that the poem does more than display textual "ambiguity" arising from the relation of poem to urn[42] or the tension between art and reality;[43] it displays acute historical anxiety arising from actual human struggles and atrocities that it has repressed and forgotten, but that will not remain completely submerged.[44] What Phyllis Chessler says against Freud's theory of hysterical amnesia provides an important gloss on the historical amnesia that I believe is present in the *Urn:*

> The headaches, fatigue, chronic depression, frigidity, paranoia, and overwhelming sense of inferiority that Freud recorded so accurately about his many female patients was never *interpreted* in any remotely accurate terms. Female "symptoms" were certainly not viewed by Freud as the indirect communications characteristic of slave psychologies. Instead, such symptoms were viewed as "hysterical" and neurotic productions, as underhanded domestic tyrannies manufactured by spiteful, self-pitying, and generally unpleasant women whose *inability to be happy as women* stems from unresolved penis envy, unresolved Electra (or female Oedipal) complexes, or from general, intractable, and mysterious female stubbornness.[45]

Accepting Freud's general description of neurosis in women, Chessler takes strong issue with his interpretation of it. Where Freud tended to see neurosis in purely individual and private terms, Chesler recognizes it as a product of social relations, that is, as a product of the specific difficulties that women have long experienced at the hands of patriarchy. The anxieties present in the *Urn* are vulnerable to exactly this explanation. To historicize Keats's portrayal of the feminine is to expose the political underpinnings of his vision—a vision that is seemingly transhistorical and ostensibly inspired solely by sculptural beauty.[46]

To approach the poem from this direction—that is, from the assumption that it is historically implicated and that its vision of beauty and truth is fundamentally patriarchal—is to commit oneself to critically questioning Keats's poetic articulation of value, belief, and social relations. It is not a matter of attempting to let the poem speak for itself; it does speak for itself, unrelentingly, in strong patriarchal language. Rather, it is a matter of engaging in historical critical excavation to expose the bones of the dead and the blood of the beaten that are essential to this poetic expression, in the hope that just as the poem appropriates the urn for patriarchal purposes the poem itself can be appropriated for purposes of exposing human atrocity. To subject the *Urn* to the fires of a materialist feminist critique is not to say that it should be dismissed as just another display of patriarchal onesidedness—simply to dismiss articulations of patriarchy without investigation and critique is to assure its ongoing power—but rather, to argue that its poetic expression is also an historical expression, and, therefore, of absolute importance to understanding a specifically patriarchal form of social existence. It is to see that Keats's attempt to develop an alternative model of hope outside the military aggression, ideological conflict, and economic hardship of his own day entailed significant elements of social domination. The valorization of the agrarian past in the *Urn* is at the same time the valorization of patriarchal values that prevailed in Keats's world.

In historicizing and politicizing the *Ode on a Grecian Urn,* I have not sought to denigrate the considerable beauty and achievement of Keats's poetry, his ambition "of doing the world some good," or his individual integrity; to the contrary, I believe that his struggles and contributions must be honored by all who come after him. Rather, my purpose has been to argue that Keats's poetry is vitally important in our history and still has a great deal to teach us, even if it may not teach us exactly what Keats had in mind, because it provides glimpses of the power relations with which people must struggle, and expressions of hope that endure through history and that can and should be recognized as a hope for a better world. The importance of his work is not that it allows us to see beyond history, but that, as a response to and product of specific historical contexts, it provides us with a means of resisting historical amnesia.

6
"The Great Basement of All Power"
OTHO THE GREAT

KEATS'S poetic ventures into the real historical past were often less successful than his astonishingly beautiful short lyrics and highly imaginative longer narratives derived from myth and legend. But they are no less important, for they articulate an array of concerns and issues that inform all of his poetry in fundamental ways. While *King Stephen,* his only independent attempt at historical drama, never moves very far "into times past," breaking off after only little more than three scenes, *Otho the Great* provides a startlingly full picture of the social dimensions of political power. This drama, whatever its poetic shortcomings (which, in my opinion, are not as severe as some critics maintain), articulates the specific material workings of state authority—particularly the ideological processes within that authority—in a way that the most abstract and symbolic renderings of social life in *The Eve of St. Agnes* and *Hyperion* had not, and belongs alongside Byron's *The Two Foscari, Sardanapalus,* and *Marino Faliero* as an important dramatic formulation of history and politics. Further, in its steady attention to these matters, *Otho* provides a more compellingly critical vision of social relations and social institutions than the aesthetically superior (and roughly contemporary) *Ode on a Grecian Urn.*

Otho was coauthored with Charles Armitage Brown for the express purpose of making money. Unfortunately, these two facts—the partnership with Brown and the pecuniary motive—along with several slighting comments Keats made regarding the play, have led most readers to dismiss it without serious critical investigation as one of his most inferior works.[1] Brown's account of his role in composing the play has been particularly damaging, for it emphasizes the potboiler nature of the work and suggests as well that Keats played only a secondary role in the project: "I [Brown] engaged to furnish him [Keats] with the fable, characters, and dramatic conduct of a tragedy, and he was to embody it into poetry. The process of this work was curious; for, while I sat opposite him, he caught my description of each scene, entered into the characters to be brought forward, the events, and everything connected with it. Thus he went on, scene after scene, never knowing nor inquiring into the scene which was to follow, until four acts were completed."[2] It is likely, however, that even if this statement is accurate, Keats's role in the composition of *Otho* was not entirely passive. As Robert Gittings notes, once Keats began the project, he became very much committed to it: "[Keats's] wry reference to the play whose plot Brown fed to him was not a good augury for its quality; yet as its 'plots, speeches, counterplots and counter speeches' began to work him to a fever of composition, he began to put more and more of himself into it. 'The Lover is madder than I am', he announced to Fanny Brawne. It would be more true to say that he projected much of his own irrational and suppressed feeling into the hero Ludolph. Even quite idiosyncratic obsessions of his were repeated in the play." Indeed, it is fairly clear (as even Brown himself acknowledged) that Brown's influence diminished as the play proceeded, so much so that Keats rejected entirely Brown's idea for the final act, writing it (as Gittings puts it) "according to his own scheme."[3] To emphasize these facts is not to deny Brown's contribution, but to argue that Keats's growing enthusiasm for the project should encourage serious critical investigation of it in terms of Keats's developing intellectual, poetic, and political interests.

Further, Keats's occasional comments slighting the play should not obscure its real significance. He was no more critical of this work, for instance, than he was of several others, including the great odes,[4] and in fact, despite the doubts he occasionally voiced about the play, he believed that it was an important new beginning for him in poetry. As he told Bailey during the latter stages of its composition: "I sincerely hope you will be pleased when my Labours since we last saw each other shall reach you—One of my Ambitions is to make as great a revolution in modern dramatic writing as Kean has done in acting" (*LJK* 2:139). After completing the play, too, he wrote to his brother George that he hoped it would improve his reputation as a writer: "Were it [the play] to succeed even there it would lift me out of the mire. I mean the mire of a bad reputation which is continually rising against me. My name with the literary fashionables is vulgar—I am a weaver boy to them—a Tragedy would lift me out of this mess. And mess it is as far as it regards our Pockets" (*LJK* 2:186).

One of Keats's hopes respecting the play probably was that it would establish him as a writer of historical and intellectual sophistication, even while it earned him money and popularity. This is suggested by the fact that it de-emphasizes the "abstract" (Keats's word; see, e.g., *LJK* 2:132) features of his earlier works, and draws directly on history for its subject matter, stressing the significance of specific circumstances and of the network of relations arising from them. Any serious consideration of the play must acknowledge this focus and proceed from a knowledge of Keats's historical sources. To learn these sources and to understand the imaginative use he made of them is to learn much about why he may have considered the play to be a first step in revolutionizing dramatic writing.

Although he never actually documents his sources, his letters provide an excellent guide to his reading, making it fairly easy to speculate what they must have been. During 1818 and 1819 he noted that he had been reading Voltaire and Gibbon, both of whom give accounts of the reign of the German Otho I (912–973, A.D.), the first of the Holy Roman Emperors. Another source, not mentioned in the letters during this period but probably of even greater significance, is William Fordyce Mavor's *Universal History, Ancient and Modern* (in twenty-five volumes), which Keats had read avidly at the Clarke residence during his last months of school.[5] This work not only describes in greater detail than the accounts of Voltaire and Gibbon the revolt of Ludolph against his father, Otho; it also contains several names—e.g., Sigifred and Albert—that Keats uses in his play. (Keats's Sigifred and Albert, however, are not assigned their actual historical roles.) Further, the striking parallels in description and even in phrasing suggest that Keats had Mavor before him while he was writing the play. To note only one example, in presenting the reconciliation between Ludolph and Otho, both Keats and Mavor emphasize the emotional intensity displayed by father and son, and even use similar phrasing in describing this reconciliation. (Mavor refers to a "paternal embrace," while Keats has Otho remark: "Nor let these arms paternal hunger more / For an embrace.")[6]

These histories are strikingly similar in their evaluations of Otho, not only in their agreement that he was the first European ruler since Charlemagne to unify Europe under one rule, but more importantly in their descriptions of how and to what end he did this. In *The Decline and Fall of the Roman Empire*, for instance, Gibbon states: "In the North [of Germany] Christianity was propagated by the sword of Otho."[7] This is virtually identical to Voltaire's comment in his *Ancient and Modern History* that "Otho, who restored a part of the empire of Charlemagne, like him propagated the Christian faith in Germany, by conquest."[8] Mavor's account follows suit. In describing the coronation of Otho in 936 he remarks: "The archbishop [presiding at the coronation] . . . girded on the emperor's sword, saying—'Receive this sword, and use it against the enemies of Jesus Christ.' "[9] Keats would not have been oblivious to such consistency in these descriptions; as I hope to show, he actively integrates them into the dramatic action of the play, using them as the basis of an important unstated system of values governing the conduct and thoughts of all the characters.

A second and equally important characteristic of Otho that these historians stress is his blending of extreme violence and tyranny with equally extreme displays of mercy and benevolence. For example, in describing the initial invasion of Germany by the Hungarians early in Otho's reign, Mavor notes: "the invaders were defeated with prodigious slaughter."[10] He follows this almost immediately with a lengthy account of the unsuccessful revolt of Ludolph against Otho, his father, stating:

> After some time the prince [Ludolph] was made sensible of this error, and took an opportunity, while his father was hunting, to throw himself at his feet, and implore his clemency. "Have pity," said he, "upon your misguided child, who returns like the prodigal son to his father. If you permit him to live after he has deserved death, he will assuredly repent of his folly and ingratitude, and the residue of his life shall be marked by exemplary fidelity and obedience." To this affecting appeal Otho could only reply by a flood of tears and a paternal embrace; but when his agitation subsided, he assured the penitent of his warmest favor, and generously pardoned all his adherents.[11]

Voltaire makes the same point in the *Annals of the Empire*, describing the glory that came to Otho in "having re-established the empire of Charlemagne,"[12] the mercy he showed to his rebel son, Ludolph, and at the same time the absolutism that characterized his reign: "The more Otho effects absolute power, the more he is opposed by the noblemen of the great fiefs.... The despotism of Otho alienates the minds of men to such a degree that his own brother, Henry, duke of one part of Lorraine, had united with several noblemen to deprive him of his throne and life."[13]

These sources demonstrate the ideas that permeate Keats's play. In dramatizing the conflict between Otho and Ludolph, and then in describing Otho's world after this conflict has been resolved, Keats consistently focuses the politics of power in all public and personal relations. Specifically, he brilliantly shows the contradictions that arise when benevolence and mercy exist within a context of absolute domination. Following Voltaire and Mavor, he emphasizes that Otho is capable of compassion, but only after he has militarily defeated and completely humiliated those toward whom he is being compassionate. Implicit in this portrayal is a commentary on the religious and political institutions that sanction and make Otho's personal character and public power possible, and Keats addresses these issues as well. In dramatizing history, however, he does not simply duplicate his sources; he evaluates the ideas and issues they describe, insisting that a system of benevolence and power, such as the one controlled by Otho, is execrable and ultimately destructive of all social and human ties.

One final point about Keats's use of his historical sources bears stressing before I turn to an analysis of the play. Although he draws directly and in discernible ways on Gibbon, Voltaire, and Mavor, Keats was faced with the difficult task of dramatizing the diverse and complex issues that he encountered in his reading. Rather than attempting to detail the literal conflicts that plagued Otho's thirty-seven-year rule, he chose instead to interiorize them—that is, to focus them within Otho's family after the revolt of Ludolph has been suppressed. In so doing, he abandons his sources and places a love interest at the center of the play. This strategy is obviously calculated to appeal to the theater-going public of the early nineteenth century, but it also serves several important additional functions.

First, by beginning the play as the revolt is winding down, and by offering a brief sketch in the opening act of the disturbances that have plagued Otho's reign, Keats effectively establishes the central thematic importance of public political concerns: Otho's violence, his absolute rule, the connivings of other characters for position within Otho's regime, and so on. Second, by following these matters with an essentially domestic situation in the heart of the play, he not only creates a manageable context for the dramatization of large political subjects that otherwise would be impossible to handle, but, more importantly, he shows directly the impact of social conflict on personal life. That is, interiorization of the action does not disturb the play's historical focus; quite the reverse, it sharpens this focus by showing the ineluctable presence of political reality in every aspect of human experience.[14]

I want now to turn to the play itself, using the ideas that characterize Keats's sources as the basis for analyzing the system of values and the network of social relations that, I believe, underpin its dramatic action.

The action of the play compellingly demonstrates not only Keats's deep understanding of his historical sources but also his ability to recreate imaginatively a significant historical situation. In reconstructing Otho's world, he makes public and personal power the issue that encompasses all other issues; moreover, he shows how this power underlies all value in the world of the play. The connection between power and systems of value is seen fully in Otho, who appears almost consistently to be a good ruler and a good father who has been wronged. His many displays of affection towards his prodigal son, his displays of mercy towards his enemy, his open embrace of Erminia after she has been proven innocent: all these actions imply his fundamental honesty and benevolence.

The apparent integrity of his character, however, must be weighed against the sort of world he rules and against what he demands in return for his kindness. We begin to understand that political expediency motivates his benevolence when he publicly releases Gersa, one of the leaders of the Hungarian invaders. Brought before Otho in chains, Gersa initially believes he is being mocked in public, and complains loudly to Otho about this humiliation. To everyone's surprise, Otho responds to these charges by setting Gersa free, an act that entirely humbles Gersa:

> I am wound up in deep astonishment!
> Thank you, fair lady [Auranthe]—Otho!—Emperor!
> You rob me of myself; my dignity
> Is now an infant;—I am a weak child.
>
> (1.2.117–20)

Gersa's emotional response here at once illustrates and obscures the political significance of his release. Extravagantly grateful for his freedom, he cannot see that he is being manipulated to strengthen Otho's rule. Otho knows that to release Gersa is to gain his loyalty and to assure that there will be no further invasions by the Hungarians. As Otho himself explains, Gersa's presence among the Hungarians will serve as a "healing presence" (1.2.132), thus strengthening Otho's political position. More than this, Otho grants Gersa his freedom because the Hungarian, Otho knows, is not a true enemy, having opposed his countrymen's plan to invade Germany. Otho tells him:

> Though I did hold you high in my esteem
> For your self's sake, I do not personate
> The stage-play emperor to entrap applause.
> To set the silly sort o' the world agape,
> And make the politic smile; no, I have heard
> How in the Council you condemn'd this war,
> Urging the perfidy of broken faith,—
> For that I am your friend.
>
> (1.2.142–49)

This side of Otho's power is presented even more compellingly in the reconciliation scene with Ludolph. When the two first meet after the long civil war, Otho begins by toying with and humiliating his son, threatening to keep him "cag'd up" (2.1.88) to avoid further rebellion, and only eventually grants him pardon, eliciting from the surprised Ludolph cries of complete submission and gratitude. But again this scene arises from more than "paternal hunger . . . / For an embrace"

(2.1.123–24); it arises from political considerations, and serves at least two political purposes. First, by pardoning Ludolph and allowing him to marry Conrad's sister, Otho aims to advance the political fortunes of Conrad, who has helped Otho to defeat the Hungarians. And, more importantly, Otho knows (although Ludolph has attempted to hide the fact) that Ludolph has fought in disguise with the Germans against the Hungarians (see 2.1.127). In other words, the situation here is identical to the events in the Gersa scene: Otho is merciful only when he knows his son is already on his side, so that the show of mercy actually costs him nothing and stands to protect him politically.

Otho's statements of self-evaluation and self-congratulation demonstrate these same discrepancies between apparent integrity and actual political motive. For instance, in describing the rule of good politics (after the release of Gersa), he remarks:

> I know how the great basement of all power
> Is frankness, and a true tongue to the world;
> And how intriguing secrecy is proof
> Of fear and weakness, and a hollow state.
>
> (1.2.175–78)

While this statement is innocent enough in the abstract, in the context of Otho's political conduct it is strikingly repulsive and blackly ironic, empty of the political honesty it professes. As shown above, Otho is concerned only with securing and extending absolute political power. Like his mercy, his honesty is simply another political weapon, no different from the violence, manipulation, and deceit that prevail in his world, and it is implemented only when it serves "to prop my empire's dome" (1.2.161). This grating reality behind his statement is made explicit by the fact that he is speaking to the most vile character in the play, Conrad, and expressing his deep gratitude to Conrad for his loyalty: Otho's is a virtue that attracts support from the devious, who are willing to practice violence and call it nobility.

This contradiction at the center of Otho's character (and, I hope to show, at the center of the world he controls) is described literally by Ludolph just before the reconciliation scene; as Ludolph explains, it accounts in large measure for his alienation, his rebellion, and even for the particular way he eventually works to preserve his father's empire. In speaking with Sigifred, he vacillates from admiration of his father's "noble nature" (1.3.55) to condemnation of his "hot, proud, obstinate" temper (1.3.89), and is driven virtually to distraction by these conflicting characteristics. Unable to resolve in real terms his difficulties with his father or to find a way to live with the political and personal implications of his father's character, he resolves them by idealizing the past and by disguising himself when he defends this idealized past. Explaining his use of this disguise when he helps his father defeat the Hungarians, he tells Sigifred:

> —Twas done in memory of my boyish days,
> Poor cancel for his kindness to my youth,
> For all his calming of my childish griefs,
> And all his smiles upon my merriment.
> No, not a thousand foughten fields could sponge
> Those days paternal from my memory,
> Though now upon my head he heaps disgrace.
>
> (1.3.40–46)

Such idealization marks the terrible distance between what human relationships should be and, as Ludolph perceives them, what they really are in Otho's empire. What Ludolph learns in adulthood is what he could not see as a child, namely, that his father represents and works for the advancement of a deceitful social system and that the principles governing his father's conduct are necessarily bound to this system. That he rationalizes his own efforts to preserve it, while at the same time literally disguising himself during combat, shows his own deep-rooted sense that any honor that he might win by serving his father would be vile and hypocritical. And that this is in fact the case is revealed when Otho grants him Auranthe's hand, ostensibly as a show of love for his son but in fact as a reward to Conrad for his loyalty: ". . . for my own / Preeminence and safety [Otho remarks], I will strive / To keep thy [Conrad's] strength upon . . . [my state's] pedestal" (1.2.163–65).

In such a world, where all values are subject to the demands of political absolutism, true virtue is impossible, and human potential is inevitably defeated, as is evidenced in the character of Albert. According to everyone in the play, Albert's honesty is his distinguishing feature, setting him apart from those around him. For example, when Erminia entrusts him with the letter that will exonerate her and expose the devious plot of Conrad and Auranthe, she says, ". . . he [Albert] was ever known to be a man / Frank, open, generous; Albert I may trust. / . . . Albert's an honest man" (2.2.22–24). But his honesty, however widely it is known and respected, is not exempt from the engulfing events of his world, and his effort to remain honest in the face of the events surrounding him focuses the unavoidable and shaping influence of circumstance even on those aspects of human character deemed most personal and sacred.[15] Through no malice of his own, and despite his effort to lead a life of principle, he finds himself embroiled in a situation that will both make him dishonest (or, put differently, that will make him honest in the way that Otho is honest) and that will finally destroy him:

for the letter that will show Erminia's honesty will also show that Albert slept with Auranthe, whom he loves, but who, it turns out, is plotting to win Ludolph and social position. In a world which comprises intrigue and deceit, his virtue is not simply a handicap, but, in fact, the central agent in his downfall. As he states it:

> Is it for this, I now am lifted up
> By Europe's throned Emperor, to see
> My honour be my executioner,—
> My love of fame, my prided honesty
> Put to the torture for confessional?
> . . . .
> I must confess,—and cut my throat,—to-day?
>
> (3.1.20–31)

Faced with the impossible choice of either deceiving his emperor and thereby destroying the innocent Erminia, or of speaking honestly and thereby destroying himself, he is driven to become as manipulative as those around him, to deceive in an effort to preserve at least the semblance of honesty. His plan is to withhold Auranthe's secret initially, to use it to bribe her to leave the country with him, and then, after he has preserved himself and won her, to reveal the secret (by turning the letter over to Otho), an act that would redeem Erminia's reputation. But his plan cannot work; rather, it dooms him by dragging him ever further into the manipulative and violent world of Conrad, Auranthe, and Otho, where human life is always expendable and where honesty and mercy are nothing unless they contribute to the advancement of one's position and power.

The distortions of value that figure so prominently in the play inevitably raise questions about the social role of religion. In some respects, Keats's handling of religion does not appear to draw on the accounts contained in his historical sources. Keats indeed seems to play down any substantive connection between Christianity and political violence and political power. The one religious figure in the play, Ethelbert, is, like Albert, fundamentally honest and is committed to defending the innocent Erminia, whom everyone else deems guilty. However, I believe that Ethelbert cannot be fully understood in purely personal terms, but must be placed within an institutional context and assessed in terms of his social role. That is, however much we may applaud specific attributes evident in his character, we must recognize the connections between the religion he represents and the larger network of social and political relations that control his world. What we see from this perspective is that there is no conflict between Christianity and Otho's tyranny, and that Otho sees in his defense of Christianity a sign of his own benevolence and righteousness. In other words, political power and Christianity work together for the security and extension of the empire, exactly in the way Voltaire and Mavor suggest in their histories of Otho's reign.

To see this political dimension of Christianity, we need look no further than the several exchanges between Ethelbert and Otho. When he comes initially before the emperor to plead for the release of captive women (including Erminia) after the conclusion of the war, Ethelbert greets him by proclaiming, "The benison of heaven on your head, / Imperial Otho" (1.2.185–86). Otho's responses are equally complimentary, as he refers to the monk as "good Ethelbert" and as "old Ethelbert" (1.2.189, 199). Further, to add authority to his statements when he is speaking to others, Ethelbert addresses them "in the Emperor's name" (2.2.128). And even when circumstances generate friction between Otho and Ethelbert, there remains mutual respect for the institutional positions of each (see, for instance, 3.2.107–10, and 117–27). Finally, after Auranthe and Conrad have been exposed as villains, and after Ludolph has gone mad, Ethelbert is one of the main sources of comfort for the distraught Otho.

These exchanges and scenes establish the fundamental social role of religion in the play. They also obligate us to assess the value system espoused by Ethelbert in terms of the network of social relations that support it and which, in turn, it works to preserve. Far from being a representative of an abstract set of principles, the religious institution is shown consistently to be humanly engaged, at one moment absorbing the contradictions and injustices of Otho's reign into a rhetoric of high purpose and morality, and, at another, working to preserve the innocent Erminia (not simply for the protection of innocence, but also for the protection of the empire from the plottings of Conrad and Auranthe). While Ethelbert certainly is not malicious, and while personally he might be regarded as honest and admirable, he is not independent of the world around him, nor is he free of the political demands that his religion places on him.

In elaborating the power relations inherent in the systems of value that control the world of the play, Keats gives extensive treatment to the social role of women. This subject is both complex and significant; for, as I have shown in my discussion of the *Urn*, he had difficulty coming to terms with women, and in trying to treat them intelligently and fairly in the play he exposes not only the limitations of his own thought but also the expectations and assumptions of patriarchal culture. Early in the play, when Ludolph is madly in love with her, Auranthe is described as a "pearl" (1.3.103) warranting the highest praise and worship; but, as her maliciousness is discovered, she becomes (in the eyes of Ludolph) a "demon" (5.5.153) who must be sacrificed (5.5.155) for her sins. Conversely, the play presents Erminia as a "pollution to / . . . holy rites"

(3.2.58), and then, when her innocence is discovered, as an "angel's voice" (5.5.168) and as the embodiment of "sweet innocence" (5.5.169). While in one respect these characterizations commendably illustrate society's gradual ability to distinguish between innocence and guilt, as well as the willingness of a ruler to admit to the wrong he has done, in terms of social relations they display exactly the point Keats makes in his letter about women, quoted in the previous chapter (see *LJK* 1:341). As the play presents them, women are either goddesses (or, at the very least, helpless creatures who need the protection of men), or they are worthless; either way, they are entirely subject to the whims of a patriarchal system, and are totally without social or even human rights and power.[16]

The portrayal of women goes a long way toward explaining the allotment of power and the system of values in Otho's world, focusing a fundamental and utterly destructive network of personal relations at the very center of the social fabric. Both Otho and Ludolph, representatives of the ruling order, objectify women, selecting or discarding them on the basis of their abilities to serve the ends of masculine power. Irrespective of the moral earnestness expressed by these men as individuals, their actions expose the abuses inherent in the patriarchal society that they unquestioningly support and work to extend. It is a society whose structure insists on absolute division along gender lines, both in terms of power and value, and even if the governing system of beliefs professes benevolence and moral integrity, the material fact of this division sows seeds of corruption and renders the value system inhumane. Put differently, the values to which all characters in the play subscribe are not transcendent and pure, but, rather, ideological; moreover, they concentrate all power in the hands of patriarchy while at the same time eliding the political basis of this allotment of power. This contradiction is at once a manifestation of the social structure encompassing the dramatic action, in the same manner that Otho's mercy and honesty are manifestations of this structure, and also, like them, a source for the tragedy that the play describes.

Clearly, the world Otho controls and the principles he defends do not begin to match self-representations of them by virtually every character in the play. This is emphasized strongly in the portrayal of physical violence, which is so deeply rooted in the social fabric of the play that all the characters take its pervasive presence for granted. In the very opening scene we are told that thousands have just been slain; yet, because the passage is spoken by a villain, we overlook its real significance—namely, that it reveals the vast human slaughter that accompanies Otho's benevolence. Further evidence of the violence used to secure and extend Otho's power is presented when Sigifred celebrates the disguised Ludolph's military accomplishments: "Ludolph and the swift Arab are the same; / Still to rejoice that 'twas a German arm / Death doing in a turban's masquerade" (1.3.3–5). Such violence carries over directly to the daily experiences of the characters, becoming a central ingredient in their lives. When Ethelbert accuses Auranthe of plotting against Erminia, Ludolph responds immediately with threats of violence: "O that that dull cowl / Were some most sensitive portion of thy life, / That I might give it to my hounds to tear!" (3.2.92–94). And later, when Ludolph believes that he will be unable to find and punish the fleeing Auranthe, he laments: "O, where is that illustrious noise of war, / To smother up this sound of labouring breath, / This rustle of the trees!" (5.1.28–30). Further, Albert's threat to Conrad and Auranthe is returned with murder (5.2 passim), and Auranthe's guilt drives her to suicide. Even the positive values presented in the play are described in terms of violence. For instance, as he affectionately watches his son and Auranthe express their love for one another, Otho remarks that compared to their happiness military conquest is nothing, "unless perchance I might rejoice to win / This little ball of earth, and chuck it them / To play with!" (3.2.23–25). These and other descriptions effectively establish the context within which all of the action and moral issues are presented, and they make violence a central part of the political and domestic troubles in the play.

The various issues sketched above are drawn together and exposed in all their horror in the final act, in which Ludolph goes mad. Structurally, this final episode is compelling, for it represents yet a further compression of the action. That is, the issues that are described initially in terms of public political life and military struggle, and which are then focused in a domestic context, are here concentrated in a single character, a dramatic strategy that allows us to see literally the contradictions and destructiveness of the world Otho controls.

One telling feature of this final scene is the domestic solidarity and compassion that are combined with religious sincerity. Otho, Erminia, and Ethelbert comfort one another as they watch Ludolph's demise, and in their displays of emotion, hope, and despair they embody and project fully the principles governing their world. Ethelbert here is no longer despised as a "rebel-priest" (3.2.219) as he had been while defending Erminia, but is now a "holy abbot" (5.4.6) (both of these comments are made by Otho); Erminia is no longer an outcast, but is now a "gentle girl" (5.4.7); and Otho, according to Erminia, deserves the prayers of saints (5.4.9). This would seem to suggest that the turmoil that has run through the play is now over and that the only remaining tragedy lies in watching a loved one die. In fact, however, nothing of substance has changed. Ludolph, in his madness, holds up the elements of their world for all to see, and yet they see only a mad man who is to be pitied: they do not see that his madness is also their madness, comprised of human sacrifice, religious cant, abuse of power, gross injustices against the innocent, and warped notions of peace, mercy, and justice. All of this is brought home in the final scene of the play:

> *Ludolph.* Oh! thou good man [Otho], against whose sacred head
> I was a mad conspirator, chiefly too
> For the sake of my fair newly wedded wife,
> Now to be punish'd,—do not look so sad!
> Those charitable eyes will thaw my heart,
> Those tears will wash away a just resolve,
> A verdict ten-times sworn! Awake—awake—
> Put on a judge's brow, and use a tongue
> Made iron-stern by habit! Thou shalt see
> A deed to be applauded, 'scribed in gold!
> Join a loud voice to mine, and so denounce
> What I alone will execute!
> *Otho.*   Dear son,
> What is it? By your father's love, I sue
> That it be nothing merciless!
> *Ludolph.*   To that demon?
> Not so! No! She is in temple-stall
> Being garnish'd for the sacrifice, and I,
> The priest of justice, will immolate her
> Upon the altar of wrath! She stings me through!—
> Even as the worm doth feed upon the nut,
> So she, a scorpion, preys upon my brain!
> I feel her gnawing here!—Let her but vanish,
> Then, father, I will lead your legions forth,
> Compact in steeled squares, and speared files,
> And bid our trumpets speak a fell rebuke
> To nations drows'd in peace!
>   (5.5.140–64)

In madness, Ludolph expresses directly and uncompromisingly the realities that undergird Otho's power, exposing the prevailing social principles for what they are—vicious and mad. The spiritual justification (5.5.156) for absolute power; the bold judgment of and extermination of human life (5.5.155); the military exploits aimed at achieving peace; the mercy that ostensibly will triumph over all: these cannot sustain a culture indefinitely, and in fact they corrode it by either denying or confusing the true human (social) needs and desires upon which a strong culture must be built. This is the conclusion that the play draws finally from the actions and values that characterize Otho's world.

Otho the Great portrays an array of religious, political, and domestic issues, integrating them into a complex and yet discernible social framework. It is an ambitious play that offers a synthesis of many of the concerns uppermost in Keats's mind during 1818 and 1819, and demonstrates powerfully the historical dimension of his poetic vision. This is not to suggest that the play is one of his finest productions. Many of the complaints against it that have been made since the time of its first publication are valid. But it is better than many critics have been willing to admit, especially in its ability to portray the contradictions that often exist between a system of social values and the actual practices that those values both give rise to and sanction. Moreover, in its portrayal of the power relations within society, the play is critically important to our understanding of the romantic period. It deserves to be placed alongside the dramas of Byron as an example of the romantic tendency to interiorize historical, political, and social issues—that is, to project them symbolically and in compressed fashion, a strategy that frees the poetry from purely empirical historical data and allows it to focus the ideological dimensions of culture.[17]

7
"This Mighty Cost and Blaze of Wealth"
LAMIA

SHORTLY before he began writing *Lamia* and *Otho the Great,* Keats remarked in a letter to his sister: "Still I cannot affo[r]d to spend money by Coachire and still my throat is not well enough to warrant my walking" (*LJK* 2:121). Later in the same letter he mentions that he has been "prepa[r]ing to enqu[i]re for a Situation with an Apothecary, put [sic] Mr Brown persuads [sic] me to try the press once more" (*LJK* 2:121). Over the next three months—that is, during the time he was working on *Otho* and *Lamia*—he continued to speak frequently and sometimes bitterly of his financial difficulties and of his need of employment. In a subsequent letter to his sister he noted that "I have enough knowledge of my gallipots to ensure me an employment & maintainance" (*LJK* 2:125), and to Fanny Brawne he wrote in August 1819 that "my cash-recourses are for the present stopp'd, I fear for some time—I spend no money but it increases my debts" (*LJK* 2:141). Also in August he noted to John Taylor (in a letter asking for a loan) that "I have been rather unfortunate lately in money concerns. . . . For these three Months Brown has advanced me money: he is not at all flush and I am anxious to get some elsewhere" (*LJK* 2:143).[1] One of the most interesting and telling of his many comments about money involves his realization that writing—including the writing of poetry—can never escape the control of economic reality. In a letter to Reynolds in July 1819 (a letter that notes his progress on *Otho* and *Lamia*), Keats states: "I have of late been moulting: not for fresh feathers & wings: they are gone, and in their stead I hope to have a pair of patient sublunary legs. I have altered, not from a Chrysalis into a butterfly, but the Contrary. having two little loopholes, whence I may look out into the stage of the world: and that world on <my> our coming here I almost forgot. The first time I sat down to write, I cod [sic] scarcely believe in the necessity of so doing. It struck me as a great oddity—Yet the very corn which is now so beautiful, as if it had only <taken> took to ripening yesterday, is for the market: So, why shod [sic] I be delicate" (*LJK* 2:128–29).

While *Lamia* need not be viewed only as a poetic allegory of these personal difficulties, concerns, and insights, neither should it be viewed as entirely exempt from them. What Keats says in his letters and what he writes in his poetry always intersect with ideological structures of authority and economic realities larger than his private desires or individual intentions, and many of his letters and poems are articulations of this fact and attempts to understand and come to terms with it. To recognize this is to situate *Lamia* within a set of interpretive controls very different from those which traditionally have defined criticism of the poem; it opens the poem up not only to literary historical investigation but also to social historical, economic, and ideological investigation.

Criticism has most often occupied itself with two major problems in interpretation of *Lamia*, both thematic and formal in nature. First is the problem of the relation between the opening section of the poem, which recounts the exchange between Hermes and Lamia, and the remainder of the narrative, which charts the activities of Lamia, Lycius, and Apollonius. The apparent disjunction between these two episodes is most often explained in terms of Keats's beliefs that, while gods (in this case, Hermes) may achieve realization of an absolute ideal (presented here as the Nymph), ordinary mortals may not hope for such fulfillment (as is illustrated in the death of Lycius at the end of the story). Thus, according to this line of argument, the opening scene provides a framework that gives human significance to the remainder of the narrative.[2] The second problem involves the apparent conflict in the narrative between philosophy, which in Apollonius appears cold and rigid, and the imagination. While there is less of a consensus about how this conflict should be understood, Walter Evert's explanation has generally been regarded as balanced and plausible. In the story of Lycius and Apollonius, Evert argues, Keats dramatizes the power and importance of philosophy as a limit "on what it is possible for poetry to be or do in the world for which it is intended."[3] Thus the poem does not reject philosophy, but, rather, views it as a necessary safeguard against the potential dangers of the unleashed private imagination.[4]

Without denying the importance of these interpretive problems, and without questioning the very real contributions of critical efforts to come to terms with them, I want to stress that previous critical focus has been largely centered on the text and has ignored the economic, ideological, and historical pressures that Keats himself recognized as important shaping influences on poetic activity.[5] When criticism has drawn upon extratextual information, it has usually been to bring the poem in line with certain of Keats's remarks in his letters about the poetic imagination, or to comment on the poet's reading of Burton's *Anatomy of Melancholy*. Seldom has it investigated the extent to which Keats's knowledge of and reading in history—and his sensitivity to imaginative renderings of human experience down through history—control the meaning of his poetry.

Sketching some matters relevant to the characters and settings of *Lamia* can illustrate Keats's possible awareness of, and poetic concern with, issues beyond those usually brought to bear on the poem, issues that can be used as at least a partial context for examining the poem's historical dimensions. The aim here is to broaden the points of reference of certain key elements in the poem, not simply to establish Keats's historical sophistication and authorial intention—although these certainly are matters that should be investigated—but, more importantly, to provide a basis for a critical historical reassessment of the narrative in terms that may include but finally extend beyond both biographical/intentional concerns and formal/thematic concerns.

It is a commonplace that Keats was an avid reader of both history and mythology, and that he knew virtually by heart Andrew Tooke's school book *The Pantheon* (see the discussion of Tooke in chapter 4), published in 1698 and running through many editions during the eighteenth century.[6] Tooke offers many descriptions of Hermes (Mercury), and likely is one source for Keats's thinking about this god. Hermes is presented by Tooke alternately as a thief, as the inventor of letters, as a master of eloquence and of interpretation, and as the inventor of the lyre. Moreover, the "serpent rod" (1:89) that Keats associates with Hermes is in Tooke noted for its "wonderful Faculty of deciding all Controversies. This Virtue was first discover'd by Mercury, who seeing two serpents fighting, as he travell'd, he put his Rod between them and reconciled them presently, and they mutually embraced each other, and stuck to the Rod, which is call'd Caduceus."[7] That this rod had a known power over serpents may have been one inducement for Keats to include a reference to it in his description of the exchange between Hermes and the serpent Lamia.

But perhaps the most significant—and certainly the most interesting—feature of Hermes, as Tooke describes him (and as Lempriere describes him as well in his *Classical Dictionary*, which Keats read in his youth), is that he was the god of profit. According to Tooke, Hermes was believed "to have taught the Art of buying, selling and trafficking first, and to have receiv'd the Name of Mercury, from his understanding of Merchandize. Hence he is accounted the God of the Merchants, and the God of Gain, so that all unexpected Gain and Treasure, that comes of a sudden, is from him call'd . . . [Hermeson or Hermaion]." Later in his account of this god, Tooke says of the statues of Mercury that "a Purse was usually hung to the Statues of Mercury, to signifie, that he was the God of Gain and Profit, and presided over Merchandizing, in which because many times things are done by Fraud and Treachery, they gave him the Name of Dolius."[8] The "serpent rod," too—though Tooke does not state this point directly—was often described as the rod of wealth. The connection between Hermes and profit is seen in other accounts of the god, which do not appear in Tooke. For instance, the lyre that Hermes invented on the day he was born was sold to Apollo, who later became the god of poetry,[9] and the knowledge that Hermes dispensed was usually sold to the highest bidder (a fact revealed in Philostratus's life of Apollonius). In ways that I want to suggest momentarily, these are significant details in the connection between the opening scene with Hermes and Lamia and the subsequent narrative of Lamia, Lycius, and Apollonius.

I want to turn now briefly to the historical background of Apollonius, the "trusty guide / And good instructor" (1:375–76) of Lycius. Keats appended to Lamia the brief account in Burton's *Anatomy* of Apollonius's exorcism to preserve a young Corinthian named Mennipus Lycius, and this is usually seen as the immediate source for the narrative. I do not wish to suggest that Keats was intentionally misleading readers by directing attention to Burton, but neither do I believe that Burton is his only source. While the account in the *Anatomy* gives a fairly accurate version of Keats's plot, many details in *Lamia* do not appear in Burton, although they do appear in other historical works to which Keats had access. Moreover, Keats mentions several times in his letters during the summer of 1819 his desire to find an adequate library (e.g., *LJK* 2:137), and in August of that summer he "removed to Winchester for the convenience of a Library" (*LJK* 2:139)—facts that suggest his desire to give his poetry historical sophistication, or at least factual authenticity.

It is possible that Keats would have read the actual (and much longer) account of Mennipus Lycius, the serpent woman, and Apollonius in Philostratus's *Life and Times of Apollonius of Tyana*, which had been translated into English in 1811. If he did indeed consult this work, he would have known that Apollonius himself, no less than Lamia, was deemed a wizard of sorts and was even tried before the emperor Domitian for sorcery. Keats certainly suggests his awareness of this fact near the end of the poem, when he has Lycius rage against Apollonius's

> Impious proud-heart sophistries,
> Unlawful magic, and enticing lies.
> Corinthians! look upon that grey-beard wretch!
> Mark how, possess'd, his lashless eyelids stretch
> Around his demon eyes!
>
> (2:285–89)

Keats also would have known that over against the view of Apollonius as a wizard or demon was the fact that he was a contemporary of Christ and was thought by many to be the true Messiah: his birth was attended by miracles, he raised someone from the dead, and he appeared after death before those who had doubts about an afterlife. Moreover, Apollonius practiced a rigid asceticism, refusing to wear clothes made from animal skins and refusing to make animal sacrifices to the gods. He also despised money, and understood that knowledge was inextricably linked to money, as is illustrated not only in his descriptions of the god Mercury,[10] who made it a practice to sell knowledge to the highest bidder, but also in his statement that "all arts and sciences existing among men, while they have different activities, agree in this, that they are universally carried on to make money. . . . True philosophy is the only exception to this rule. Among learned professions I would class poetry, music, astronomy, higher education, and oratory other than forensic."[11] All of these details find their way into Keasts's narrative in one form or another, as Apollonius is at once to be revered as a philosopher, damned as a sorcerer, recognized as an ascetic, and so on. None of these details appear in the account from Burton appended to the poem.

The case of Lamia is both simpler and more complex than that of the other characters. Like Hermes, she is described in Tooke's *Pantheon* in a way that is roughly consistent with Burton's descriptions and with Keats's poetic rendering. Lamiae, Tooke notes, "had the Faces of Women, and also the Necks and Breasts: But below they were cover'd with Scales, and they had the Tails of Serpents. They us'd to entice Men and then devour them. Their Breasts were naked, and their Bosom was open: they looked on the ground as it were out of Modesty; thus they tempted Men to discourse with them, and when they came near, these *Lamiae* us'd to fly in their Faces, and strangle them, and tear them to pieces barbarously. And what more plainly expresses the devilish Arts of wicked Women?"[12] This description, of course, is not entirely consistent with the specific details presented in Keats's poem, but it does offer a fairly precise account of the association between serpent and woman—and the threat to masculine security inherent in that associatoin—that Keats seems to be exploring on one level of the poem.

Less obvious but no less significant is the historical role assigned to lamiae by popular myth. John Brand's *Observations on the Popular Antiquities of Great Britain* (which is one source for Keats's *Eve of St. Agnes*) offers a lengthy account of "Fairy Mythology." Brand notes in the very beginning of this account that "Bourne supposes the fairy superstition to have been conveyed down to us by tradition from the lamiae, who were esteemed so mischievous as to take away young children and slay them; these, says he, together with the fauns, the gods of the woods, seem to have formed the notion of fairies."[13] This observation becomes very compelling in light of the opening lines of *Lamia:*

> Upon a time, before the faery broods
> Drove Nymph and Satyr from the prosperous woods,
> Before king Oberon's bright diadem,
> Sceptre, and mantle, clasp'd with dewy gem,
> Frighted away the Dryads and the Fauns
> From rushes green, and brakes, and cowslip'd lawns,
> The ever-smitten Hermes empty left
> His golden throne, bent warm on amorous theft.
>
> (1:1–8)

Keats is careful here to set the opening scenes in an age prior to fairy mythology—in an age, that is, preceding the mythology that, according to Brand, came to be expressed by the British imagination. Several matters become evident if we see Brand's comments as a possible source for the opening lines of *Lamia*. First, it seems apparent that the connection between lamiae, fairy mythology, and England inscribes a British historical concern in the story of Lycius and Lamia. This is not to say that the poem is intended as a simple allegory of British historical concerns, but rather that the specific historical realities of the British situation are on some level to be found in the narrative. Second, by insistently setting the opening scenes at a time before the advent of fairy mythology, only to follow this by the story of Lamia, Keats may be suggesting that one of his poetic interests is in the paradigm shift from Greek to British mythology, that is, in the demise of one mythic expression of human experience and the ascent of another—an interest that preoccupied the poet in *Hyperion* and other poems as well. To see the poem in terms of Brand's observations, in short, is to understand that the role of Lamia extends well beyond simple serpentry; she is made to carry symbolic historical significance, as she is one symbol of a major shift in historical reality, embodying and focusing the clash between ideologies within the processes of history.

This view of Lamia also helps to focus the important shift in time and setting in the narrative. The poem begins in Crete, the "sacred island" (1:13) peopled by nymphs, satyrs, dryads, and fauns, and then later shifts to Corinth at the time of Apollonius, or roughly the time of Christ. Keats never provides a specific date for the actions in the narrative, but it is probable that he would have known from his reading in Mavor and elsewhere that Cretan society reached its high point sometime between 1800 and 1400 B.C., and that as it declined prosperity shifted to mainland Greece, first to Mycenae and eventually to Corinth around the time that the subsequent portion of the narrative is set.[14] It is important to stress this because, as Keats himself emphasizes in the opening lines of the poem, one focus of the narrative is on the shift from prehistory into history, and from a relatively rural, idyllic (and idealized) moment out of time to a more frantic moment within a highly competitive, demanding, and manipulative situation. Early Crete was and is often thought of as somehow purer than subsequent historical periods, as a place where desire could be both expressed and fulfilled. As William Mitford describes it in his ten-volume *History of Greece:* ". . . in the large and valuable iland [sic] of CRETE, a regular free government, under the presidency of an hereditary prince, was established almost before Grecian history can be said to begin."[15] In their more recent work, Botsford and Robinson report that "the life of the people [of Crete] was extraordinarily gay and carefree. A royal gaming board, with inlays of ivory, crystal, and blue paste has been found. Gems and seal-stones, exquisitely cut, reveal a love of nature. . . . Both men and women wore jewelry. Nor should the children be forgotten, with the pull-carts and other toys."[16]

As mainland Greek civilization developed, Corinth was for hundreds of years one of its most important cities—"the greatest emporium of Greece," as Mitford describes it.[17] According to Botsford and Robinson, Corinth "from early time [was] renowned for her wealth," which was gained and manifested in many ways. For instance, it was one of the greatest colonizing states of Greece; it was one of the earliest states to develop coinage; it was one of the leading commercial states ("the two harbors, one on the Saronic Gulf, the other on the Corinthian, afforded easy commerce with east and west"); it was known for its metalwork, tiles, and rugs; and around the time of Apollonius it "was famous for its bronzes [which had been the primary metal in Crete centuries before] and had a great transit trade."[18] Or, as Mitford puts it, "Corinth . . . had perhaps the happiest government of Greece. The local circumstances of the city appear indeed to have influenced the disposition of the people; directing it to commerce and arts more than to politics, arms, or science; tho in these also they acquired their share of fame."[19]

But it was not an entirely blissful and idyllic civilization, despite Mitford's optimistic views. It was clearly a very different world from the earlier Cretan civilization; in many ways it was strikingly similar to Keats's England with its trade problems, military threats, racial tension, class division, and so on.[20] The "sacred island"—Crete *and* England—of perpetual love and love-play was to be overcome by a world of getting and spending, where art and the imagination were active but mediated by gain and profit; that is, by the god Hermes.

These preliminary matters are of crucial importance because they point toward the significant historical dimensions of the narrative action. Keats creates a kind of historical tension or anxiety in the very beginning by pushing his narrative action back into prehistory, only to rush forward, after one-hundred seventy lines, thousands of years when he introduces Lycius. That is, he sets the initial scene of the poem at a moment before fairy mythology has emerged—at a time when Greek and Roman myths were dominant—and then sets the main action of the narrative at the time of the emergence of Christ, when Greek and Roman mythology were beginning to be challenged. Moreover, he stresses the conflictual relationship between the various mythologies, which in turn reflects the conflictual nature of historical change itself: the fairies "drove Nymph and Satyr from the prosperous woods" (1:2) and "frighted away the Dryads and the Fauna / From rushes green" (1:5–6). This strategy effectively denies that myth is exempt from historical struggle—the poem does not suggest that myth collapses into history (as Sperry argues), but rather that it emerges from within history—showing instead that if the historical moment is one of anxiety (as it is in *Lamia*), mythic expression inevitably will embody this anxiety.

In other words, the shift from Crete to Corinth early in the narrative is at the same time a shift of historical moment and a shift in systems of belief: personal relationships as they were believed to have existed in Cretan prehistory are not the same as they are within Corinthian history, nor is the wealth that characterizes Crete the same as the wealth found later in commercial Corinth—in fact, Cretan wealth used in celebration of the beautiful nymph is "unknown to any Muse" (1:19). This rapid historical shift from the old to the new creates a narrative space wherein the anxieties of personal life and belief, of the intellect, and of cultural and social demands, are laid bare. Rather than concentrating on the "Hermes episode" in an attempt to explain its connection to the remainder of the narrative, as most critics do, it makes more sense, I believe, to notice the shift from Crete to Corinth, from prehistory into history, for this allows us to see immediately that change and conflict are at the center of the story.

Once we recognize this historical dimension of the narrative, it is easier to explain the specific thematic significance of Hermes. To state it bluntly, Hermes performs the necessary godlike function not only of transforming Lamia from a serpent into a beautiful woman, but also of moving her out of her Cretan past into the Corinthian present, and thus he is thematically connected to the kinds of historical change described in the narrative. As I have already mentioned, that change involves the disolution of a precommercial society and the emergence of a new commercial society in which wealth, private desire, and self-gratification become culturally dominant. Thus it is that Hermes is described as possessing a "passion new" (1:28)—one that, when used to transform

Lamia, provides her with a "new voice" (1:167, "beauty new" (1:172), and "new lips" (1:294), as well as "sorrows, soft and new" (2:74).

The specific importance of Hermes to Lamia's later actions is suggested most clearly by the fact that the two negotiate to obtain their respective wishes and then strike a bargain, or make an exchange. Hermes swears upon his "serpent rod" (1:89)—the rod of wealth, among other things—to uphold his part of the bargain, an act that seals both the economic and ideological significance of commercialism into the narrative. Lamia is transformed into a woman, of course, but this plot-level development entails as well her transition from Crete to Corinth and the accompanying transformation of precommercial life into commercial life. In Corinth, she tells Lycius, she "led / Days happy as the gold coin could invent" (1:312–313), and the abundant wealth of her palace is dazzling, even godlike:

> . . .so new,
> And so unsullied was the marble hue,
> So through the crystal polish, liquid fine,
> Ran the dark veins, that none but feet divine
> Could e'er have touch'd there.
> (1:382–86)

The interior of her palace, too, is described in terms of extraordinary opulence. When the people of Corinth begin to file in to witness the marriage of Lamia and Lycius, all are struck by the wealth and luxury of the scene, which is marked by "minist'ring slaves" (2:193), "silken couches" (2:197), "gorgeous dyes" (2:205), "the splendour of the draperies" (2:206), and "baskets of bright osier'd gold" (2:217), leading the guests to wonder "whence all this mighty cost and blaze of wealth could spring" (2:198).

This emphasis on private wealth is accompanied by an ideology of self-interest, which also is established in the opening bargain negotiated by Hermes and Lamia. In the deal that is struck, Lamia in effect sells a nymph whom before she had attempted to protect from satyrs and fauns, keeping her free from all domination:

> Free as the air, invisibly, she strays
> About these thornless wilds. . . .
> . . . .
> And by my power is her beauty veil'd
> To keep it unaffronted, unassail'd
> By the love-glances of unlovely eyes.
> (1:94–95, 100–102)

Hermes changes this attitude utterly, persuading Lamia to give the nymph up for his sexual consumption with the promise that Lamia too will be empowered to consume in the same way, fulfilling the most cherished of personal desires. The transformation of Lamia, in this view, is one that destroys public, mutually protective life, replacing it with private, consumerist life. That is, once touched with the power and spirit of Hermes, her old power dissolves and she is "left to herself" (1:146) to pursue her private interests, which, the narrative shows, now entail a complete denial of public exchange and public responsibility. Surrounded by wealth, and in possession of Lycius, she secludes herself from the remainder of the world, which has become invisible to her: ". . . they [Lamia and Lycius] resposed, / Where use had made it sweet, with eyelids closed, / Saving a tythe which love still open kept, / That they might see each other while they almost slept" (2:22–25). Privatization of life in this manner cannot survive, however great the wealth accompanying it, and the plot-level concerns of the narrative emphasize this fact by showing that an ethic in which the consumption of love and people are seen and valued equally with the consumption of wealth must eventually destroy itself and society as well: "Love in a palace is perhaps at last / More grievous torment than a hermit's fast" (2:3–4).

It should be remembered of course that when Hermes descends to Crete in the beginning of the poem, it is Lamia who calls to him and who effectively manipulates him so that he grants her wish. At the level of plot, she is not entirely innocent, and I do not mean to insist that she is. My point is simply that neither the opening nor subsequent sections of the poem are simply about love, but that they touch on themes of consumerism, ideology, public life, economics, and history as well. Hermes represents the driving force of gain and profit that pushes forward into history from Crete to Corinth, from past to present, from man to woman (in ways that we shall see), making itself felt not only in the material trappings of life—with its extreme wealth, its servants, its slaves—but also in the most personal dimensions of human relationships. Love is not exempt here, or elsewhere in Keats's poetry, from the force of history, and in fact the poem does not seem to be concerned so much with love in the abstract as with love-as-self-gratification in an alienating consumerist world where competition and envy (1:218), blood sacrifices (1:228), and isolation (1:232–33) define everyday experience. Thus, while Lamia is certainly implicated in the opening episode—and while she is clearly self-willed subsequently—the important point is that the opening scene of self-interest, possession, wealth, desire, and envy carries over and gives meaning to the actions which follow. If Hermes as a character disappears from the poem, the characteristics that

Tooke attached to the god remain to become the defining features of Corinth.

To understand Hermes in this way helps to explain the Lamia-Lycius-Apollonius relationship, as well as certain modifications that Keats makes to the original story. In describing Corinth as a culture of "the gold coin," "markets" (1:391), "thronged streets" (2:63), and so on, Keats establishes a world of self-interest, privatization, and consumerism. Lycius participates in "the envious race"; he is weary of verbal exchange with his fellow citizens; he desires to triumph over others, letting "my foes choke, and my friends shout afar" (2:62); and even his relationship with Lamia becomes "perverse" (2:70). As other details in the narrative illustrate, these are not simply personality traits but rather are the conditions of life in a market culture such as the one in which Lycius lives, a life predicated upon division.

The form that this privatization takes is seen most immediately of course in the withdrawal of Lycius and Lamia from the public world into the serpent's palace; but it is seen most compellingly in the definitive features of Lamia and Apollonius, characters who occupy opposite and extreme positions within a common matrix of social and cultural relations. Lamia is characterized by her call for complete self-indulgence and self-gratification, by her appeal to the senses, while Apollonius is characterized by a devout asceticism, by an absolute denial of the senses. These respective positions are not dialectically related, but rather exclude one another: each would destroy the other. Lamia's curious strength is her "sciential brain," which can

> ... unperplex bliss from its neighbour pain;
> Define their pettish limits, and estrange
> Their points of contact, and swift counterchange;
> Intrigue with the specious chaos, and dispart
> Its most ambiguous atoms with sure art.
>
> (1:191–96)

Apollonius' power lies in his denial of pleasure and in his exercise of sheer intellect. When he enters Lamia's palace uninvited and inspects the scene of wealth and self-gratification,

> ... something too he laugh'd,
> As though some knotty problem, that had daft
> His patient thought, had now begun to thaw,
> And solve and melt.
>
> (2:159–62)

His is the power of "cold philosophy" (2:230) that would make "all charms fly" (2:229), that would

> . . . clip an Angel's wings,
> Conquer all mysteries by rule and line,
> Empty the haunted air, and gnomed mine—
> Unweave a rainbow, as it erewhile made
> The tender-person'd Lamia melt into a shade.
> (2:234–38)

Without retracing the many critical explanations of these lines, it can be noted that Keats is not here setting up in Lamia and Apollonius two equally powerful ways of viewing the world and asking Lycius to choose between them; rather, he is describing two reductions of the world that occur under specific economic and ideological conditions. As Clarence DeWitt Thorpe puts it, "An error that most critics of *Lamia* have made is to assume that Keats meant either Lamia or Appolonius [sic] to be in the right. The facts rather seem to be that Keats was here dealing with two falsities. Lamia and Lycius represent an existence of phantasy—pure dream. Apollonius, on the other hand, stands for cold factual and reasoned knowledge." But even this description is limited by its abstraction of the issues from the material conditions that produced them in these particular forms, leading Thorpe to suggest that while Keats fails to do so in *Lamia,* in other poems he effectively combines these "falsities" into a "truth" where "the conflict between reality and dream is . . . resolved."[21]

The positions represented by Lamia and Apollonius do not have unchanging significance. They are products of historical reality, responses to and representations of life within a market economy. They are absolute gratification and absolute denial, and they see nothing but their own private visions of these respective values. Such reductions of life are dualistic rather than dialectical, and as such necessarily become mutually destructive rather than mutually supportive. That this is an economic and ideological issue, rather than simply a question of philosophy versus sensual pleasure, is illustrated not only by the fact that Lamia is surrounded by wealth, but also by the fact that it is this wealth that Apollonius seeks to penetrate and oppose. Seeing "that royal porch, that high-built fair demesne" (2:155), Apollonius "walk'd in austere" (2:158), and as he is led by his pupil through the display of extreme wealth (2:172–220) his position hardens in opposition to "the alarmed beauty of the bride" (2:247) until "pleasure ceased" (2:265).

But under the conditions set down in the narrative—in a world energized and shaped by Hermes—asceticism and self-gratification become increasingly difficult to distinguish, as both are private responses to—

indeed, forms of retreat from—all public exchange. Although in Corinth "men, women, rich and poor, in the cool hours, / Shuffled their sandals o'er the pavement white, / Companion'd or alone" (1:355–57), and although the streets are "thronged" (2:63) with people, the "busy world" (1:397) is an imposition rather than a support, and it is somehow less real than one's solitude, whether that solitude takes the form of philosophy or of pleasure. Thus, as Apollonius gains authority within Lamia's palace, he becomes indistinguishable from her, no less a serpent than she is, with "juggling eyes" (2:277), "lashless eyelids" (2:288), and "demon eyes" (2:289)—he is, in short, "possess'd" (2:288). And while his rhetoric is characterized by his desire to preserve Lycius from "a serpent's prey" (2:298), the effect of his power is not to destroy Lamia (who vanishes) and preserve Lycius, but to destroy Lycius himself, so that the young Corinthian in the end becomes a serpent's prey, although the serpent is Apollonius rather than Lamia.

To put the matter somewhat differently, Apollonius's response to Lamia—and to Lycius—is undialectical in that it seeks simply to destroy her. And this is why, in fact, it destroys Lycius, who is torn between apparently irreconcilible forces within his culture. He is taught by his "trusty guide" that only philosophy is of value, yet he is surrounded by a thoughtless and commodity-rich world that would promise him bliss and power. Even if Apollonius is correct in his perception that the extreme wealth and private pleasure characteristic of Corinth are potentially destructive, his solution is faulty, and in fact is no less a product of Corinthian culture than the actions of Lamia and Lycius. Like them, Apollonius is blind to the busy world, absorbed entirely in his own solitude, and desirous of reducing the world to his personal sense of what it should be. In this he is serpentine.

The serpentine qualities of both Lamia and Apollonius, and the conflict between them for the loyalty of Lycius, again recall the unifying role of Hermes in the narrative, although here the presence of the Greek god has an ironic dimension to it. According to Tooke, the "serpent rod" (as Keats calls it) of Hermes "had a wonderful Faculty of *deciding all Controversies.* This Virtue was first discover'd by *Mercury;* who seeing two Serpents fighting, as he travell'd, he put his Rod between them and reconciled them presently, and they mutually embraced each other, and stuck to the Rod, which is call'd *Caduceus.*"[22] In Keats's narrative, of course, Lamia and Apollonius are the fighting serpents, although their differences are never reconciled within the narrative and indeed cannot be reconciled because they are the fundamental contradictions within commercial culture (in this case, Corinth): self-gratification in the form of Lamia, and asceticism in the form of Apollonius. This is a culture that claims to value restraint, reason, and the intellect, while at the same time displaying an absolute immersion in everything (including the flesh) that is capable of being consumed. Still, the rod of Hermes may be said to emblematize their struggle, because they both embrace ideologically the commodity culture that has assigned them their respective positions. Theirs is not an embrace of peace but an embrace of mutual distaste and hatred, and although the positions they represent endure as long as Hermes' authority endures, the lives of others—in this case, Lycius—are destroyed, as Keats's revision of his source material (which never describes the death of Lycius) shows. In the end, Lamia and Apollonius vanish, their combat presumably to surface and resume subsequently, and all that remains is the dead Lycius, whose corpse is made—in terms similar to Blake's bitter conclusion to his poem *London*—to demonstrate the black and bitter irony of the social situation: "On the high couch he lay!—his friends came round— / Supported him—no pulse, or breath they found, / And in its marriage robe, the heavy body wound" (2:309–11).

Having traced some of the economic and ideological dimensions of the narrative, I want now to turn to a consideration of the significance of gender relations, prefacing my argument with the observation that Keats seems to complicate the matter here in ways that he does not in many of his other poems. Part of the difficulty in assessing relations of gender in *Lamia* arises from the fact that the title character seems to be portrayed inconsistently, undergoing confusing change through the story: she appears at first truly serpentine, but is later sympathetic and compassionate. While some critics (for instance, Bernice Slote) have explained this in terms of Keats's dramatic sensibility, this does not satisfactorily account for the many interesting and problematic portrayals of gender in its social context. Lamia is initially portrayed as a protector of feminine liberty against masculine domination, and yet she ultimately gives over that which she would protect, apparently out of selfishness; she seems to deceive and entrap Lycius—"she saw his chain so sure" (1:256)—and yet she ultimately becomes Lycius' victim; and as Lycius gains in power, she seems to take pleasure in the "tyranny" (2:81) that he exercises over her, even though in the beginning she is portrayed as an opponent to such tyranny. Such contradictions can be explained only in terms of the conditions of her world, which exact an extraordinarily high price from men and women alike.

Keats's portrayal of women here elucidates important contradictions within patriarchal and commodity culture. At the very center of the problem lies the question of domination. In a world broken and divided in ways described above, where the gain and profit of Hermes are culturally dominant, where the individual subject appears autonomous, and where (as Philostratus notes) even poetry and learning are subservient to money, all relations without exception are relations of domination, and are shown here to emerge within a patriarchal context. From the very beginning, profit and gain are represented in masculine terms in the form of Hermes, who descends to possess and stamp his identity on the nymph, who "like a moon in wane, / Faded before him, cower'd, nor could restrain / Her fearful sobs" (1:136–38). The ideological dimension of this process of domination is seen clearly in the fact that once he triumphs over her he becomes worshipful, presenting himself virtually as her servant, "fostering her chilled hand" (1:140) and giving "her honey to the lees" (1:143). As I have shown in the examination of the *Ode on a Grecian Urn*, this is tyranny that becomes ideologically converted into spirituality: as innocent and idyllic as it may appear, it is nonetheless a relation of power and domination.

This same process of domination is seen in the relation between Lamia and Lycius, where both the economic and the ideological dimensions of gender relations are developed fully. After Hermes transforms and empowers Lamia, then departs with his prize (the nymph), his presence, as noted above, continues to be felt everywhere in the narrative, not only in Lamia's beauty but also in the association of her beauty with private and unaccountable wealth. This is important to an understanding of the relationship between Lamia and Lycius, because, by identifying Lamia with wealth in this way—by placing the imprint of Hermes clearly on her character—the narrative dramatizes the process whereby the masculine ego, in the character of Lycius, feminizes wealth, becomes enamored of it, and then appropriates it. Hermes transforms Lamia into a woman, providing a feminine representation of his power, and Lycius (with the knowledge that she "led / Days happy as the gold coin could invent" [1:312–13]) desperately desires to win and experience her as a "delight" (1:327), a "pleasure" (1:327), and finally as a "treat" (1:330).

While these early scenes are admittedly descriptions of young love and on some level are innocent and admirable, they are ultimately socially constituted, part of the process of masculine appropriation and domination of the feminine. The fullest revelation of this dimension of the narrative appears in the description of Lycius' attempt to persuade Lamia to accept a public wedding:

> ... The lady's cheek
> Trembled; she nothing said, but, pale and meek,
> Arose and knelt before him, wept a rain
> Of sorrows at his words; at last with pain
> Beseeching him, the while his hand she wrung,
> To change his purpose. He thereat was stung,
> Perverse, with stronger fancy to reclaim
> Her wild and timid nature to his aim:

> Besides, for all his love, in self despite,
> Against his better self, he took delight
> Luxurious in her sorrows, soft and new.
> His passion, cruel grown, took on a hue
> Fierce and sanguineous as 'twas possible
> In one whose brow had no dark veins to swell.
> Fine was the mitigated fury, like
> Apollo's presence when in act to strike
> The serpent—Ha, the serpent! certes, she
> Was none. She burnt, she lov'd the tyranny,
> And, all subdued, consented to the hour
> When the bridal he should lead his paramour.
>
> (2:64–83)

That she is subdued and that she is said to love the tyranny exercised over her in this scene are not simply signs that she has undergone a character change—though certainly she has, as various critics have noted[23]—but also signs of the particular kind of possessiveness and objectification that emerge from within the culture of Hermes. What Lycius does here to Lamia (i.e., establish his absolute domination over her), Hermes before had done to the nymph, illustrating that the "wealthy lustre" (2:173) of this new world brings with it a reduction of people to things and a reification of human relationships.

The nymph and Lamia are objects to be won, possessed, and controlled—and worshipped when they are brought under control. In this process, love itself becomes dislodged from the actual exchanges of human experience, transformed into an apparently independent and abstract object which has power over people:

> Love, jealous grown of so complete a pair,
> Hover'd and buzz'd his wings, with fearful roar,
> Above the lintel of their chamber door,
> And down the passage cast a glow upon the floor.
> For all this came a ruin.
>
> (2:12–16)

This atomization and reification of personal relations is a symptom of a network of social relations grounded in the admittedly tremendous power of masculine wealth, and it cannot be reduced to the evil nature and intentions of Lamia. She herself—like Lycius—is transformed by the emergent culture, and that transformation entails the disempowerment of the feminine. Initially in the narrative the feminine, if not free in any transhistorical sense, at least has some means of self-protection, and hence some degree of relative freedom in a world already crawling with masculine wealth and masculine desire for domination (see, for instance,

1:14–21). The change of the world irrevocably into a sphere of gain and profit entails the appropriation—literally and ideologically—of the feminine, as it must come to endorse and even love masculine control if that control is to be complete. This is what happens to Lamia.

Once the world changes it is controlled entirely by the masculine ego, by patriarchy, and the only space left where the feminine retains at least the appearance of control and integrity is the private sphere, which is precisely why Lamia so strongly resists a public wedding. But even here, the belief that the private can be insulated from the public is ideological, as is illustrated not only by the fact that Lycius gets his way, but also by the fact that the private space at every turn is underwritten by the getting and spending of the public world. The private sphere, no less than the motivating assumptions of Lamia, Lycius, and Apollonius, is a historical and cultural construct, constituted by the demands of money. To see it as an alternative, as Lamia does, or to attempt to live invisibly, as the nymph in the opening scenes of the narrative does, is to seek and proclaim freedom under the conditions of true domination.

This is not to say, however, that Lycius is correct and that Lamia is wrong, for the public entrance that Lycius wishes to make is defined by the same privatized value scheme that motivates Lamia's desire for isolation. He seeks public endorsement but not public exchange; that is, he wishes to proclaim his "prize" (2:57) before "other men" (2:57), to "triumph" (2:60) as his "foes choke" (2:62). This is the identical approach that we see in Hermes early on, when he learns that others are competing for the affections of the invisible nymph. Hermes is "full of painful jealousies" (1:33), which subside only when he has triumphed over the "Wood-Gods" (1:34) in his pursuit of the invisible nymph. Such attitudes do not reflect a view of the world as a place of public exchange and social responsibility and solidarity, but rather a view of the world as marketplace, where each individual is thought to be entirely autonomous, free to enter the public sphere at will to compete for what he can win—this is the "envious race" in which Lycius participates and which he hopes to win by possessing Lamia. But he cannot win, because his world is predicated upon domination and division. While he worships Lamia, he tyrannizes over her; while he seeks public endorsement for his actions, he detests public life—thus while he seeks marriage, he finds death.

The clearest representation of this fundamental contradiction at the center of the world of the poem comes rather early on, when the narrator describes Lamia as the ultimate prize for Lycius. She is "a virgin purest lipp'd, yet in the lore / Of love deep learned to the red heart's core" (1:189–90). Here are the opposite extremes, presented in sexual terms, vying for control in the world of the poem, and Lycius—as well as

Lamia—naively believes that they are autonomous, of equal value, equally capable of being indulged, and that somehow they can persist unquestioned and unchallenged by the various social networks within which they abide. As virgin and whore, Lamia is made to represent discrete culture values; she is the paradigm of the atomization and division of people in the poem. Individuals are divided both internally (as we see here) and socially, as is demonstrated in Lycius's desire to triumph over his foes, in his triumph over Lamia, and in the conflicts between Apollonius and Lamia, between Apollonius and Lycius, and so on.

I want to return briefly now to the question of the nymph and Lamia at the beginning of the narrative in an attempt to explain them against the various ideological currents traced above. Both characters are, in their different ways, invisible to the world in the beginning, the nymph literally and Lamia by virtue of her serpentine shape. The nymph's invisibility, while affording her the freedom to roam unthreatened outdoors, assures that her existence is entirely private, just as Lamia's shape assures that she can never enjoy human exchange. Lamia is motivated, as she puts it, by a desire for "a sweet body fit for life, / And love, and pleasure, and the ruddy strife / Of hearts and lips!" (1:39–41). The only means of entrance into the public world for her requires that she turn against, or yield up, femininity (in the form of the nymph, whom heretofore she has protected) and place herself squarely in the hands of Hermes. This means that from the very beginning she is masculine-dependent; her pleasure in life depends upon her ability to attach herself to masculinity, which controls the world, and the way to do this, she knows, is by making herself into a prize that the masculine ego would want to win. The point here is that the transformation of Lamia from a serpent into a woman at the same time entails her transformation from a feminine personality into a serpentine personality, for she comes to be divided from her own femininity and to accept that meaning for her life requires manipulating for the attention of the controlling masculine ego. Thus it is that "she lov'd the tyranny" (2:81) exercised over her by Lycius; though it is tyranny, it is at least attention.

A point that has been implicit in this discussion of gender relations bears explicit comment here, namely, that Lamia should not be seen in some simple allegorical way as identical with wealth or money. Rather, she is made to carry multiple significance in the narrative, although her significance always involves her role as object or as Other in a masculine world. She is identified with wealth when that is the item to be cherished; she is identified as virgin when that is the virtue to be esteemed; she is identified as whore when that is the feminine quality most desired: but she is always an object and always, finally, submissive. This objectification of the feminine and the feminization of wealth, the narrative suggests, accompany the emergence of the culture of Hermes.

Also subject to Hermes are knowledge and learning; indeed, one theme of the narrative is the competiton between ideas for control of the minds of the various characters. Lamia is of "sciential brain" (1:191), once apparently a student in, and a "graduate" (1:198) of, "Cupid's college" (1:197); Lycius is "a scholar" (1:279); Apollonius is a "sophist" (2:291) as well as Lycius's "trusty guide" (1:375) and "good instructor" (1:376). Through the course of the narrative the ideas and thoughts of these characters are laid bare (as Lycius puts it at one point: "My thoughts! shall I unveil them?" [2:56]), and it is the "cold philosophy" (2:230) of Apollonius that apparently triumphs in the end. Once again, Hermes provides a unifying point of reference for the various dimensions of this theme, for, as Apollonius notes (in Philostratus), Hermes was "the dispenser of knowledge and wealth": "Many . . . came to Mercury to ask for the same gift [wisdom], and offered for it gold, or silver, or an ivory wand or some other precious thing. . . . All the suppliants having met on the day appointed for the distribution of wisdom, Mercury . . . said to one of them, 'you take philosophy,' and to the one who had offered most he said, 'you shall sit with orators,' and to the next in liberality he said, 'I give you the province of astronomy.'" While at one point in the life of Apollonius it is noted that "true philosophy" is exempt from the power of money, most philosophers are unable to escape its grip: "Aeschines the son of Lysanias sailed all the way to Dionysius in Sicily to get money, and Plato is said to have dared the passage of Charybdis three times for the sake of Sicilian wealth."[24] In *Lamia* this is seen clearly, despite the fact that Apollonius is "austere" (2:158), and despite the fact that in Philostratus's life of the philosopher he is said to have led a long life of extreme asceticism. The point is not that Lamia possesses wealth, Lycius desires wealth, and Apollonius abhors wealth, but rather that wealth is at the center of the conflict, defining in an important sense the thought processes and ideological commitments of the various characters. That is, wealth—and the beauty and demonism associated with it—governs the ideas of Lycius's world, and none of the characters is exempt from its influence.

That Lamia vanishes under the onslaught of Apollonius should not be regarded as a sign of the defeat of wealth, although certainly it must be regarded as a denial of it and, on a biographical level, a sign of Keats's own extreme frustration in the face of poverty. Rather, the concluding scene, which would seem to value austerity over wealth, points up once again the contradictions of a world grounded in profit and gain and characterized by domination, whether in the form of men dominating women or masters dominating slaves (2:193). In the end, both Lamia and Apollonius have vanished, and Lycius is left dead, despite the fact that Apollonius professes to be concerned to save the young scholar: ". . . from every ill / Of life have I preserv'd thee to this day, / And shall I see thee made a serpent's prey?" (2:296–98). If the philosopher saved Lycius from the serpent, he destroyed him with his own radical rejection of life, a fact that shows, once again, that there is no true alternative within the world of new money that has come to prevail. The retreat into cold philosophy, the retreat into a luxurious and isolated palace, the retreat into private and intensely sensual relationships: none of these escapes the structures of social authority which inspire them. Further, the struggle between Lamia and Apollonius takes place entirely within these structures and ends only with the death of those, such as Lycius, caught up in it.

A final comment on the presence and role of the supernatural in *Lamia* may help to draw together some of the threads of argument pursued above. Lamia, the nymph, and Hermes are all seen in terms of the supernatural, and Apollonius is suspected by Lycius of having connections with the supernatural as well. But unlike some of Keats's earlier works (for instance, *Endymion*), here the supernatural elements are not presented as embodiments or representations only of positive value. In *Endymion,* Cynthia represents a definite alternative to the disappointments experienced by Endymion in the everyday world. But in *Lamia,* there is uncertainty from the very beginning about the status and intentions of anything supernatural: Hermes is described initially as a thief ("Hermes empty left / His golden throne, bent warm on amorous theft" [1:7–81)[25], and his motives are never described as noble; Lamia, while reasonably sympathetic in part 2 of the narrative, is a serpent who withholds her true identity from Lycius, and indeed Keats's sources suggest that her intentions are demonic rather than romantic; Apollonius poses as the protector of Lycius, and yet his demonic gaze is responsible for the destruction of the young Corinthian. In short, the supernatural elements in the narrative do not so much express hope or possibility as anxiety; they embody and project those forces and energies of the world that cannot be seen in their full complexity but which are, nonetheless, controlling. Lycius wishes his idealization of Lamia in part 1 to be consistent with his everyday life, as is evidenced in his desire for a public wedding, and yet his wish is grounded in a refusal or inability to see the true dimensions of that idealization. As Donald Reiman puts it, "Lycius dies—unable to live in a world stripped of its mythology."[26] To extend this idea a bit further, Lycius dies as the historical struggles, which give rise to myths intended to pacify those struggles, push to the foreground and overwhelm myth. In Corinth, gain and profit prevail and the mythology that would offer personal protection from their ravages cannot finally withstand the contradictions generated within commercial culture. The status of the supernatural in *Lamia*, then, is always tentative at best, expressing at once the desire for the reconciliation of conflict and the awareness that reconciliation is impossible. This is consistent with the handling of the supernatural in many of Keats's mature works, where the emphasis is seldom on myth as an alternative to history and often on the collapse of mythic structures.

Lamia is marked by many inconsistencies—these show up in its characterization of Lamia, in its attitude toward sensual pleasure, in its view of the imagination, in its handling of philosophy, and so on—and it is probably impossible to know with certainty what Keats's actual intentions were in the poem. Nevertheless, it is likely that one of the poet's concerns was with the contradictory status of the human imagination in a world dominated by gain and profit. Keats seems to have been working intensely in 1819 to formulate and articulate poetically the strange connections between the imagination, myth, money, individual life, and knowledge, connections that are noted briefly in his "Robin Hood" poem and then explored in even greater detail in *The Fall of Hyperion*. In 1819, the year of Peterloo and the year after Tom's death—and a year in which Keats's personal financial situation reached an unprecedented low point—Keats's youthful idealism seems to have been completely cast aside, and he seems to have been prepared to face (much as Shelley does in the *Ode to the West Wind,* also written in 1819) the uncertainties and contradictions of the historical situation within which he was caught. Just as Shelley was unable to see the wind addressed in his famous poem, but only the products of its power, Keats could not speak concretely of the driving force behind the world as he was coming to know it. But he seemed to sense—or at least he was haunted by—the tremendous controlling power of history and its many contradictions and accomplishments. Certainly his poetry discloses the anxiety of living in a culture where the important gods were Hermes and Moneta, where Apollo had actually bought (from Hermes) the lyre that would make him the god of poetry, where "the very corn which is now so beautiful, as if it had only <taken> took to ripening yesterday, is for the market" (*LJK* 2:129).

8
"Twing'd with Avarice"
THE FALL OF HYPERION

SOME years ago K. K. Ruthven argued that conventional accounts of Moneta as an admonisher and as the goddess of counsel do not fully explain her significance in *The Fall of Hyperion*. In addition to these roles, Ruthven shows, she also was in classical mythology the goddess of money; indeed, our word for money comes from her name. Ruthven establishes not only that Keats must have known Moneta's role as the supreme treasurer among the gods and included her in his poem with this role in mind, but, further, that his poetic interest in money did not begin with the *Fall* but extended back to his very earliest writings. This information is critical to any full understanding of Keats's poetry—and certainly points toward a very different critical orientation to the *Fall* from that which currently prevails—because, at the very least, it suggests that underneath the large and abstract themes that pervade his work there lingers an uncomfortable sense of the way abstractions and ideals arise from, are made possible by, and are even destroyed by something as mundane and yet as powerful as money.[1]

I want to build upon and extend Ruthven's argument, using it to develop a more specific analysis of the *Fall* than Ruthven offers, and also a more explicitly political interpretation of the connection between Keats's poetry and the structure of social life during the romantic period. A necessary starting point in such a task requires not so much an extensive examination of Keats's personal financial hardships, or of the actual literary sources for his work, as it does an elaboration of the encompassing network of social relations within which he produced his poetry. To this end I want to offer initially an elementary survey of some of the broader historical and socioeconomic conditions of the age which would have had a general bearing on Keats's poetic practice, and specifically on the *Fall*. Presentation of this information is extremely condensed and selective, and the interpretative comments I offer are not original;

still, it is necessary to cover this (for many) old ground by way of prelude because much of it has not yet been connected satisfactorily to Keats studies. My aim will be first to sketch the general theory of economics and society that prevailed during Keats's day, and then to historicize this theory by providing a very brief and schematic materialist account of matters that it fails to explain satisfactorily, namely, the connections between economics, society, and personal life. This dual focus will allow a glimpse of the intellectual and ideological framework within which Keats's poetry was produced, while at the same time providing a historical basis for interpreting its socio-aesthetic dimensions.

In discussing the economic and social relations of the romantic period, it is important to bear in mind that the most powerful analyses and interpretations of the marketplace—despite frequent and intense voices of opposition—were by and large supportive of a free market economy, and that in fact the theories of the marketplace that proliferated were often presented as discoveries of natural law and not at all as political arguments about how society should be governed. These theories were so powerful and their most deeply held assumptions so pervasive that they effectively set the terms of economic and social debate, determining almost absolutely the structures of discourse that were intellectually admissable in the age. While, as Catherine Belsey puts it, many romantic poets and intellectuals rejected "an alien world of industrial capitalism,"[2] they rarely, if ever, developed a true oppositional theory of economics. Even such politically and intellectually sophisticated writers as Hunt, Hazlitt, and Cobbett, who wrote often and critically about economics, shared certain fundamental assumptions with the structures of authority they wished to criticize.[3] There was no work by a romantic writer that was accorded the respect or that carried the weight of, say, Adam Smith's *Wealth of Nations*.[4] Any discussion that hopes to account for the specific points of contact between romantic poetry and social reality must begin with an acknowledgment of this historical fact.

The theory of the marketplace in the late eighteenth and early nineteenth centuries may be schematized in the following way. According to Adam Smith, society is made up of individuals who are motivated entirely by self-interest rather than by a desire for social good: "It is not from the benevolence of the butcher, the brewer, or the baker, that we expect our dinner, but from their regard to their own interest. We address ourselves, not to their humanity but to their self-love, and never talk to them of our own necessities but of their advantages. Nobody but a beggar chuses to depend chiefly upon the benevolence of his fellow-citizens."[5] But this self-interest, as Smith understood it, is not socially destructive, and in fact is the key to social survival. As Robert Heilbroner points out, for Smith self-interest is a constituent ingredient of human nature, and when it is allowed to operate freely in an environment of other self-interested individuals—that is, within the marketplace—competition results, which in turn produces "those goods that society wants, in the quantities that society desires, and at the prices society is prepared to pay." Society can never become victim to a few vicious and greedy individuals because they are always regulated, not by government but by competition: ". . . each man, out to do his best for himself with no thought of social cost, is faced with a flock of similarly motivated individuals who are in exactly the same boat. Each is only too eager to take advantage of his neighbor's greed if it urges him to exceed a common denominator of acceptable behavior. A man who permits his self-interest to run away with him will find that competitors have slipped in to take his trade away. . . . Thus . . . the selfish motives of men are transmuted by interaction to yield the most unexpected of results: social harmony."[6]

In this view, the key to social strength is absolute individual freedom from social restraint, for such freedom alone allows one to compete—economically and otherwise—to one's fullest ability and thus to be truly socially productive. For Smith, in other words, the marketplace is the key to social organization itself, the necessary starting point from which any investigation of all other social institutions and activities must begin. He acknowledges the critical social significance and function of religion, education, public works, and defense, for instance (and sees the latter two as essential to the survival of a market economy), but he argues that these institutions must be established and conducted in a manner that is consistent with the marketplace; that is, all institutions are defined in terms of their economic relation to society, a fact illustrated clearly in his very chapter titles themselves: "Of the Expence of Justice," "Of the Expence of the Institutions for the Education of Youth," "Of the Expence of the Institutions for the Instruction of People of All Ages" (i.e., religion). This perspective alone, he claims, can assure the preservation of individual freedom, which, again, he understands as one's freedom to "purchase whatever part of the produce of other men's talents he has occasion for."[7] The cultural pervasiveness of this ideology of individual autonomy manifests itself outside the immediate economic sphere in Keats's day not only in the popular celebration of Napoleon's genius and in the general cultural commitment to individual talent, but also in the burst of emotionally charged and highly personal lyrics that characterize the poetic output of the age. The constituent elements of romanticism (including the "belief in the autonomy of the subject")[8] are themselves connected in fundamental ways to the encompassing power of the marketplace.

Before leaving the theory of the marketplace that dominated the romantic age, it might be helpful to touch glancingly upon one other writer whose ideas significantly shaped and influenced the economic debate of the period, and whose name was before the public more frequently than Smith's during Keats's adult life. David Ricardo's writings are of major importance not only because they reflect the prevailing understanding of economics in the early nineteenth century, but also because they investigate in a detailed way the workings of the marketplace and at the same time explicitly attempt to influence public economic policy. While his general theory begins from the same premises as Smith's (for instance, it assumes that "the produce of the earth— . . . is derived from its surface by the united application of labour, machinery, and capital"),[9] his specific contribution is directly relevant to our purposes both because it appeared largely in the periodical literature of the age (of which Keats, of course, was an avid reader)[10] and because it addresses questions of banking and, specifically, the connections between money and other commodities. Ricardo recognized that the role of money in culture had changed radically throughout history, and that older interpretations and definitions of money, based largely on an agricultural community, were no longer sufficient. He wanted to define the specific role of money in a market economy and to use this definition to influence British monetary legislation. Specifically, he argued that within a market economy money is essentially passive, an epiphenomenon, as it were, of the production of goods: "Money cannot call forth goods, but goods can call forth money. . . . Here again it is supposed that the augmentation of money precedes the augmentation of goods. I am of opinion however that it would seldom cause any augmentation of goods, . . . [and] that the augmentation of goods is the only legitimate cause for an increase of money."[11] If money has an essentially passive role in the economy, as this suggests, then the supply of money can only be equal to, not greater than, the production of goods; otherwise, an economic imbalance occurs, as money takes on a power likely to disrupt the free nature of the marketplace. This argument developed directly out of the controversy over how to finance England's war against Napoleon without disabling the domestic economy. To assure funds for paying the military, England had gone off the gold standard in 1797 with the Bank Restriction Act. Ricardo believed that this was dangerous because it would allow currency to expand too rapidly, thus causing prices to rise, which in turn could cripple the general economic development of the nation. (The issue of the gold standard continued to be a major economic problem in 1818 and 1819, and was addressed frequently in the pages of the *Examiner,* when Keats was writing his *Hyperion* poems.)

These ideas are important because they constitute an analysis from within the ideology of a market economy, and, from this position, raise significant questions about the role of government in such an economy. While Ricardo's analysis may appear to diminish the role of money per se in the marketplace, this finally is not the case; to say that money is essentially passive is not to say that it is insignificant. Like Smith, he argues simply that the market should be free, and that to use currency rather than gold bullion as the measure of money is potentially to jeopardize this freedom. This understanding of the connection between the government, money, and commodities is likewise the basis for his opposition to the new Corn Law legislation of 1815 (which was intended to protect wealthy landowners from the vicissitudes of the marketplace), even though other economists in his ideological camp (Malthus, for instance) supported it.[12] In other words, Ricardo's writings show clearly a historically specific understanding of the role of money in a market economy; his is not a position that casts money as capital in some abstract sense, or as the absolute key to economic strength, but which, rather, shows that money is one vitally important ingredient within a much larger economic and even cultural framework. (Specifically, like Smith, he sees it as a part of production.)[13] For this reason, Ricardo's work provides an important basis for understanding Keats's portrayal of money.

These are some of the key ideas governing thinking about economics during the period. To stress them, however, is not to say that there was no intellectual resistance to the ideology of the marketplace. As noted above, numerous radicals of the period spoke eloquently against the political and economic injustices of the day. The romantic poets themselves were highly cognizant of the contradictions and oppression in the world they inhabited. While they never developed a coherent and fully explanatory critique of the economic relations within their culture, to varying degrees they recognized that to pass off economic freedom as human liberty was in fact a form of liberticide, and that what in one way appeared to be the advance of culture through an accumulation of wealth was in another a weakening of culture through the conversion of people into economic units.[14] But within the larger and dominant structures of romantic society, these were, more often than not, moral voices in the wilderness, unable to mount a serious theoretical or political challenge to the ideas of Smith and Ricardo. Further, despite the very real integrity and contribution of intellectual radicalism in the period, there is a sense in which both the voices of resistance and the voices of the status quo existed within a single historical and ideological framework—a framework dominated entirely by the marketplace. To understand this is to see that subjectivity and revolutionary individualism themselves—the powerful signs of the romantic spirit—are historically implicated, shaped in significant ways by an economy that required the absolute dismantling of public life as it was once understood and lived.

I want to develop this idea briefly not only because it establishes more clearly the social and cultural significance of the ideology of the marketplace, but also because it extends the discussion of a romantic poetics of subjectivity mentioned above. Eli Zaretsky has shown that there is an absolute connection between economic relations, social values, and the nature of individualism. Focusing his analysis on the development of capitalism in the late eighteenth and early nineteenth centuries, he notes, like Fekete and Belsey, that there emerged at this time a culturally pervasive idea (which still persists) that personal life is separate from and even contradictory to public life (see the discussion of *Isabella*, above). But this idea, he argues, is itself a product of the capitalist power structure that had come to prevail during the period. Under capitalism, which leaves nothing in its path unchanged, the horizon of human potential within society recedes, and value, meaning, and freedom become increasingly privatized, themselves transformed into commodities to be pursued privately by self-interested individuals.[15] Carol C. Gould, summarizing Marx's critique of the rise of capitalism, describes this historical phenomenon precisely in *Marx's Social Ontology:* "For Marx, the era of capitalism introduces a distinctive mode of objectification, which he characterizes as alienation. . . . [T]he [individual] subject appears to be an isolated self or pure 'subjectivity' standing against an object that is taken to be wholly other than it."[16] In this view, what the classical political economists such as Smith, Ricardo, and Malthus present as a discovery of natural law is in fact the result of historical development, and specifically the result of capitalist economic relations that had come to prevail.

Before turning directly to the *Fall*, I will return for a moment to several of the source materials for the poem that Ruthven mentions, because they gain significance in the light of the economic issues presented above and help to elucidate the vision of social reality presented in the poem. As Ruthven points out, one possible source for Keats is Tooke's *Pantheon*, which gives Moneta as one of the variant names of Juno.[17] More significant for the specific role of Moneta in the *Fall*, however, is Burton's *Anatomy of Melancholy,* a work that Keats read avidly. In the *Anatomy*, Burton speaks explicitly of Moneta in terms of money: "Our *summum bonum* is commodity, and the goddess we adore *Dea Moneta,* Queen Money, to whom we daily offer sacrifice, which steers our hearts, hands, affections, all: that most powerful goddess, by whom we are reared, depressed, elevated, esteemed the sole commandress of our actions, for which we pray, run, ride, go, come, labour, and contend as fishes do for a crumb that falleth into the water. It is not worth, virtue,... wisdom, valour, learning, honesty, religion, or any sufficiency for which we are respected, but money, greatness, office, honour, authority."[18] This account of the Roman goddess is perfectly consistent with Keats's poem because, for one thing, in its discussion of money it leaves no aspect of human life and experience untouched. For Burton, money is directly connected not only to how we conduct our life, but also to how we *value* it; this idea, I shall argue, stands at the center of the *Fall*, informing in vital ways the world in which the narrator of the poem finds himself.

Keats's thinking, as Ruthven shows, was shaped not only by such literary sources as these, but also by the intellectual voices of the period. In particular he was strongly influenced by Hazlitt and Hunt, both of whom wrote extensively about politics and economics. Hunt's *Examiner*, for instance, regularly ran articles about the bullion controversy (see the discussion of Ricardo, above), the mendicant sailors everywhere in the London streets, and the problems of poverty and unemployment generally. A passage from 23 May 1819 (when Keats was most likely rethinking *Hyperion*) on England's unemployed workmen might be taken as an example of the paper's interest in economics, and as a key to the political and social nature of Keats's poem. Addressing specifically the issue of British finance, the *Examiner* states:

> We fear war in India; we fear a war with America; we fear another challenge in France, in which our Ministers would be implicated by their pledges to support legitimacy, or any convulsions in Germany, with which our Hanoverian dominions connect us; we dread any improvements of machinery on the Continent, which would injure our manufactures: at home we are alarmed lest the moneyed men should be panic-struck by the state of the finances; we tremble at the idea of the effect of the resumption of cash-payments, and the consequent limitation of the issues of Bank-notes, on the commercial body; we dread lest the distress in some parts of the country should drive the people into violence; and in short we are as sensitive as the Bulls and Bears of Change Alley to every breath of wind, because we know on what a slight foundation our present calm is built.[19]

War and money dominate this passage; further, the economic situation is presented in the broadest possible terms as being international in scope. The perspective offered in the *Examiner* was regularly this inclusive and this pointed. Even if no particular passage can be isolated as a source for Keats, it is probable that the tone and emphasis provided by the paper are an essential context for understanding Keats's mythologizing of power struggles and of the control that money exercises over society.

One of the greatest difficulties in attempting to explain the *Fall* in terms of the array of specific issues and general ideas sketched here is that a close reading shows the narrative to be extremely confusing, more so than any other narrative poem Keats produced during this period, and seemingly more concerned with things of the mind than with things of the world. Not only is it virtually impossible to account for Moneta's many blatantly contradictory statements (seldom noted by critics) and difficult to explain the narrator's changing views through the course of the narrative; the setting itself is at once so abstract and fanciful as to defy systematic inquiry. For example, Keats subtitles the poem *A Dream*, which in itself directs attention away from social and historical considerations and toward the issues that had occupied the poet, say, in *Sleep and Poetry*—poetry itself, the subtitle suggests, is the equivalent of dreams (though later Moneta will distinguish emphatically between the poet and the dreamer). From within this framework of the poem-as-dream, Keats has his narrator imagine ("Methought I stood . . ." [1:19]) himself in a sort of abandoned Spenserian bower of bliss, where what seem to be leftovers from a feast of angels or Eve attract and delight him:

> Before its wreathed doorway, on a mound
> Of moss, was spread a feast of summer fruits,
> Which, nearer seen, seem'd refuse of a meal
> By angel tasted or our mother Eve.
>
> (1:28–31)

Next, the narrator, after drinking from "a cool vessel of transparent juice" (1:42) that he finds among these leftovers, falls down into a swoon, from which he arises into yet another dream, this one bringing him into the presence of Moneta. Finally, Moneta shows the narrator a vision of "the scenes / Still swooning vivid through my globed brain" (1:244–45)—that is, a vision of the fallen Saturn and his Titans. The professed subject matter of the narrative, given in the poem's title, is at three removes from the narrator of the poem. This seems to reflect a desperate poetic retreat into the remoteness not only of the mythic past but also of the innermost recesses of the dreaming mind.

Enclosing the subject matter of the narrative within a series of dreams, however, never actually enables the poem to escape social and historical determination; in fact, the dream frame both captures the dizzying and unreal sensation of experiencing radical historical change, and dramatizes the impossibility of actually seeing the change that is so extreme. Because of the highly subjective and escapist nature of the poem, we cannot easily interpret the war of the Titans as only an allegory of the Napoleonic Wars and the state of Europe in the early nineteenth century, nor can we assert a mechanical relationship between expressions in the poem and the British economy. But these elements haunt the poem, the fear and anxiety that accompanied them stirring deep in its political unconscious and giving shape and meaning to its surface structure. The portrayal of the narrator, alone, who begins to dream, whereupon he (still alone) is shown a vision of characters and events from the mythic past, gives glimpses of a highly unstable and uninviting commercial world. This is a world where individuals are driven inward and compelled to rely on their own private resources for sustenance, a world where all of value that can be known and achieved is spun entirely from one's own head; a world, in short, riddled by fear, hope, anxiety, and the fragmentation of consciousness. In such a world, imagination is entirely privatized. The narrative not only addresses many troubling features of this world, ranging from the nature of subjectivity to the loneliness of the isolated individual; it also discloses the structures of authority and belief that control it.

The values and assumptions that emerge within this context of isolation, anxiety, fear, and desperate hope are necessarily beset by contradiction: manipulation and self-interest govern much of the narrative action, despite the fact that the principle characters (Moneta and the narrator) are almost without exception portrayed as sincere, benevolent, and well-intentioned. In the beginning, for instance, the narrator is described as self-indulgent but innocent, motivated to appropriate the world around him for his own pleasure but at the same time reluctant to engage with it. He drinks the enticing potion he finds in the bower and then "struggled hard against / [It] . . . but in vain" (1:53–54); shortly after this scene he approaches the steps leading to Moneta's altar, striving "hard to escape / The numbness" (1:127–28) created by the "tyranny" (1:119) exercised over him by Moneta. The ambiguity and relative innocence of these scenes describing conflicting sentiments—as well as the narrator's repeated statements of his own unworthiness, offset by his intense desire to produce something of worth—modulate gradually into a more aggressive stance when the narrator finally learns who Moneta is and what she may be able to offer him. At this point, the self-effacement that before had characterized his speeches diminishes, and, much like a character out of Gothic fiction, he desperately conjures her to give him a vision of what she knows:

> . . ."Shade of Memory!"—
> Cried I, with act adorant at her feet,
> "By all the gloom hung round thy fallen house,
> By this last temple, by the golden age,
> By great Apollo, thy dear foster child,
> And by thyself, forlorn divinity,
> The pale Omega of a wither'd race,

> Let me behold, according as thou said'st,
> What in thy brain so ferments to and fro!"
>
> (1:282–90)

Following, as they do, immediately upon a lengthy lesson in the nature and role of true poetry and on a picture of Moneta as a benevolent goddess, these lines are ironic and disturbing, undermining much of the sympathetic innocence and idealism that were prominent in the poem's beginning, and displaying a darker set of attitudes implicit in the narrator's character. The arbor of Edenic bliss and the desire for noble poetic visions here give way to a gloomy, decaying, and death-riddled setting and to expressions of desperate personal need. Every plea that the narrator makes to persuade Moneta to grant him his wish is colored by death, isolation, and loss of hope. From the description of Moneta as a "shade" and her house as "fallen," to the description of Apollo as a "foster child," the passage imagines that "ferment" comes from desolation. The Gothic tone of the passage and the "devout" (1:292) attitude of the narrator are suggestive of one deploying every strategy to bring power to himself as the world around him dies or shrinks into insignificance.

This is an extreme assessment of the narrator, far removed from the mainstream critical view of him as a representative of Keats himself sincerely wishing to find value and meaning in a world of pervasive misery, and clearly it would be wrong simply to condemn him as a sort of Gothic villain or even as the ethical equivalent of Byron's Manfred; the sympathy, compassion, and relative innocence that are seen in his character are to be taken seriously as reflections of his (potential) integrity. My aim here is simply to suggest that he is not merely a neutral or perfectly unchanging character. He abides by a discernible system of values present in the narrative, just as Moneta herself (as a product of his imagination) does, values which both reflect and produce numerous contradictions throughout the narrative. Moneta, for instance, is presented in the beginning not only as a "Holy Power" (1:136) but also as a "tyrant" (1:119) who appears at times quite heartless, as when she taunts the narrator for his unworthiness and slowly burns his poetry while ignoring his pained expressions. The struggle to manipulate, to preserve self-identity, to consume what belongs to others, accompanies the admittedly very strong desires of the characters to be moral and compassionate. The tensions and contradictions between these two extreme tendencies in the narrative suggest a world wherein the desire for self-fulfillment and meaningful commitment often becomes the very ghost of itself, much like the Spectres who haunt Blake's poetry.

I want now to turn directly to Moneta and consider the way her role as the goddess of money shapes and informs the political unconscious of the narrative and explains the desires, tensions, and self-interest just described. Moneta is the central unifying symbol in the poem, assigning social meaning to every issue, character, and action. To understand her full significance and complexity, it is necessary to revise some of Ruthven's claims about her—most importantly, his inclination to see her mainly as a benign and benevolent goddess whose role is to show the poet what he must do to survive in a world controlled by money (". . . in her capacity as Moneta, her purpose is to advise modern poets on how to survive in the terrible dispensation of the age of gold, where misery is the norm and money an indispensable commodity").[20] As her name suggests, she is not set apart from the world of money, presiding over the economic trials and tribulations of those below her: she is money. The poem establishes this as the narrator enters her sanctuary, passing numerous symbols of the pure wealth and power associated with it, symbols that apparently represent permanence and beauty previously unknown to the narrator, but that in fact represent the material and ideological forces that control the narrator's thoughts and imagination:

> Upon the marble at my feet there lay
> Store of strange vessels, and large draperies,
> Which needs had been of dyed asbestos wove,
> Or in that place the moth could not corrupt,
> So white the linen; so, in some, distinct
> Ran imageries from a sombre loom.
> All in a mingled heap confus'd there lay
> Robes, golden tongs, censer and chafing-dish,
> Girdles, and chains, and holy jewelries.
>
> (1:72–80)

Associated in this way with money, Moneta is implicated directly in the world through which she would guide the poet, both in the value schemes that she debates with him and in the assumptions underlying the discussions and debates about history, political power, and even the craft of poetry. Nothing escapes her pervasive presence.

To see Moneta in this light is to recognize that, like the narrator, she is not a neutral or transparent character. It is true of course that she displays great sorrow when the Titans are overthrown, that she offers to show the sensitive poet a vision of the past, and that there is something of "a benignant light" (1:265) about her. It is true, too, that the poet adores, even worships, her, struggling desperately to climb the difficult steps that lead to her altar. It is even true, or at least arguable, that her stated intentions are never malicious, that her decision to grant the troubled but courageous poet a vision of the past is intended to help mankind. Despite these isolated characteristics and impulses, however, the social definition of her character is traceable to a Hobbesian and Smithian world of individual warfare where only the blessing of money makes survival possible. Her presence and actions show that in a world governed by the marketplace, everything—even the most personal and sacred elements in life—is commodified and thus controlled by money. In this view, the poet is not so much guided (at least in a benevolent sense) by Moneta as subjected necessarily to her incredible power—to her "tyranny" (1:119).

This dimension of Moneta's character becomes evident when she is considered apart from her own representations of herself. In the very beginning, for instance, she is described in terms of her willingness to allow and to watch individuals die in great pain. Her attitude, in fact, is even taunting. As she tells the desperate and struggling young narrator who attempts to approach her altar: "If thou canst not ascend / These steps, die on that marble where thou art" (1:107–08). Further, when the poet sees her initially, she is engaged in a sacrificial offering that is left unexplained by her and unquestioned by the poet, but which apparently involves the burning of poetry (an activity which might be said to promote forgetfulness of the products of human labor and, thereby, of history itself, replacing these with visions of sheer "bliss" [1:104]—though what stands behind this vision of bliss cannot be seen by the narrator [1:102–5]). When she finally allows herself to be seen, moreover, she proves to be less than appealing, as she is characterized by her "hollow brain" and by the "dark secret chambers of her skull" (1:276, 278). In short, while the narrator himself displays an astonishing naivete and seriousness in these early passages, questioning virtually nothing about Moneta, the narrative allows us to see that, despite the narrator's blind commitment to her, she is at least potentially deceptive. (Poetically, this is a highly effective yet disturbing strategy that suggests the significance of her role as the goddess of money by stressing the way money lures us on even while it enslaves us.) Indeed, this first revealing picture of Moneta is charged with elements that seem to make her character vicious, while at the same time establishing convincingly, despite these elements, her absolute power over art (she burns poetry as a pastime) and life (the narrator is entirely at her mercy). The portrayal of Moneta and of the narrator's unquestioning respect for and commitment to her offer a condensed symbolic formulation of commodity culture, presided over by money even as the surrounding world is plagued ever-increasingly by struggle and difficulty, as can be seen in the pain and defeat of the Titans.

If the initial descriptions of Moneta and the narrator are fairly simple, the actual relationship that develops between the two is highly complex. One of the key ingredients of Moneta's "Holy Power" is her ability both to hide her true nature (her altar is "clouded . . . with soft smoke" [1:105]) and, at the same time, to avoid clear explanations of herself and her world. The confusion she is capable of generating is seen in her early conversation with the narrator about why she has allowed him to live and about the difference between poets and dreamers. For instance, while she taunts and belittles him, at the same time she favors him because, as she puts it, he is unworthy to be favored (". . . thou art here, for thou art less than they" [1:166]), which of course confuses and flatters the narrator: "That I am favour'd for unworthiness, / By such propitious parley medicin'd / In sickness not ignoble, I rejoice" (1:182–84). The issue is confused further when the two discuss the difference between poets and dreamers, the former apparently being the superior breed, and Moneta explains that the narrator is no poet but a dreamer: "Thou art a dreaming thing, / A fever of thyself" (1:168–69). Again, he is favored apparently because he is *not* a poet, which the narrator, interestingly, does not question and in fact interprets as an "award" (1:185) rather than as an insult.

To make sense of this confusing scene it is necessary to look beyond the common assumption that the narrator is in the process of learning to be a poet to the actual details of the situation, which suggest that he is being put to use by Moneta. That is, he is belittled and maligned while at the same time being rewarded, a tactic that at once humiliates him and gives him pleasure, and, most of all, makes him quite tractable. As Moneta establishes her power over him in this way, she at the same time begins to shape his thinking about human experience, displaying an attitude that is quite unKeatsian and that the narrator uncritically accepts:

> . . . Every creature hath its home,
> Every sole man hath days of joy and pain,
> Whether his labours be sublime or low—
> The pain alone, the joy alone, distinct.
>
> (1:171–74)

This controlling and undialectical view of life—which recalls portions of *Lamia* and which should be contrasted, for instance, with the view Keats presents in *Ode on Melancholy*—clarifies considerably the ideology behind the fragmentation and isolation of the narrator's world; it is a view that divides experience into unique and autonomous components, which, Moneta implies, can never be effectively integrated. Hers is not a vision of history but of what she considers to be human nature, and her power resides very largely in her ability to hegemonize the world with this naturalistic vision.

This view of human nature involves as well a specific view of poets and poetry. In a world such as the one Moneta has just described, the poet (who also is described in terms of autonomy, as "distinct" [1:199] from the dreamer) "pours out a balm upon the World" (1:201), thus making this rigid, dichotomized experience bearable. While on the surface Moneta's comment appears sufficiently laudable, in fact it implies a very specific social and cultural role for poetry that is not laudable. Faced with a reality that is made up of isolated, unmediated, and contradictory tendencies, poetry serves the same function that Marx later was to claim belonged to religion; it is "the opium of the masses," a product intended to absorb these contradictions and to soothe the frustrations of the alienated.[21] The effect of such a poetry is (at least tacitly) to endorse the world as Moneta describes it and to "naturalize" this world, assuring that it is neither questioned nor changed.

Such unsettling glimpses into Moneta's character notwithstanding, the narrator nonetheless assumes that she deserves his allegiance and even reverence. His conversion to her vision and to her cause is effected not only by her apparent integrity, the rhetorical persuasiveness of her arguments, and the mysteriousness of her character; it is effected as well by the lure of material gain, a not very pleasant but nonetheless significant fact in the narrator's developing character. Images are presented frequently in passing to suggest that the worshipper of Moneta stands to gain wealth (note, for instance, the references, mentioned above, to the "golden tongs" and "holy jewelries" in Moneta's sanctuary), but the most explicit statement of the determining influence of money on the modern poet comes after Moneta offers her view of human nature and of poetry, and while the narrator is looking "upon the offerings" (1:239) being made to the sacrificial fire. At this moment, when Moneta grants a boon to the narrator in the form of a vision of the past, he realizes (in a moment that marks a turning point in his character) that he stands to gain considerably from his worship of the goddess:

> . . . As I had found
> A grain of gold upon a mountain's side,
> And twing'd with avarice strain'd out my eyes
> To search its sullen entrails rich with ore,
> So at the view of sad Moneta's brow,
> I ach'd to see what things the hollow brain
> Behind enwombed: what high tragedy
> In the dark secret chambers of her skull
> Was acting, that could give so dread a stress
> To her cold lips, and fill with such a light
> Her planetary eyes.
>
> (1:271–81)

If in the earlier passages Moneta manipulated the narrator in an effort to convert and control him, here the process begins a reversal of sorts, one that is not entirely arbitrary. The narrator's eye to gold is nourished, as in his speech: his attitude does not simply materialize, as though by magic. His new attitude is the direct result of being empowered by Moneta. In order for him to be of use to her, she knows, he must have some power (in the form of the impending vision), and yet this power at the same time enables him to attempt to use her just as he is being used—hence the efforts at mutual manipulation that begin at this moment in the narrative. This is Adam Smith's world perfectly represented. Would-be poets are lured into activity by the possibility of self-gain, and where the poetry that is to be produced—the poetry that will find a market—is that which "pours out a balm upon the World," thereby serving Moneta and the marketplace.

It should be clear from what has been presented thus far that the narrative offers a developing rather than a static perspective, one that gradually unfolds the power and workings of the goddess Moneta. Beginning with the poet's stated doubt about whether the story to be told is poetry or fanaticism, and with the admission that only history can determine this (1:16–18), it proceeds to an almost parodic description of the narrator in a Spenserian or Wordsworthian world of pure and serene nature (the feast, on close inspection, is likened to "refuse of a meal / By angel tasted [1:30–31]), from where he has a vision that brings Moneta into the poem. At this moment, casting the worlds of Spenser and Wordsworth behind, the narrator enters a qualitatively different world of material wealth, confused debate, and aspirations unlike any that have characterized him before. And these aspirations, the poem implies, are related to the fact of Moneta's hollow brain, to the fact that her eyes remind him of gold, and to the fact that she possesses secrets that he believes can benefit him. With new aspirations driving him, the narrator loses his initial innocence and performs the conjuring act, discussed above, which is meant to persuade Moneta to divulge her secrets and to share her power. These developments effectively set the tone that prevails when Moneta finally presents the narrator with her vision of the war of the Titans.

An important point, implicit in what has been presented above, should be stressed before considering the actual vision of the war of the Titans—namely, that during the exchange of ideas between Moneta and the narrator about human nature, poetry, the past, and so on, the narrator's self-interested motives continue to develop, coming increasingly to the forefront of his character, illustrating the extent to which he has come under Moneta's power. For instance, when he begins to look closely at Moneta, he is clearly terrified of her ("And yet I had a terror of her robes, / And Chiefly of the veils" [1:251–52]), and when at last he actually sees her face, worn by the pressures of "an immortal sickness which kills not" (1:258), he feels a strong urge to run away. That he remains despite these fears and apprehensions, encouraged by her eyes, which attract him with what he calls a "benignant light" (1:265), does not mean that he believes Moneta is looking on him with compassion. Her eyes, after all, are "half-closed, and visionless entire they seem'd / Of all external things;—they saw me not (1:267–68). Even though he likens her to the moon, "Who comforts those she sees not, who knows not / What eyes are upward cast" (1:270–71), the fact remains that she appears here as a sort of private head, utterly blind as it spins visions out of itself. Deeply human compassion does not come from this sort of blindness. What attracts him, what he imagines as comfort, he admits, is the thought of "gold" (1:272), which her eyes call to his mind, and this makes him a worshipper of her power: "'Shade of Memory!'— / Cried I, with act adorant at her feet" (1:282–83). The desperation involved in such adoration is seen immediately when we recall the images, previously noted, repeatedly associated with Moneta; her divinity and her benignity must be measured against the presentations of her "blank splendor" (1:269), "hollow brain" (1:276), "secret chambers of her skull," and "cold lips" (1:280). Sickness, death, and dread surround her.

An additional determining feature of Moneta's character involves her relationship as a goddess from the past with a poet (or dreamer) of the present. Two issues emerge from this situation. First, she states explicitly that she belongs to an order of gods who have sought to preserve hierarchy:

> . . . This temple, sad and lone,
> Is all spar'd from the thunder of a war
> Foughten long since by giant hierarchy
> Against rebellion: this old image here,
> Whose carved features wrinkled as he fell,
> Is Saturn's; I Moneta, left supreme
> Sole priestess of his desolation.
> (1:221–27)

This confession of course emphatically distances Moneta from Keats's own political sympathies, evident everywhere in his letters, which placed him on "the liberal side of the question" and not at all on the side of hierarchy; but it also indicates the context out of which Moneta's character develops, associating her with a past of political conservativism, which, once defeated, she converts into a nostalgic vision for an old and superior order.

More importantly than this, Moneta's statement helps to identify the new world that has come to prevail and of which she is now a part. As the "sole Priestess of his desolation," she is the spirit and power that have survived the collapse of hierarchy, not unscathed (as the descriptions of her attest) but reshaped and redefined. She does not, after all, any longer represent hierarchy, at least in the old sense—this has been destroyed—but has begun to take on the features of a goddess of consumerism and self interest. Money existed prior to the modern world, but it did not exist in the same form and it did not carry the same power. In the modern world, Moneta both offers and controls the visions of the past, serving an entirely new role that requires ever greater sacrifices from her followers ("the altar's blaze / Was fainting for sweet food" [1:232–33]). Just as in *Isabella* Keats rewrites the medieval romance so that it speaks directly and bitterly to the modern world, here he recreates a minor figure from classical mythology as a major figure in his own age, one who controls even our most private dreams and highest aspirations to save the workings of the imagination.

The actual vision of the war of the Titans—the ostensible center of the narrative—reveals further the complex and often contradictory struggles between the narrator and the structures of authority governing his world, and presents yet another development in the narrator's character. The central facts of the vision are that it arises entirely from "the dark secret chambers of . . . [Moneta's] skull" (1:278), and that it is of an utterly fallen world, one devoid of all hope (1:463). The narrator, Moneta claims, will behold this vision of desolation "free from all pain, if wonder pain thee not" (1:248), and at the same time share her enormous powers. While he does indeed in the very beginning imagine himself as transformed—". . . there grew / A power within me of enormous ken / To see as a God sees" (1:302–4)—his experience is finally very different from what Moneta had promised. During the course of the vision he feels intense pain, a pain that does not deify him but rather humanizes him, generating true compassion for the suffering Titans. Describing the fallen Saturn, Thea (the wife of Hyperion), and his guide, Moneta, he notes:

> . . . Without stay or prop,
> But my own weak mortality, I bore
> The load of this eternal quietude,
> The unchanging gloom, and the three fixed shapes
> Ponderous upon my senses, a whole moon.
> For by my burning brain I measured sure
> Her silver seasons shedded on the night,
> And every day by day methought I grew
> More gaunt and ghostly. Oftentimes I pray'd

> Intense, that death would take me from the vale
> And all its burthens. Gasping with despair
> Of change, hour after hour I curs'd myself.
>
> (1:388–99)

The point here is not that Moneta's promise of a painless vision proves false. It is not necessary to condemn her as a demon conspirator intent on fooling the narrator at every turn; in fact, her sorrow and her loss are real. The point is rather that the vision transforms the narrator in ways that Moneta does not intend; the power that comes to him with the vision creates a certain independence and a new sort of intellectual inquisitiveness in him (". . . More I scrutinized" [1:445]), which threaten to lead him away from Moneta. As this happens, Moneta's voice becomes noticeably more shrill and insistent that the narrator interpret the vision as she means it to be interpreted. After closely inspecting the despair-ridden Thea and Saturn, for instance, the narrator notes:

> Ere I could turn, Moneta cried,—"These twain
> Are speeding to the families of grief,
> Where roof'd in by black rocks they waste, in pain
> And darkness, for no hope."—And she spake on.
>
> (1:460–63)

The extreme shift in narrative strategy in canto 2 elucidates very well the developing tension that I am describing. Canto 1 is characterized by Moneta's recollective powers—she is the "Shade of Memory" (1:282)—and by her presentation to the narrator of her memories in visionary form. At the end of the canto, however, when she interrupts the vision to interpret the fates of Saturn and Thea for the narrator—her first comments since the beginning of the vision—the vision itself recedes and in fact is converted by Moneta into a story, which the narrator must himself now recollect:

> . . . And she spake on,
> As ye may read who can unwearied pass
> Onward from the antichamber of this dream,
> Where even at the open doors awhile
> I must delay, and glean my memory
> Of her high phrase: perhaps no further dare.
>
> (1:463–68)

The effect here is not simply to test the narrator's recollective powers, but, more importantly, to assure that Moneta controls and directs the story of the war entirely. No longer does the narrator examine events for himself, as Moneta initially had said he would do (1:241–48), and no longer are the gods allowed to speak for themselves; now Moneta both describes and interprets the vision for him. If she "humanize[s]" her "sayings" so that the narrator "may'st understand aright" (2:1–2), at the same time she severely redefines her relationship to him and redefines as well the vision she has promised him. His role now is simply to listen to a compressed, intense, and nearly unbearable narrative characterized by "melancholy," "sorrow," "woe," "doom," "fright," "horrors," and more (2:7–19)—a narrative that seems bent on the destruction of all nobility and high purpose.

The final lines of the poem mark yet another development in the narrator's character, a development that provides a humane and compassionate perspective on the events Moneta has related and that begins to pull the various strands of the narrative together. His description of Moneta (Mnemosyne) when she concludes her monologue is chilling:

> . . . Now in clear light I stood,
> Reliev'd from the dusk vale. Mnemosyne
> Was sitting on a square edg'd polish'd stone,
> That in its lucid depth reflected pure
> Her priestess-garments.—My quick eyes ran on
> From stately nave to nave, from vault to vault,
> Through bowers of fragrant and enwreathed light
> And diamond-paved lustrous long arcades.
>
> (2:49–56)

He seems here to have developed beyond simply sympathizing with the struggling Titans to understanding, in some real and deep sense, the nature of the goddess who has presented him with their demise. What he describes here is a priestess in full splendor, ruling over an empire of death offset by exorbitant wealth and comfort. Her narrative recounts the horrors facing her race, and yet she remains ". . . sitting on a square edg'd polish'd stone, / That in its lucid depth reflected pure / Her priestess-garments." She is genuinely sorrowful for her race, but she is also preserved from their fate, transformed into a goddess who will endure in a new and even more powerful role.

Moneta's position at the end of the poem[22] begins to point toward the real significance of the connection between poetry and the marketplace. Ironically, the narrative rises to a noble and compelling poetic account of the "tyranny" (1:119) that commodity culture exercises over the poetic imagination. As Moneta presides sorrowfully yet comfortably over all visions of the past, Hyperion, the old god of the sun and hence of the imagination, rushes headlong to certain destruction. He is destroyed not by a demonic and conspiratorial Moneta, but rather by the same powers—the powers of buying and selling—that have brought her to the forefront of the modern age, enabling her to bestow and control the visions of even the most innocent would-be poets.

In abandoning his original *Hyperion* poem and rewriting it as the *Fall,* Keats was not simply abandoning an objective art form for a subjective one and hence "attempting something intrinsically inferior."[23] He was, rather, acknowledging the impossibility of the old poetic forms and myths, however noble they may have been, and rewriting them in the terms of his own age.[24] To do this, as the poem amply demonstrates, meant recognizing that poetry in the modern world necessarily passes through the marketplace, which determines in large measure not only the degree of its visibility and accessibility in society but also its values and critical powers. Even historical vision—the vision of the past—does not escape the realities and influences of commodity culture. In making this argument, I do not wish, however, to suggest that there is a mechanical relation between poetry and the marketplace, with the former being more or less automatically produced in pure capitalist form by the latter. The connection, as I have tried to show, is much more complex than this. Even as we show, for instance, that the narrator's vision in the *Fall* is directly underwritten by the goddess of money, we also must recognize the correctness of such scholars as Walter Evert, for instance, who argue that "Moneta . . . schools the visionary poet in the lessons (insofar as poetry is a social act) of social responsibility."[25]

On this view, the important issue is not whether Moneta is absolutely good or evil, or whether the narrator is either purely honest or manipulative—indeed, to see them as absolute opposites would entail accepting a priori Moneta's definition of the autonomy of individual life. Rather, the significant point is that the poem embodies and projects the dialectical nature of human history. Various needs and desires conflict with and develop from other needs and desires presented in the poem. Sometimes the result is a display of strength and integrity on the part of the characters, and, at others, a display of deceit or naivete. The dialectical process itself shows an actual and discernible historical change taking place, a dismantling of one power system that leaves another standing, one that is presided over by money.

One final point on the biographical dimension of this argument may help to clarify the critical orientation to the literary text that I have assumed. That Keats, throughout his life, was troubled by money and by getting a living, and that he even tried writing verse for the sake of making money at the very time he was working on the *Hyperion* project (*Otho the Great,* which did not sell), has been ably discussed not only by Ruthven but by others as well.[26] Further, as we have seen, abundant biographical evidence exists to support a view of *The Fall of Hyperion* as a poem about money and poetry. But this is at best an anecdotal consideration in a historical investigation of the poem. The decisive point, which goes back to the argument of Lowy and Sayre, noted in the preface to this study, is that the poem is ineluctably grounded in the world of capitalism, and that its multilayered textual elements give us a way into this world. To argue that it looks finally and most significantly toward the world is not to slight its aesthetic dimension but to acknowledge its achievement as a moving document of our own history, not a "fanatic's" dream but a "poet's."

9
"All Things Turn'd Topsy-turvy"
JEALOUSIES AND *GRIPUS*

DURING the latter months of 1819 Keats complained in a letter to his brother George that his friends were no longer engaged in literary pursuits but were settling instead into the boring routine of daily life. Reynolds, he lamented, "has turn'd to the law," and "Dilke is entirely swallowed up in his boy" (*LJK* 2:190). Their new interests and commitments came at a time when Keats himself had made a strong commitment to intellectual pursuit, going so far as to move to Winchester "for the convenience of a library" (*LJK* 2:184). His concerns now, as he remarked to Brown, were "entirely literary" (*LJK* 2:176). The sharp contrast between his own dogged pursuit in an area where he stood to make little if any money ("I could not raise any sum by the promise of any Poem" [*LJK* 2:185]) and the more settled and secure direction that his friends were beginning to take brought home to him the ironies of his situation and of the age in which he lived. The political machinery of the Regency government; the developing industrialization of the economy and its destructive impact on many old, agrarian communities; and the increasing commercialization of literary-intellectual endeavor—these were, for Keats, part of those ironies. Even while he was pleased that in Winchester "there is not one loom or any thing like manufacturing beyond bread & butter in the whole City" (*LJK* 2:189),[1] and even while his commitment to literature was perhaps now stronger than ever before ("I am fit for nothing but literature" [*LJK* 2:179]; "My hopes of success in the literary world are now better than ever" [*LJK* 2:237]), he did not escape the politics of age, and, in fact, felt besieged by the expanding authoritarian measures of the Regency and by the larger crosscurrents of sociohistorical change of which those measures were a part. He continued to be seriously concerned about how he might ease his very difficult financial situation in such a climate.[2] His letters from late 1819 into early 1820 return repeatedly to these matters, with money, local and national politics, the struggles of literary activity, and the nature of historical change fusing into a single area of intellectual concern that seemed to isolate him from the new and safer interests of his friends.

Keats's intense intellectual involvement in history and politics during this period is illustrated by his reading of "Holingshed" [sic] (*LJK* 2:234), his attendance at Hazlitt's lectures, and his continued regular reading of the *Examiner*. But his interests were not historically and politically restricted to his own country and his own day: he studied these within the context of larger historical developments. For example, in one of his most important letters on the nature of historical development, he describes to his brother and sister-in-law the halting and contradictory way that history unfolds:

> Three great changes have been in progress—First for the better, next for the worse, and a third time for the better once more. The first was the gradual annihilation of the tyranny of the nobles. [W]hen kings found it their interest to conciliate the common people, elevate them and be just to them. . . . The change for the worse in Europe was again this. The obligation of kings to the Multitude began to be forgotten—Custom had made noblemen the humble servants of kings—Then kings turned to the Nobles as the adorners of the[i]r power, the slaves of it, and from the people as creatures continually endeavoring to check them. Then in every kingdom therre [sic] was a long struggle of kings to destroy all popular privileges. The english were the only people in europe who made a grand kick at this. They were slaves to Henry 8th but were freemen under william 3rd at the time the french were abject slaves under Lewis 14th[.] The example of England, and the liberal writers of france and england sowed the seed of opposition to this Tyranny. (*LJK* 2:193)

These comments are followed by remarks on contemporary activities by British radicals to challenge the authoritarian and repressive measures of the Regency: Carlisle the bookseller, Keats notes, was selling "deistical pamphlets" (*LJK* 2:194), including the works of Thomas Paine, in a challenge to the government to prosecute him; Orator Hunt, after the Peterloo Massacre, marched through London to the great applause of 30,000 people (Keats's figure). Such remarks demonstrate Keats's attempt to think seriously and systematically about British and European history from the Renaissance through the period of the war with France and to articulate his (occasionally confused) ideas on historical progress, to which he had probably been introduced by William Robertson, Hazlitt, and others.[3]

Such seriousness, however, was occasionally offset by whimsical, even cynical, references to the politicians of the day. Writing to his sister-in-law in America, for instance, Keats remarks that "T wang dillo dee . . . is the Amen to nonsense," and that "My Lords Wellington, Castlereagh and Canning and many more would do well to wear T wang-dillo-dee written on their Backs instead of wearing ribbands in their Button holes" (*LJK* 2:246). Much like Byron, he recognized the pressing reality of the political moment and seemed unable to reconcile intellectually its extreme contadictions or to sustain for very long at a time a systematic analysis of those contradictions. When consideration of these contradictions did not drive him to despair it drove him to laughter, not only in his letters, as in the one quoted above, but also in his poetry. While this laughter assuredly is less skillfully managed in Keats's poetry than in Byron's, it is no less important as a point of entry into Keats's vision of politics, history, and society, and into the way the politics of the age changed the problematic of literary activity.

The Jealousies is Keats's fullest satirical response to the radical transformations of the world that were daily taking place around him; with Byron's *Don Juan,* it is perhaps one of the last attempts in British literary history at extended political verse satire, an eruption into serious laughter that would give way to the more somber articulation of crisis and contradiction in the high Victorian poetry of Tennyson and Arnold. Drawing upon the example of Byron, Keats attempts to develop a poetic strategy capable of formulating and articulating the historical crosscurrents of his age. The result is a fascinating, if at times clumsy, distillation of many of the topics found in his letters and of the themes found in his more serious and more successful poetry. Consisting of a thinly veiled allegory of the actions of leading political characters of his day, and of vague, abstract, but sweeping portrayals of the material and ideological contexts within which these characters moved, the poem is critical to understanding the social context of Keats's intellectual and poetic activity.

Robert Gittings, one of the few scholars to take *The Jealousies* seriously, attempts to redeem it from critical disrepute by explaining it in terms of the contemporary political scene, tracing the various poetic characters to their actual counterparts in Keats's world.[4] Because Gittings has pursued this dimension of the poem exhaustively, I intend to omit it here, situating the poem instead within a larger framework of ideas that disclose many of the social relations governing the romantic period. In approaching the poem from this direction, I do not wish to diminish the significance of Gittings's contribution, but to elucidate the material contexts within which his findings should be placed.

In an important respect, this poem is a logical sequel to *The Fall of Hyperion.* Whereas the earlier poem had addressed and questioned things of the spirit in a serious fashion, the *Jealousies* openly attacks them, subjecting them to a bitterly humorous treatment. In his portrayals of Emperor Elfinan, Bellanaine, Hum, and the other spirits Keats is not abandoning the principle of beauty and the power of the imagination that he so often celebrated in both his poetry and letters; what he is rejecting here is a naive conception of them. The most telling feature of Keats's spirits in this poem is that they are distinctly unhappy as spirits, and long for the warmth and passion of mortals, that is, of things that die. This is a complete reversal of Endymion's quest, and arguably a radically different theme from that which appears in the great odes, *Hyperion, La Belle Dame Sans Merci,* and other poems that display intense yearning for enduring spiritual beauty.

But the plot of *The Jealousies* reveals more than a rejection of Keats's earlier themes. It is an extension of the *Fall* in that it emphasizes the claim of materiality on all life, spiritual and otherwise. If in the earlier poem Keats dramatized the conflict between an imagined world of permanence and beauty, on the one hand, and, on the other, the constraints placed on imaginative activity by a market economy, implying that historical reality limits the higher aspirations of human life, here he asserts directly that all meaningful exchange is to be found within the human community and nowhere else. On this view, the search of Elfinan and Bellanaine for earthly lovers is not simply a play on the classical and neoclassical themes of the gods dallying with mortals for passing pleasure (the plights of these spirits are much too desperate and desperately funny for this); it is a criticism of the insistent spiritualizing and idealizing of value, as is made clear by the consistent description of the spirit world of the poem as petty and silly. This satirical critique of the world of spirits provides the necessary basis for understanding the politics of the narrative, which reveal that Keats had been following the lectures and essays of his mentor, Hazlitt (see, again, Keats's references to Hazlitt's essay on Gifford in *LJK* 2:71–76). Gittings rightly sees in the story of Elfinan and Bellanaine an allegory of Regency politics and personsalities, but he does not consider the larger significance of Keats's strategy of situating the political story within a spiritual framework. This strategy is critically important, for it not only provides a poetic means of criticizing both Regency England and things spiritual; it enables Keats to illuminate the connections between these two topics and to enlarge his satirical vision to include the ideological structures of authority and systems of belief and value within which the politics of Regency England played themselves out. To place Elfinan, Bellanaine, their servants, and the institutions of religion and government among the spirits is to call attention to the extent of their removal from actual, human experience and to show that, removed or isolated from that experience, the forms of social life become a mere parody of themselves. This becomes immediately apparent in Crafticant's description of the Royal Palace as "the strangest sight—the most unlook'd-for-chance—/ All things turn'd topsy-turvy in a devil's dance" (755–56). Put simply, the politics of the age are played out within an utterly hollow framework of absurdity and chaos.

That the institutions of social life and the structures of social authority described in the narrative are situated away from the humanity for which both Elfinian and Bellanaine long is not, of course, to say that they are without real political consequence. Quite the reverse: political consequences arise from the division and fragmentation of life, and especially from the isolation and invisibility of social authority. In the opening sections of the poem, Keats describes an emperor (Elfinan), the law, religion, and parliament, as well as the political nature of personal relationships, effectively establishing the structures and relations of social life that he is most immediately concerned to portray. In describing these, he emphasizes the insistent institutional refusal to be integrated into everyday life. The "law" (10) denies Elfinan the right to consort with mortals; the "priesthood" (11) proclaims the emperor's activities a "sin" (13); "parliament" (19) petitions him not to violate his responsibilities to his position. Clearly, rule of the spirit-kingdom depends upon the containment and isolation of power, and every institution contributes directly to these. Even Elfinan, against his consuming desires, pays lip service to them.

This division of social life into a spiritual world of rulers and the institutions that surround them, and a mortal world of men and women, is also a class division—one that shows the boredom of the aristocracy and, at the same time, the social contradictions and situation responsible for that boredom. Moreover, Keats implies, this class division cannot last; in fact, it is in the process of disintegrating. The lines between those with authority and those without (spirits and mortals) are ideologically absolute, yet the very life of those with power (as the actions of Elfinan and Bellanaine vividly illustrate) depends for its energy and purpose upon those who are subordinate to them: while denying mere mortals any real worth, spirits use them for their own ends. This is much like Byron's point in his poems on Napoleon, which maintains that Napoleon falls precisely because he comes to see himself as a god, independent of the very forces that have made his power possible in the first place. Keats most certainly understands this point, for he makes social division and social blindness the central issue of the narrative.

To approach the poem from this perspective is to understand that the fading hierarchies with which Keats is concerned in his poetry from *Hyperion* onward are weakened not only by external resistance but also by their own internal withering, which results from a refusal to acknowledge the proper sources of power and even of value. The anxiety that characterizes the opening sections of the narrative arises from the conviction that by consorting with ordinary, mortal people, Elfinan will destroy the kingdom: "And all the priesthood of his city wept, / For ruin and dismay they well foresaw" (11–12). Much of the remainder of the poem traces the social disintegration that arises from this persistent attitude, recalling again the laments voiced in *La Belle Dame Sans Merci, Ode to Psyche, The Eve of St. Agnes, Hyperion,* and elsewhere. The characters in *The Jealousies,* in other words, dramatize vividly what in *Endymion* was called "the latter end of some strange history," which of course are the latter days of the aristocracy; but Keats seems here to recognize an important reason for this historical development, which he had not before pursued: the aristocracy neither acknowledges nor understands the sources of its own power. This ideological blind spot creates contradictions that cannot be overcome. In the attempt to reconcile these contradictions from within the institutions of aristocratic-spiritual life, hypocrisy (in the character of Crafticant), alienation, drunkenness, debauchery, and deception take over, blinding those who rule. Crafticant matter-of-factly expresses this obliviousness of those with power to those without when he describes his journey with Bellanaine to the Royal Palace: "Onward we floated o'er the panting streets, / That seem'd throughout with upheld faces paved" (730–31). While Keats does not stop to dwell on the human and political dimension of this description, he makes it clear through the subsequent narrative that in walking on and running over the general populace the aristocracy becomes ever more ridiculous, ever more hollow at the core. Within the Royal Palace, for instance, ". . . the Chief Justice on his knees and hands doth crawl" (765); "A Poet, mounted on the Court-Clown's back, / Rode to the Princess swift with spurring heels" (775–76); "Powder'd bag-wigs and ruffy-tuffy heads / Of cinder wenches meet and soil each other" (770–71).

In this world turned topsy-turvy the problem, then, is not simply that there are rulers, but that social and political leadership is entirely severed from social life itself. This produces a system and structure of values that touch every facet of life—not only the ruling institutions, such as religion, law, and government, but also the daily arrangements and activities of personal and social exchange. One of the most significant examples of this is the urbanization of social life, the crowding of people together to the point where they seem to lose their humanity. The "crowds of people" (544) in the narrative, for instance, are seen as "monsters" (545), as a "swarm" (575), and as a "mighty coil" (565). The urbanization of social life in turn constricts movement, a point that is emphasized in the one section (on travel by coach) of the poem printed before Keats's death. Elfinan's servant, Eban, angered because the coach which he has hired is barely moving through the crowded streets, is told by his coachman:

> Certes, monsieur were best take to his feet,
> Seeing his servant can no further drive
> For press of coaches, that to-night here meet
> Many as bees about a straw-capp'd hive,
> When first for April honey into faint flowers they dive.
>
> (257–61)

These descriptions of massive urbanization and of the transformation of people into swarms, bees, and monsters are accompanied by descriptions of the power of a corrupt publishing industry ("those sly compeers / Who raked up ev'ry fact against the dead" [88–89]), the power of money in the world ("It was a time when wholesale houses close / Their shutters with a moody sense of wealth" [208–9, see also 289–97]), and the connection between race and slavery. This latter point is made emphatically in the description of Eban, Elfinan's slave:

> [Eban] was his [Elfinan's] page,
> A fay of colour, slave from top to toe,
> Sent as a present, while yet under age,
> From the Viceroy of Zanguebar,—wise, slow,
> His speech, his only words were "yes" and "no."
>
> (181–85)

Together, these dimensions of social life provide not so much a glimpse of the future as a sign of social perversion that turns the world virtually upside down and threatens to send it spinning toward ever greater inhumanity. The most telling image of social insanity and possible historical regression in the narrative is the description of Hum the Magician descending the stairs backwards with "one shoe / . . . off, and one shoe on" (304–5), to greet Eban. "[R]etrograding careful as he can, / Backwards and downwards from his own two pair" (309–10), Hum points the direction of the entire social world being described and calls to mind Byron's comment in the letter, noted in an earlier chapter, written after the defeat of Napoleon: "And we are retrograding to the same, dull, stupid old system" (*BLJ* 3:218). Indeed, while the narrative is a satire of Regency England, as Gittings shows, it is at the same time a lament for what must inevitably be the social and political consequences of the Regency.

The understanding, pursuit, and very concept of love, the ostensible subject matter of the narrative, are all shaped and determined by this material context of individual struggle and institutional corruption.

Within such a context, Keats suggests, love—one of the major themes in many of his earlier poems—can become quite confusing, for it is not only touched by the reality around it but indeed cannot be defined apart from that reality; it is not an unmediated category. Recognition of this fact causes love to appear quite comical and drives the narrative to cynical laughter.

The descriptions of social fragmentation, and of the inability of love to escape this fragmentation, mark a significant departure from the vision presented in many of Keats's other poems. Far from offering simply a more realistic view of the material world, *The Jealousies* constitutes a changed vision, one that shifts the relation of the poetic subject to the world that it would articulate. In other words, in many of Keats's earlier poems the fundamental poetic assumption was, as Stillinger has convincingly elaborated in *The Hoodwinking of Madeline and Other Essays,* that while mortality hangs over us we can have glimpses of an unchanging and transhistorical beauty, and in these glimpses we discover the meaning and value of life. In these poems, poetic value is situated in terms of a principle that apparently transcends conflict and mortality and that in fact would reconcile at the level of imagination or spirit the turmoils and struggles facing everyday mortal existence. In *The Jealousies,* on the other hand, Keats attempts to shift the burden of poetic vision from reconciliation at the level of imagination to conflict at the level of material life. This move is arguably one reason the poem is unsuccessful. Unlike Byron, Keats was unable to direct his full poetic energies toward a frontal attack on the bourgeois dream of spiritual unity or transcendental beauty. But the effort in this direction in *The Jealousies* begins to release or articulate those anxieties just beneath the surface of such a beautiful poem as the *Ode on a Grecian Urn,* and constitutes the fullest pronouncement we have of the material conditions of social life haunting all of Keats's other work.

* * *

While scholars are not agreed on whether *Gripus* was actually written by Keats, the dramatic fragment raises many of the same issues set down in *The Jealousies.* Thus, I want to offer a few remarks about it that may help to elucidate Keats's growing confusion about poetry and politics in the latter period of his life. This confusion, as I have suggested, pressed to the foreground in *The Fall of Hyperion*—although it is implicit earlier— and erupts in *The Jealousies;* it points explicitly to Keats's need to rethink the nature and possibilities of poetry in a socially fragmented world in which older forms of social authority are both oppressive and doomed, and in which the bourgeois system emerging to replace aristocracy is characterized by self-interest and money. *Gripus* does not, in its 189 lines, explore this crisis in any real detail, but it effectively and humorously comments upon it, showing, as *Isabella* had done, the extent to which money, personal life, and social authority are intertwined.

The plot of *Gripus*—the story of Lord Gripus's decision to send his servant-paramour, Bridget, out of house so that he may wed a woman of wealth—not only focuses on the depravity of an aristocracy (and patriarchy) that takes sexual advantage of the classes below it, but also addresses the crisis of the aristocracy as a class doomed to extinction. The invasion of the aristocracy by the bourgeoisie is seen from the very beginning in Lord Gripus's distaste for money (the symbol and means of bourgeois power) and at the same time his desire for it as the only means of assuring that his family name will endure through history. As he tells his servant Slim, money itself is filthy unless it can be harnessed to serve aristocratic authority and value:

> And gold and silver are but filthy dross.
> Then seek not gold and silver, which are dross,
> But rather lay thy treasure up in heav'n!
> . . . .
> But I must lay up money for my children,
> My children's children and my great–grand children,
> For, Slim! thy master will be shortly married—.
> (1–3, 7–9)

Even as Gripus prepares to secure his name and authority through a favorable marriage, he betrays the changing nature of the world in his many references to money and marriage, all of which reflect bourgeois or capitalist, rather than aristocratic, values. His marriage, he says, is "downright venture and mere speculation" (22), a risk greater than "what the merchant trusts / To winds and waves and the uncertain elements" (23–24). Further, to marry is to run the risk of legally binding oneself to one "who will . . . spend far more than she has brought" (29), a fact that again leads Gripus to compare marriage with capitalism:

> . . . the broker cannot tell
> He is not cheated in the wares he buys;
> And to judge well of women or the seas
> Would oft surpass the wisest merchant's prudence,
> For both are deep alike—capricious too—
> And the worst things that money can be sunk in.
> (31–36)

Even so, Gripus understands clearly that capital is the historically necessary means for him to preserve his authority. Unlike Byron's Manfred, who, as the last of his race (i.e., aristocracy), refuses to make any compromises whatsoever, dying in utter isolation, Gripus is more realistic, maneuvering carefully and persistently to assure that he will have both money and "a little heir to leave my little wealth to" (64).

The question of money in the drama also raises the issue of rank, or class—especially the relation of the serving class to the changing aristocracy. Bridget, the servant and mistress of Gripus, exemplifies both the workings of aristocratic hegemony and the reality of the human sacrifices resulting from historical change. The hegemonic power of aristocracy becomes apparent, of course, in Bridget's misunderstanding of Gripus's wedding plans. Believing that the lord and master intends to marry her, Bridget indulges herself in visions of personal grandeur, proclaiming that as Gripus' wife she "shall be another woman quite" (79): "Great Lady Gripus—O lord!— / The lady of the old and rich Sir Gripus!" (82–83). And to Slim, a fellow servant, she says of his personal affection and familiarity: "Ruffin, begone, or I will tell my lord. / Do you not care for difference of rank, / Nor make distinction between dirt and dignity?" (124–26). The point here is not simply that she is mistaken about her fortunes, but rather that she has all along identified herself entirely in terms of Gripus, succumbing to his sexual advances to attach herself, however insignificantly, to his power, assuming that as his wife she will attain real social status and hence power. All along she consents to his authority because she believes that in his power is to be found her own.

That this in fact is not the case is a surprise to herself only. In her discovery of the truth of the workings of aristocracy we see the readiness with which individuals are discarded to serve the ends of social authority in a class-divided society. When she is told by Gripus that she must "seek and get a situation elsewhere" (152), because he does not want her in his estate when his new wife arrives, she faints and then, upon recovering, embraces her servant status wholly. Once she is driven out of Gripus' life, the real monetary, labor, and power relations entailed in her situation surface. To Gripus, she and other laborers are simply "thieves" (171) whom he can "discard" (171) at will. She, on the other hand, voices at last the real point of connection between herself and Gripus, insisting that before she will leave the premise she must have her wages: "I'll have a month's full wages or my warning! / I'll not be left at non-plush for a place" (173–74). This bitter, comic scene reveals the significance of the title character's name: Bridget, Slim, and other laborers are in the grip of those with power and money (or who have access to money), and that grip is tightened and even made possible by the fact that under ordinary circumstances the lower classes consent to that power under the illusion that somehow they share in it. Only at moments of crisis, such as the one presented in *Gripus,* does it become clear that the interests of the ruling class are not the same as those of the laboring class.

While we may never know with certainty whether Keats actually wrote *Gripus*, we should recognize that thematically it is consistent with the direction that Keats's thought had been moving over the past few years, as the social significance of money became uppermost in his mind. Further, the satirical thrust of this dramatic fragment, and its focus on social turmoil rather than on transhistorical beauty, is consistent with the thematic interest of *The Fall of Hyperion* and with the thematic and formal interests of *The Jealousies*. For these reasons, despite its fragmentary status and despite its inferior poetry, the poem should be included in any critical investigation of Keats's developing intellectual and social poetic vision. What he seems to be working toward in the final years of his life is redirecting his poetic effort not simply to the mortal but to the social, with its myriad struggles, conflicts, and class and economic realities. Such a poetic direction is consistent with his many comments in his letters that he needed to know much more about the world to be able to produce the sort of poetry that he believed was capable of enduring over time. If *The Jealousies* and *Gripus* are not successful efforts in this direction, they are nonetheless a testament to the sort of socially aware writing to which he had come to commit himself.

10
"The Truth of the Imagination"
CONCLUSION

In a letter written to Fanny Brawne during the period of his last illness (presumably early 1820), Keats betrays intimations of his imminent death, laments that he will not leave behind him any work that will endure, and remarks that, even so, "I have lov'd the principle of beauty in all things" (*LJK* 2:263). Any careful study of his poetry, whether materialist or idealist, will show that this comment is true. Indeed, it is this commitment to the principle of beauty that sustains his poetry and makes it important not only to literary history but to social and political history as well. For if Keats never abandoned his commitment to the principle of beauty, neither did he view it through the same eyes across the span of his short life. What he did not see clearly early on, but what he came to learn, is that beauty is never exempt from history, but is mediated and constituted by it in quite specific ways. If in his later poems Keats seemed to speak less enthusiastically on the themes that had occupied him earlier, this is not because he rejected the ideals at the center of those themes but because he shifted his poetic focus to the contexts and relations to which those ideals were ineluctably bound. *Otho the Great*, *King Stephen*, *The Fall of Hyperion*, and *Jealousies* are efforts in the direction of a poetry focusing on the historical, political, and economic contexts of beauty, while works such as *Sleep and Poetry* and some of the great odes are efforts to define beauty independently of these contexts, as an ideal set against human mortality and individual suffering. Keats's poetic development, I have tried to show, is marked by this maturing vision of the contexts within which beauty—and, more generally, human meaning—must be understood and articulated.

To approach Keats's poetry from this direction is to recognize that even at its most escapist and desperately idealist moments it remains socially and historically important, for it provides a point of entry into the conflicted cultural situation in Keats's day that threatened to annihilate or (what, for Keats, was the same thing) to co-opt all beauty. Put differently, the love of beauty that is everywhere apparent in Keats's work is a key to understanding the historical dimension of the poetry of the period, because it displays that utopian longing which emerges from within a context of historical contradiction and hardship. The persistence with which Keats pursued his theme is a sign of the extent to which the avenues of human investment had narrowed during the romantic period, forcing individual responses to the world into increasingly privatized and subjectivized domains of pursuit.[1] And as a sign, it can be used to open up historical investigation of the situation within which Keats was caught. By following the thread of beauty through Keats's poetry, we discover the highly complex nature of the historical contradictions of Keats's world, seeing, for instance, in *Isabella*, the horrors of a capitalist social authority, and, in the *Ode on a Grecian Urn*, the patriarchal connections of Keats's concept of beauty. In other words, Keats's poetry is too important to be dismissed as an example of bourgeois idealism. Whatever Keats's poetic intentions, and despite the specific direction of individual poems, he produced a body of work saturated with historical significance; having as their genesis the historical moment of bourgeois triumph, his poems are an important literary representation of the many ideological dimensions of that triumph.

One way of understanding the multidimensional nature of Keats's poetic interest in beauty is by situating it at the historical moment of Napoleon's defeat at Waterloo. Much early romantic poetry is characterized by the historical energy of revolutionary hope, fed by the French Revolution and by the intellectual, artistic, radical response to it in England.[2] Even after the initial faith in the Revolution was dampened by the horrors of Robespierre and by the drawn-out war between England and France, a more realistic commitment to historical progress was maintained by many who witnessed the emergence and meteoric rise of Napoleon. As John Kinnaird puts it in his account of Hazlitt's support of the French general: "The fact is that when we examine Hazlitt's 'idolatry' in the context of English liberal attitudes in the early years of this decade (1810–20), we soon discover that Napoleon's regime was often seen and judged, even by lukewarm onlookers, as perhaps the only 'enlightened' alternative to the hoary anachronisms that opposed his power."[3] The defeat of Napoleon at Waterloo destroyed this enlightened alternative, producing a period of extreme anxiety among British intellectuals and artists. It now seemed to many that Europe would return to an older, conservative, and potentially oppressive and violent political situation. (The return of Ferdinand VII to the throne of Spain was one sign of this, and Hunt in the *Examiner* made much of it.) Even Keats, who was no avid supporter (and indeed was a frequent critic) of Napoleon, was concerned that the "good" accomplished by Napoleon would be destroyed by the "divine right Gentlemen" (*LJK* 1:397).

Keats's greatest poetry, written during this period of historical anxiety, carries this anxiety within it, offering glimpses of human hope and moments of despair and loneliness, and articulating a persistent need for values and principles worthy of commitment. The limitation of much Keats criticism, I believe, is not that it has failed to recognize the hope and loneliness in his poetry, but that it has failed to explore their full historical context, and thus has overlooked their specific, historically differentiated significance. Keats's poetry is not simply a record of the human condition, unmediated by the material world within which it moves; it is a representation of human response to the intellectual, political, and military developments of the age. The period from 1815 to roughly 1820, the period of Keats's maturity, is a critical historical moment, a moment of uncertainty when it looked as though social change, in England and abroad, could break in any one of several different directions. Keats was on some level aware of this, writing letters about the nature of historical progress, speculating on the likelihood of national bankruptcy, and criticizing those who stood to gain from Napoleon's defeat (even as he criticized Napoleon). While his poems do not always address such matters directly, neither do they escape them entirely; indeed, they are constituted by these matters, which are the necessary material conditions determining Keats's poetic activity. To read Keats's poetry in terms of material history is not to lose sight of the principle of beauty, but to understand why that principle is critically important to Keats and how it became an energizing force in his writing.

But the moment of historical anxiety is not the only historical feature of Keats's poetry, and I do not wish to situate my argument entirely within the immediate context of post-Waterloo developments. Keats's poetry achieves greater significance within the much larger context of the historical development from feudalism to capitalism. The defeat of Napoleon and the triumph of England and the Holy Alliance did not mark a simple return to that "dull, stupid, old system," as Byron dreaded, nor did it mark the restoration—at least at the level of ideology—of the "divine right Gentlemen" whom Keats so detested. One effect of the long Napoleonic Wars was to usher in the world of industrial capitalism, which included not only the redefinition of political apparatuses but also of ideological structures of authority and systems of belief.[4]

The moment of England's war with Napoleon was also the moment of the demise of an entire historical age: feudalism, a social structure constituted by land, agriculture, inheritance, aristocracy, institutional religion, and monarchy (divine right), succumbed finally to capitalism, a social structure ruled by money, property, industry, talent, secular belief, parliament, the middle class, and an industrial class of laborers. The poetry of the age is both a product and a record of this giant historical shift; as such, it reflects many of the values of the emergent bourgeois world while looking nostalgically, from a position of modern isolation and loneliness, to a past world where human integrity and meaning were possible.

Thus Keats's poetry, while riddled with the historical anxiety of the post-Waterloo years, also articulates the early venture into this modern world. The nearly obsessive poetic concern with things, people, stories, and poetic forms of the past—the Elgin Marbles, Endymion, Spenser, Psyche, St. Agnes, St. Mark, Otho the Great, King Stephen, Apollonius, Hermes, Milton, epic poetry—is a concern with that which is socially and culturally lost. Moreover, for Keats, writing from the perspective of a sordid world ruled by finance, factories, and military strength, these lost emblems represent the highest achievements and possibilities of human meaning. Further, the values at the center of Keats's poetry (i.e., beauty and truth) are consistently presented as being under fire, as threatened with extinction, and the poetry presents this fact in moving language; it also seeks to preserve those values by converting them into universal principles, free from every onslaught of history and mortality. Keats's poetry, from this perspective, is a record of the loneliness, fear, and desperate hope that result from the dissolution and disempowerment of the known forms and symbols of social life and social meaning; it is a record of the belief that history has ended as the world moves into isolated, privatized, subjectivized modernity.

The search through past history and past legends and myths for things and values that are pure, meaningful, and "true," then, is one sign of the radical historical change of the romantic period, a sign of the last moments of feudalism and the early, powerfully resonant moment of industrial capitalism; it is a sign, in short, of the latter end of some strange history. Keats's poetry must not be understood only as a nostalgic longing for a past world; within the nostalgia and escapism that characterize so much of his poetry are traces of the real history that both enables and constrains his poetic vision. In the folds and seams of nostalgic poetic expression, history discloses itself, the political unconscious energizes and structures the textual surface, and "the truth of Imagination" (*LJK* 1:184) becomes visible. That is, Keats's expressed intentions, in both his letters and his poetry, are not the ultimate key to poetic and interpretive meaning; historical genesis encompasses and constitutes both, providing the necessary basis and starting point of critical investigation. This is not to say that what Keats tells us about beauty and truth in his letters and in his poetry should be discarded by the historical critic, but to insist that subjective self-representations must be seen as objective historical categories, as elements within certain material structures of social life. To understand this is to begin to understand the historical meanings of what was for Keats the principle of beauty in all things, and the historical importance of the critical investigation of that principle.

Notes

Preface

1. See *Studies in Romanticism* 25 (1986). For a discussion of Keats's poetry in historical terms, see June Koch, "Politics in Keats's Poetry," *Journal of English and Germanic Philology* 70 (1972): 491–501; Clarence DeWitt Thorpe, "Keats's Interest in Politics and World Affairs," *PMLA* 46 (1931): 1228–45; Philip J. Eggers, "Memory in Mankind: Keats's Historical Imagination," *PMLA* 86 (1971): 990–98; Renée Winegarten, *Writers and Revolution: The Fatal Lure of Action* (New York: New Viewpoints, 1974), 68–81; Carl Woodring, *Politics in English Romantic Poetry* (Cambridge: Harvard University Press, 1970); and Jerome J. McGann, "Keats and the Historical Method in Literary Criticism," *Modern Language Notes* 94 (1979): 988–1032.

2. I do not mean to suggest here that mainstream Keats criticism is not valuable, or even that it misrepresents Keats's poetry (at least insofar as Keats himself understood and described it)—Keats has been blessed with excellent readers and critics. I am suggesting merely that criticism, like poetry, has its own agenda, whether or not it is explicitly stated, and that in the case of Keats that agenda has entailed in very large measure the writing out of a conventional set of cultural values. My aim is to gain critical distance on those values in an attempt to define more fully the possible historical and political significance of Keats's poetry.

3. I am here drawing on Lukács's comments on realism. Writing in a different context, Lukács remarks that the realist's "goal is to penetrate the laws governing objective reality and to uncover the deeper, hidden, mediated, not immediately perceptible network of relationships that go to make up society. Since these relationships do not lie on the surface, since the underlying laws only make themselves felt in very complex ways and are realized only unevenly, as trends, the labour of the realist is extraordinarily arduous, since it has both an artistic and an intellectual dimension." See Georg Lukács, "Realism in the Balance," trans. Rodney Livingstone, in *Aesthetics and Politics,* translation editor Ronald Taylor (London: Verso, 1977), 38–39.

4. John Fekete, *The Critical Twilight* (London: Routledge and Kegan Paul, 1976), 6. For a view of Keats's poetry similar to that offered by Fekete, see Christopher Caudwell, *Illusion and Reality: A Study of the Sources of Poetry* (1937; reprint, New York: 1973). According to Caudwell, "Keats is the banner bearer of the Romantic Revival. The poet now escapes upon the 'rapid wings of poesy' to a world of romance, beauty and sensuous life separate from the poor, harsh, real world of everyday life, which it sweetens and by its own loveliness silently condemns" (108). See also E. P. Thompson's *William Morris: Romantic to Revolutionary* (1955; reprint, New York: Pantheon, 1976), 10–21.

5. M. I. Finley, "Utopianism Ancient and Modern," in *The Critical Spirit: Essays in Honor of Herbert Marcuse,* ed. Kurt H. Wolff and Barrington Moore, Jr. (Boston: Beacon Press, 1968), 6.

6. Again, see Caudwell, *Illusion and Reality,* 107–13; see also G. V. Plekhanov's general account of romanticism as escapism in *Art and Social Life* (Moscow: Progress Publishers, 1977), 12–16.

7. Robert Sayre and Michael Lowy, "Figures of Romantic Anti-Capitalism," *New German Critique* 34 (1984): 49.

8. For the significance of authorial intention in critical practice, see Jerome J. McGann, *A Critique of Modern Textual Criticism* (Chicago: University of Chicago Press, 1983), 65–80, and Robert Weimann, *Structure and Society in Literary History: Studies in the History and Theory of Historical Criticism* (Baltimore: The Johns Hopkins University Press, 1984), 5–7.

9. The best single essay to illustrate and elaborate this assertion is Jerome McGann's excellent "Keats and the Historical Method in Literary Criticism," *Modern Language Notes* 94 (1979): 988–1032.

Chapter 1. "Formed by Circumstance": Introduction

1. For an early instance of Keats's negative attitude toward Hunt, note the letter to Haydon of May 1817: "His [Hunt's] self delusions are very lamentable they have inticed him into a Situation which I should be less eager after than that of a galley Slave—what you observe thereon is very true must be in time. Perhaps it is a self delusion to say so—but I think I could not be deceived in the Manner that Hunt is—may I die tomorrow if I am to be" (*LJK* 1:143).

2. The fullest discussion of Keats's political and social views is by Thorpe, "Keats's Interest in Politics and World Affairs," but see also Eggers, "Memory in Mankind: Keats's Historical Imagination"; Winegarten, *Writers and Revolution* (68–81); and Woodring, *Politics in English Romantic Poetry* (77–83).

3. Garrod remarks that while Keats "was more the child of the Revolutionary Idea than we commonly suppose," and was very much interested in "the crying and striving of our politics, our social misery," he had "very little business" among such matters because they caused him to indulge in a kind of "poetry in which he was never likely to be competent." *Keats,* 2d. ed. (1926; reprint, Oxford: The Clarendon Press, 1962), 27–29.

4. Note, for instance, the essays in the issue of *Studies in Romanticism* 25 (1986): 171–229, devoted to "Keats and Politics."

5. John Barnard, *John Keats* (Cambridge: Cambridge University Press, 1987), 1.

6. Note John D. Kinnaird's comment that "Napoleon's regime was often seen and judged, even by lukewarm onlookers, as perhaps the only 'enlightened' alternative to the hoary anachronisms that opposed his power. And even the Emperor's campaigns of conquest in the Near East, Spain, the Tyrol, and Russia appeared, however ruthless in specific instances, to be advancing the cause of modern civilization and the rule of cosmopolitan law against the darkest strongholds of superstition and despotic 'barbarism.'" *Hazlitt: Critic of Power* (New York: Columbia University Press, 1978), 83–84.

7. George Rudé, *Revolutionary Europe: 1783–1815* (1964; reprint, New York: Harper Colophon Books, 1975), 263.

8. For a full discussion of romanticism in these terms, again see Sayre and Lowy, "Figures of Romantic Anti-Capitalism."

9. For a discussion of Keats's reading see Walter Jackson Bate, *John Keats* (Cambridge: Harvard University Press, Belknap Press, 1963), 25–32, and Charles C. and Mary Cowden Clarke, *Recollections of Writers* (London, 1878).

10. B. Ifor Evans, "Keats's Approach to the Chapman Sonnet," *Essays and Studies by Members of the English Association* 16 (1931): 26–52.

11. In addition to Evans, see Joseph Warren Beach's excellent source study, "Keats's

Realms of Gold," *PMLA* 49 (1934): 246–57. Like Evans, Beach does not consider the significance of Robertson's description of Cortez, nor does he consider Keats's reading of history in critical terms, emphasizing rather "with what solid blocks of history Keats built up the airy fabric of his fancy" (256).

12. William Robertson, *The History of America*, 3d ed. (London: W. Strachen and T. Cadell; Edinburgh: J. Balfour, 1780), 3:101–2.

13. Robertson, *History of America*, 1:286–90.

14. Robertson, *History of America*, 2:452–53.

15. Aileen Ward also observes that Keats in all likelihood is in his sonnet combining two scenes from Robertson: "Balboa's discovery of the Pacific and Cortez's first view of Mexico City." *John Keats: The Making of a Poet* (1963; reprint, New York: Viking, 1967), 75.

16. For more conventional discussions of *Sleep and Poetry*, see, for instance, M. A. Goldberg's *The Poetics of Romanticism: Toward a Reading of John Keats* (Yellow Springs, Ohio: The Antioch Press, 1969), 80–83, and James Land Jones's *Adam's Dream: Mythic Consciousness in Keats and Yeats* (Athens: University of Georgia Press, 1975), 93–94. These studies focus on Keats's desire for "the ethereal and the immortal" (Goldberg 80) and on his "deep religious feeling associated with process" (Jones 94), rather than the fact of anxiety.

Chapter 2. "The Latter End of Some Strange History": *Endymion*

1. Stuart Sperry, *Keats the Poet* (Princeton: Princeton University Press, 1973), 92.

2. Sperry's discussion appears in *Keats the Poet* on pages 90–116. For an additional survey of the critical tradition dealing with the poem's allegorical dimension, see Clarice Godfrey, "*Endymion*," in *John Keats: A Reassessment*, ed. Kenneth Muir (Liverpool: Liverpool University Press, 1969), 21–24. Note also Walter Evert's comment that "the critical tendency has been . . . to represent the poem as either a giant step toward conceptual and architectonic maturity or a puerile ramble through an unweeded and unconscionably vast garden of immature themes and forms." *Aesthetic and Myth in the Poetry of Keats* (Princeton: Princeton University Press, 1965), 89.

3. Sperry, *Keats the Poet*, 94, 113.

4. I am here of course drawing upon Jerome McGann's discussion of romantic ideology; modern criticism preserves that ideology when it manifests "an uncritical absorption in Romanticism's own self-representations." See *The Romantic Ideology: A Critical Investigation* (Chicago: University of Chicago Press, 1983), 1. For a relevant general discussion of the problem of authorial intention, see V. N. Volosinov, *Marxism and the Philosophy of Language*, trans. Ladislav Matejka and I. R. Titunik (Cambridge: Harvard University Press, 1973), 9–15.

5. To stress the determining significance of the historical situation that encompasses and energizes the poem is not to deny the significance or purposiveness of individual activity; nor is it to say that history rather than Keats produced the poem. Rather, it is to insist that human action—even the writing of poetry—is never entirely self-generating and self-defined. While Keats certainly *produces* his poem, he does so under conditions that are antecedent to him. In producing the poem, at the same time he *necessarily reproduces* certain of those conditions, and thus his poem is historically and culturally implicated. To put the matter somewhat more broadly, the critical orientation I am describing, which acknowledges the priority of historical determination, at the same time would avoid the Althusserian tendency to explain individual activity (in this case poetic production) as entirely predetermined by structures totally independent of human agency, and the Sartrean/ existentialist tendency to explain individual activity as entirely free of all determination. That is, I wish to preserve Keats's individual and poetic integrity and at the same time open

his poetic activity to explanation that extends beyond the empirical data of history and beyond the poet's own expressive intention. Poem and history are not the equivalent of object and subject, of a divided reality; rather, they exist coterminously within a single sphere, namely, the sphere of *praxis*. It is this fact that provides the conceptual framework in what follows.

This description of historical materialism draws most directly upon Jorge Larrain's recent attempt to reformulate historical materialism in such a way that resolves the fierce dispute between E. P. Thompson and Louis Althusser. See *A Reconstruction of Historical Materialism* (London: Allen & Unwin, 1986), esp. 92–106. A helpful definition of praxis is offered by Robert Weimann, who uses the term to denote "the total process and activity by which men in society (as *Subjekt*) act upon and change the world as their object. In this sense Marx and Engels, in rejecting Feuerbach's mechanical materialism, emphasized the 'active' and 'subjective' dimension of consciousness and society which, even while it reflects the material conditions of existence, helps to create them." *Structure and Society,* 3.

6. Thompson, *William Morris,* 15.

7. Caudwell, *Illusion and Reality,* 108.

8. Eric J. Hobsbawm, *The Age of Revolution: 1789–1848* (New York: New American Library, 1962), 28.

9. Hobsbawm, *Age of Revolution,* 32.

10. For a helpful discussion of the political dimension of pastoral literature in the romantic period, see Roger Sales, *English Literature in History, 1780–1830: Pastoral and Politics* (New York: St. Martin's Press, 1983). For a discussion of the tendency of many writers of the nineteenth century to look nostalgically to the preindustrial world, see Raymond Williams, *Culture and Society: 1780–1850* (New York: Harper & Row, 1958).

11. *The Examiner,* 11 August 1816, 507.

12. To cite one additional entry in the *Examiner,* this one from 25 August 1816: "On all sides, the symptoms are now fast increasing of the instability of the present state of things. It cannot possibly last. We always said so; we say so still;—the Allies, with their violated promises, would not have it otherwise; and they will inevitably see the blessed fruit of that Divine Right which they would have re-planted" (534).

13. For an excellent discussion of the connections between the Gothic and the political in *Frankenstein,* see Michael Scrivener's recent essay, "*Frankenstein*'s Ghost Story: the Last Jacobin Novel," *Genre* 19 (1986): 299–318.

14. With respect to Shelley, at least, important work is currently being done by Terence A. Hoagwood to enable more positive political readings of such poems as the *Hymn.*

15. Caudwell, *Illusion and Reality,* 108.

16. I am drawing here on Jameson's discussion of figuration. Speaking of religion, for instance, he notes that it "is not a cognitive but a figural mode, and any attempt to reappropriate it must include a meditation on the nature of figuration itself. 'Through a glass darkly,' allegory, types, figures, iconoclasm, the letter rather than the spirit—all these expressions alert us to the essential ambiguity of a plane of expression that risks fixing the mind in external trappings, thereby generating the institutional necessity of a priesthood, of the guardians of interpretation, with the monopoly of meaning and exegesis, who alone have the right to tell us what a given figure really means." See Fredric Jameson, "Religion and Ideology: A Political Reading of *Paradise Lost,*" in *Literature, Politics and Theory: Papers from the Essex Conference 1976–84,* ed. Francis Barker et al. (London: Methuen, 1986), 40.

17. For a more orthodox explanation of the poem's major concerns, one that recognizes its historical significance but, to my mind, individualizes or privatizes history, note Northrop Frye's comment that "the Romantic myth is the form in which the Romantic poet expresses the recovery, for man, of what he formerly ascribed to gods, heroes, or the forces of nature. When man is recognized to be a myth-making animal, mythical language is also

recognized to be the language, not for what is true, but for what could be made true. Mythology, thus, with Romanticism . . . ceases to be fables about the actions of superior powers and becomes a structure of human concern. It thereby takes over some aspects of religion." *A Study of English Romanticism* (New York: Random House, 1968), 126. This view would stress the concern of *Endymion* with human betterment, but would locate this concern first in the realm of desire, without considering that desire itself is a product of historical determination.

18. It is perhaps worth recalling here Jameson's insistence that "history is *not* a text, not a narrative, master or otherwise, but . . . an absent cause." Fredric Jameson, *The Political Unconscious: Narrative as a Socially Symbolic Act* (Ithaca: Cornell University Press), 35. Therefore, history is only accessible through its products.

19. Jameson, "Religion and Ideology," 39.

20. Morris Dickstein notes that "from the start *Endymion* is a poem in which the self has already fallen into division." See *Keats and His Poetry: A Study in Development* (Chicago: University of Chicago Press, 1971), 53. While this certainly is true, I want to argue that the divided self is the consequence of a divided and disintegrating social world.

21. In his excellent discussion of the poem, Walter Evert focuses on natural rather than social considerations, and sees Endymion's quest in terms of the shepherd-king's "redemption of his fall from nature." See *Aesthetic and Myth*, 136. While this line of argument provides a means of speaking coherently about the poem's structure, I would argue that the natural must be understood within the context of the social.

22. Sales, *English Literature and History*, 218.

23. Harold Bloom. "The Internalization of Quest-Romance," in *Romanticism and Consciousness: Essays in Criticism*, ed. Harold Bloom (New York: W. W. Norton, 1970), 6.

24. While he is more concerned with the psychological than the social, Edward E. Bostetter makes a similar point: Keats "would have to come to realize that what was important was the power of human beings to realize their own dreams, to control their own destinies, as he had suggested without perhaps fully comprehending in *Endymion*." *The Romantic Ventriloquists: Wordsworth, Coleridge, Keats, Shelley, Byron* (Seattle: University of Washington Press, 1963), 176.

25. Here and throughout I am drawing upon some of the ideas in Belsey, although I should stress that I do not wish to be seen as sharing her assumptions about language and the unconscious. See Catherine Belsey, "The Romantic Construction of the Unconscious," in *Literature, Politics and Theory: Papers from the Essex Conference 1976–84*, ed. Francis Barker et al. (London: Methuen, 1986), 57–76.

26. Russell Jacoby, *Social Amnesia: A Critique of Conformist Psychology from Adler to Laing* (Boston: Beacon Press, 1975), 113.

27. The critical perspective I mean to stress here is best stated by Marx in his third *Economic and Philosophic Manuscript:* "It is above all necessary to avoid postulating 'society' once again as an abstraction confronting the individual. The individual *is* the *social being*. . . . Individual human life and species-life are not different things, even though the mode of existence of individual is necessarily either a more *specific* or a more *general* mode of species-life." Quoted in *Karl Marx: Early Writings*, trans. and ed. Tom Bottomore (New York: McGraw-Hill, 1964), 158.

28. Even the induction to book 3, perhaps the most explicitly political section of the poem, expresses a denial of the ultimate priority of history, politics, and society.

29. Belsey, "Romantic Construction of the Unconscious," 64.

30. Belsey, "Romantic Construction of the Unconscious," 71.

31. William Garrett, "The Glaucus Episode: An Interpretation of Book III of *Endymion*." *Keats-Shelley Journal* 27 (1978): 23–34. In addition to Garrett, see June Koch's "Politics in Keats's Poetry" on the hidden political allusions in book 3. While my own analysis provides a

somewhat different emphasis from Koch's, it is not intended to denigrate in any way her important findings and arguments. Further scholarly work of the sort she has begun is seriously needed in Keats studies.

32. To cite only the most obvious, note the friendship between Victor and Clerval in *Frankenstein,* a friendship that is not the basis for building a better world but rather is the product of a privatized reality.

33. Edward Said, *Orientalism* (1978; reprint, New York: Vintage Books, 1979), 75.

34. Said, *Orientalism,* 76.

35. Said, *Orientalism,* 5.

36. Said, *Orientalism,* 5.

37. Edward Said, "Orientalism Reconsidered," in *Literature, Politics and Theory: Papers from the Essex Conference 1976–84,* ed. Francis Barker et al. (London: Methuen, 1986), 225.

38. On the masculine nature of the romantic imagination, see Margaret Homans, *Woman Writers and Poetic Identity: Dorothy Wordsworth, Emily Bronte, and Emily Dickinson* (Princeton: Princeton University Press, 1980).

39. Jameson's comment about aesthetics in general describes very clearly the process at work in Keats's poem: "[I]deology is not something which informs or invests symbolic production; rather the aesthetic act is itself ideological, and the production of the aesthetic or narrative form is to be seen as an ideological act in its own right, with the function of inventing imaginary or formal 'solutions' to unresolvable social contradictions." *Political Unconscious,* 79. Note also Michele Barrett's excellent chapter on "Ideology and the Cultural Production of Gender" in *Women's Oppression Today: Problems in Marxist Feminist Analysis* (London: Verso, 1980), 84–113, especially her designation of literature as "a primary site of ideological negotiation" (98).

40. For a Marxist-feminist discussion that attempts to make positive critical use of the masculine romantic portrayal of women, see Daniel P. Watkins, *Social Relations in Byron's Eastern Tales* (Rutherford, N.J.: Fairleigh Dickinson University Press, 1987), especially pages 61–64 and 83–85.

41. It should be noted here as well that the Indian maiden's song of sorrow elicits once again the significance of the East in the narrative, for it describes her travels through "Osirian Egypt" (4:257), "parch'd Abyssinia" (4:259), "Old Tartary" (4:262), and "Inde" (4:263).

42. Simone de Beauvoir, *The Second Sex,* trans. and ed. H. M. Parshley (1952; reprint, New York: Vintage, 1974), xvi.

43. *John Keats: Complete Poems and Selected Letters,* ed. Clarence DeWitt Thorpe (New York: Odyssey Press, 1935), xxii.

44. Morris Dickstein's discussion of the sonnet *To Sleep* offers a view of sleep that is relevant to this line of argument: "The passiveness that Keats exalts does not here connote . . . openness and receptivity. Nor does it imply merely, as in the sonnet on fame, an unfevered acceptance of mortality. Though 'casket' has never been a standard word for coffin in England, as it has long been in America, the last two lines nevertheless make clear that the quest for unconsciousness has become a quest for death." *Keats and His Poetry,* 19.

45. Note, for instance, Thorpe's comment, in his edition of Keats's poems, about the induction to book 4: "It is probable that as he originally conceived this passage he had intended to point again to the regeneration of poetry among the moderns, but, having lost faith in Hunt . . . , finding himself impatient of Wordsworth's sober-sided didacticism, and reading again his own lines and hating them, he had no heart at the moment to say anything of the kind. If he had gone on with this idea, the introduction would have had pertinence, serving, by implication at least, as a prologue to a presentation of the means by which its lost greatness could be restored to poetry. But since he did not thus go on, the induction stands as fragmentary, uncertain in meaning and direction." *John Keats,* 173n.

But compare Richard Macksey's remark that "the invocation of Book IV of *Endymion* . . . is not unrelated to the narrative that it introduces and that in turn introduces the resolution of the poem, for hard upon it follows the Indian Maid's lament for her 'dear native land,' a land of sorrow she has abandoned to join Bacchus' rout to faraway countries." " 'To Autumn' and the Music of Mortality: 'Pure Rhetoric of a Language without Words,' " in *Romanticism and Language,* ed. Arden Reed (Ithaca: Cornell University Press, 1984), 291.

46. McGann, *Romantic Ideology,* 1.

47. Weimann, *Structure and Society,* 6.

Chapter 3. "Love's Fev'rous Citadel": *Isabella* and *The Eve of St. Agnes*

1. Bernard Shaw, *The Collected Works of Bernard Shaw* (New York: William H. Wise, 1932), 29:192.

2. Note, for instance, Claude Lee Finney's matter of fact statement that *"The Pot of Basil* is, in short, a transitional poem." *The Evolution of Keats's Poetry* (1936; reprint, New York: Russell & Russell, 1963), 1:379. One of the few recent essays to take seriously the poem's politics is Susan Wolfson's excellent "Keats's *Isabella* and the 'Digressions' of 'Romance,' " *Criticism* 27 (1985):247–61, though her emphasis is quite different from my own. For a discussion of my differences with Wolfson, see my "Personal Life and Social Authority in Keats's *Isabella,*" *Nineteenth-Century Contexts* 11 (1987): 23–49, which is the basis for the present analysis.

3. Woodhouse corroborates this idea in his comments about Keats's dislike for *Isabella.* See *LJK* 2:162.

4. For an excellent discussion of the Keats-Hazlitt connection, see John D. Kinnaird, *Hazlitt: Critic of Power,* especially pages 228–30.

5. Robert L. Heilbroner, *The Nature and Logic of Capitalism* (New York: W. W. Norton & Company, 1985), 16–19.

6. Eli Zaretsky, *Capitalism, the Family, and Personal Life* (New York: Harper & Row, 1976), 57.

7. Two points bear stressing here. First, this transition from feudal (romance) to commercial values is rendered vividly in Keats's portrayal of the relations between the nurse and Isabella as a contrast to the relations between the brothers and Lorenzo. For instance, Lorenzo works for the brothers' money, not out of fealty. Therefore, he is not betraying a trust in the medieval sense when he seduces their sister; in fact, one accepted way for a man to rise in the commercial world was to marry the daughter or sister of one's employer. The nurse, like Angela (the beldame in *The Eve of St. Agnes*), has a different, feudal loyalty to Isabella, more significant than the manual labor they do in the forest.

It should also be noted at this point that Boccaccio's story in the *Decameron* was a particularly suitable source for a poem about the transition from feudalism to commercialism. Keats clearly recognized this fact, taking over and emphasizing the labor and class aspects of Boccaccio's story, while at the same time providing a fuller exposition of the ideological dimensions of the emerging commercial world. Donald Reiman states this point explicitly: ". . . in *Isabella* Keats rewrites not only Boccaccio's tale but *The Duchess of Malfi:* in Webster's day the pride of the aristocracy had been insufferable; by Keats's day the same vicious pride had seeped into the wealthier bourgeoisie. *Isabella,* like Webster's play, portrays the love of moral individuals set against a corrupting social system, and the corrupt nature of the brothers is as essential to Keats's purpose as is the purity of Lorenzo and Isabella. Indignation, as well as pathos, is a necessary emotional response to Keats's tale." See Reiman's review essay in *Studies in Romanticism* 20 (1981): 257.

8. For a discussion of the social dimensions of Byron's Eastern Tales, see Daniel P. Watkins, *Social Relations in Byron's Eastern Tales*.

9. Raymond Williams, *Marxism and Literature* (Oxford: Oxford University Press, 1977), 116.

10. For a discussion of *Sardanapalus* from this perspective, see Daniel P. Watkins, "Violence, Class Consciousness, and Ideology in Byron's History Plays," *ELH* 48 (1981): 799–816.

11. Stuart Sperry, *Keats the Poet*, 198. See also Walter Jackson Bates's *John Keats*, 438–51. Note also Miriam Allott's comment that "'The Eve of St. Agnes' was written in January–February 1819, a few weeks after his first 'understanding' with Fanny Brawne of Christmas Day, and celebrates the warmth of a requited passion, but characteristically cannot forget its attendant hazards nor its vulnerability to time. His young brother had just died, and love and death are inextricably bound together in his imagination." *The Poems of John Keats*, ed. Miriam Allott (London: Longman, 1970), 16.

12. Note, for instance, his comment in the same letter that "I am g[r]ieved to say that I am not sorry you had not Letters at Philadelphia, you could have had no good news of Tom and I have been withheld on his account from beginning these many days; I could not bring myself to say the truth, that he is no better, but much worse—However it must be told, and you must my dear Brother and Sister take example frome [sic] me and bear up against any Calamity for my sake as I do for your's" (*LJK* 1:391).

13. Several scholars have noted the political dimension of *Hyperion*. See for instance Kenneth Muir, "The Meaning of *Hyperion*," in *John Keats: A Reassessment*, ed. Kenneth Muir, 2d ed. (Liverpool: Liverpool University Press, 1969), 103–23, or Alan Bewell, "The Political Implication of Keats's Classicist Aesthetics," *Studies in Romanticism* 25 (1986): 220–29.

14. As Keats remarked to George and Georgiana Keats in a letter dated 14 February 1819: "I was nearly a fortnight at Mr. John Snook's and a few days at old Mr. Dilke's—Nothing worth speaking of happened at either place—I took down some of the thin paper and wrote on it a little Poem call'd 'St. Agnes Eve'—which you shall have as it is when I have finished the blank part of the rest for you" (*LJK* 2:58–59).

15. See, for instance, Claude Lee Finney, *The Evolution of Keats's Poetry*, 538–60.

16. William Robertson, *The History of the Reign of the Emperor Charles the Fifth* (Philadelphia: J. B. Lippincott & Co., 1876), 1:x.

17. Robertson, *Charles the Fifth*, 1:xi. It should be noted that Robertson subscribed to a progressive view of history that is very similar to Keats's own views of progress in literature, the arts, the intellect, and so on. Note, for instance, Robertson's remark that "I have exhibited a view of the progress of society in Europe, not only with respect to interior government, laws, and manners, but with respect to the command of the national force requisite in foreign operations." *Charles the Fifth*, 1:xi.

18. Robertson, *Charles the Fifth*, 1:220.

19. Robertson, *Charles the Fifth*, 1:220–21.

20. Robertson, *Charles the Fifth*, 1:227. For a longer view of the development of feudal society (and one which was written at a later period), see Karl Marx and Frederick Engels, *The German Ideology* (Moscow: Progress Publishers, 1976), 98–101.

21. Robertson, *Charles the Fifth*, 1:236–37 and 239. Note also Robertson's comment that "notwithstanding the immense difference between the first of these classes and the third, such was the spirit of tyranny which prevailed among the great proprietors of lands, and so various their opportunities of oppressing those who were settled on their estates, and of rendering their condition intolerable, that many freemen, in despair, renounced their liberty and voluntarily surrendered themselves as slaves to their powerful masters. This they did in order that their masters might become more immediately interested to afford

them protection together with the means of subsisting themselves and their families" (1:233–34).

22. William Hazlitt, *The Life of Napoleon Buonaparte*, in *The Complete Works of William Hazlitt*, ed. P. P. Howe (London: J. M. Dent and Sons, Ltd., 1930), 13:38–39.

23. See, for instance, John Charles Leonard Simonde de Sismoni, *A History of the Italian Republics: Being a View of the Origin, Progress, & Fall of Italian Freedom* (1807–18; reprint, London: J. M. Dent & Co., 1907; New York: E. P. Dutton & Co., 1907). While there is no direct evidence that Keats knew this work, it was very popular during the period, and influential, for instance, on Byron's writings.

24. I want to stress that my aim here is not to exempt institutionalized religion from social critique—indeed, I wish to implicate religion directly in the feudal social order—but to distinguish the social position and social role of individuals from the social significance of their activities.

25. It is worth noting that Keats was not alone in criticizing the nostalgia that he describes here and that was a popular ingredient in the literature of the period. See, for example, Hazlitt's "Sketch of the History of the Good Old Times before the French Revolution, When Kings and Priests Did What They Pleased, by the Grace of God." This bitter essay, which appeared in the *Examiner* 6 April 1817, surveys the "madness, avarice, ambition, and ferocity" of Charles VI, the avariciousness and violence of Philip VI, the faithlessness of Philip-le-Bel, and much more. In the following issue of the *Examiner*, Hazlitt included yet another essay on the same subject, with the express purpose of demonstrating once and for all that "whoever after this sketch shall have the face to talk of 'the good old times,' of mild paternal sway, and the blessings of Legitimacy, that is, of power restrained only by its own interests, follies, vices, and passions, and therefore necessarily sacrificing to them the rights, liberties, and happiness of nations, we shall pronounce to be either a consummate hypocrite or 'a fool indeed'" (*Works* 19:182–96).

26. See Sperry's *Keats the Poet*. See also Leon Waldoff, *Keats and the Silent Work of the Imagination* (Urbana: University of Illinois Press, 1985).

27. Another sort of historical anxiety is seen as well in the changes that Keats himself made in character and place names when revising the poem, changes that obscured the actual historical setting of the narrative. The most distinctive change, of course, involved Hildebrand, who was originally named Ferdinand, probably in reference to Ferdinand VII of Spain, who was written about frequently in the *Examiner* during 1818 and 1819 as one of the first rulers to return to power after the defeat of Napoleon. To note only one account of Ferdinand in the *Examiner*, in a letter to the paper on 7 August 1818, it is noted: "First on the list of those returned legitimates [after the defeat of Napoleon], appeared Ferdinand, who acknowledged the loyalty of a nation which had bled for him, by throwing into dungeons its protectors and the preservers of the crown, and by bringing back the Inquisition in the 19th century." Such abusiveness and violence are perfectly consistent with the character of Hildebrand, and provide a basis for interpreting the poem as a condemnation of the restoration of the older political systems that Napoleon had sought to destroy.

28. In an earlier draft of the poem, Keats had Porphyro promise Madeline a home "Over the dartmoor blak," but later changed this to ". . . o'er the southern moors," making vague the geographical reference.

29. Robertson, *Charles the Fifth*, 1:89.

30. Robertson, *Charles the Fifth*, 1:85.

31. Robertson, *Charles the Fifth*, 1:315.

32. Robertson, *Charles the Fifth*, 1:316. While, according to Robertson, "The English were accordingly one of the last nations in Europe who availed themselves of those commercial advantages which were natural or peculiar to their country" (1:320), these

details of commercial development are nonetheless crucial to Keats's vision of historical development as it is articulated in the *Eve,* because they indicate a general change that included England no less than Italy, Spain, and other Western nations.

33. Voltaire, "The Kingdom of Fez and Morocco," in *The Works of Voltaire: a Contemporary Version,* ed. John Morley et al (1762; reprint New York: E. R. DuMont, 1901), 27:275. See also the section entitled "Fez and Morocco" in the Supplementary Notes to Voltaire's *Ancient and Modern History,* in *Works* 30:269–72. Here Voltaire speaks about both Jews and English merchants who settled in the region.

34. Jane S. Gerber, *Jewish Society in Fez, 1450–1700: Studies in Communal and Economic Life* (London: Brill, 1980), 170.

35. Gerber, *Jewish Society in Fez,* 171, 173.

36. William Robertson also speaks directly of the sugar industry in the Middle Ages, though he does not mention Fez by name in his discussion: "Sugar is likewise a production of the East. Some plants of the sugar-cane were brought from Asia; and the first attempt to cultivate them in Sicily was made about the middle of the twelfth century. From thence they were transplanted into the southern provinces of Spain. From Spain they were carried to the Canary and Madeira Isles, and at length into the New World.... In the Middle Ages, though sugar was not raised in such quantities or employed for so many purposes as to become one of the common necessaries of life, it appears to have been a considerable article in the commerce of the Italian states." See *Charles the Fifth,* 1:315–16.

37. It should be noted here that while I am stressing the sugar trade, Fez was known for other food products as well. As Roger Le Tourneau says of fourteenth-century Fez: "Milk was also a part of the diet, in the form of fresh milk, curds, butter, or cheese," a fact that is particularly interesting in light of the reference to "curd" in the passage from the *Eve* cited here. See *Fez in the Age of the Marinidas,* trans. Bease Alberta Clement (Norman: University of Oklahoma Press, 1961).

38. Robertson, *Charles the Fifth,* 1:315.

39. Allott, *Poems of John Keats,* 471.

40. I want to quote a passage here from *Purchas His Pilgrimes* referring to silk. While it is not directly relevant to Samarkand, it has significance for my discussion, which I shall offer momentarily, of the social significance of Porphyro's name. In discussing European trade with the East Indies, Purchas says: "But I will come to the raw Silkes and Indico, this being so excellent for the dying of our woollen clothes, thereby so much esteemed in so many places of the world; that ornament, together with the great reliefe and maintenance of so many hundreds of poore people, who are continually imployed, in the winding, twisting, and weaving of the same: Insomuch, that by the cherishing of this businesse ... it may well be hoped, that in short time, industrie will make the Art to flourish with not lesse happinesse to this Kingdome, then [sic] it hath done (through many ages) to divers states in Italy, and lately also to the Kingdome of France, and to the united Provinces of the Low-countreyes." Samuel Purchas, *Hakluytus Posthumus, or Purchas His Pilgrimes: Contayning a History of the Worlds in Sea Voyages and Land Travells by Englishmen and Others* (1625; reprint, Glasgow: James MacLehose and Sons, 1906), 5:266.

41. Allott, *Poems of John Keats,* 471.

42. Purchas, *Hakluytus Poathumus,* 1:65. For a specific reference in *Purchas* to the cedars of Lebanon, see 10:478.

I want to suggest momentarily as well that the reference to Lebanon has special significance with respect, again, to Porphyro's name. But for now it will do to stress the importance of the area to the shipbuilding industry and, by extension, to trade.

43. For an additional reference to the Cedars of Lebanon in terms I am suggesting, see *Volney's Ruins:* "The second mode of carrying on the trade was by means of vessels with

decks of the size of our river-boats, which were able to pass the streight, and to weather the dangers of the ocean: but for this purpose it was necessary to bring the wood from Mount Libanus and Cilicia, where it is very fine and in great abundance. This wood was first conveyed in floats from Tarsus to Phoenicia, for which reason the vessels were called ships of Tarsus." Constantin Francois Volney, *A New Translation of Volney's Ruins* (1802; reprint, New York: Garland Publishing, Inc., 1979), 1:37.

44. Philip K. Hitti, *Lebanon in History: From the Earliest Times to the Present* (London: MacMillan & Co., 1957), 110.

45. Hitti, *Lebanon in History*, 111.

46. Hitti, *Lebanon in History*, 111.

47. While I do not intend to pursue it in this chapter, it is worth noting Edward Said's comment about writers' interest in the East after about 1800: "We may as well recognize that for nineteenth-century Europe, with its increasing *embourgeoisement*, sex had been institutionalized to a very considerable degree. On the one hand, there was no such thing as "free" sex, and on the other, sex in society entailed a web of legal, moral, even political and economic obligations of a detailed and certainly encumbering sort. Just as the various colonial possessions—quite apart from their economic benefit to metropolitan Europe—were useful as places to send wayward sons, superfluous populations of delinquents, poor people, and other undesirables, so the Orient was a place where one could look for sexual experience unobtainable in Europe. Virtually no European writer who wrote on or traveled to the Orient in the period after 1800 exempted himself or herself from this quest." *Orientalism*, 190. In Keats's poem, of course, the references to the East come precisely at that moment when sexual passion is about to be unleashed, despite the institutional restraints on it.

48. I am aware that purple originally meant crimson rather than lavender, but in the poem Keats distinguishes crimson (256) from lavender, which, I believe, justifies the argument I am advancing. It is worth noting, however, that just as Lebanon was a major producer of purple, it was also a major producer of crimson. As Hitti notes: "Besides the purple dye the ancient Lebanese were responsible for the introduction of kermes [crimson] into world commerce. This is the scarlet of the Old Testament. It was made from insects found on a species of oak growing around the Eastern Mediterranean shores." *Lebanon in History*, 111.

49. It is worth recalling here Marx's comment about his approach to individual agents within history: ". . . here individuals are dealt with only in so far as they are the personifications of economic categories, embodiments of particular class-relations and class-interests." See Karl Marx, *Capital: A Critique of Political Economy* (Moscow: Progress Publishers, 1954), 1:20–21.

50. Allott, *Poems of John Keats*, 458.

51. This picture of sexual desire is also a picture of sexual domination, very similar to Blake's description of secretive sexual activity in "The Sick Rose."

52. See for instance Ronald A. Sharp's comment that early in the narrative "Madeline is indeed 'hoodwink'd with faery fancy' (line 70); she is deceived because by surrendering herself totally to the 'lap of legends old' (line 135), she puts all her trust in a superstition that is based on a sterile conception of love. By contrast with the humanized religion she embraces later, this superstition, for all its apparent charm, is really as life-denying as the beadsman's strict asceticism. . . . The messenger of the new religion is Porphyro." *Keats, Skepticism, and the Religion of Beauty* (Athens: The University of Georgia Press, 1979), 41–42.

53. Jack Stillinger, "The Hoodwinking of Madeline: Skepticism in *The Eve of St. Agnes*," in *The Hoodwinking of Madeline and Other Essays on Keats's Poems* (Chicago: University of Illinois Press, 1971), 67–93.

54. John Brand, *Observations on the Popular Antiquities of Great Britain: Chiefly Illustrating the Origin of our Vulgar and Provincial Customs, Ceremonies, and Superstitions*, pub. 1813 in 2 vols., rev. 1841 and 1848 in 3 vols. (1848; reprint, New York: AMS Press, 1970), 1:34.

55. I am aware that there is a great deal of debate about the usefulness of the term patriarchy, and that it runs the danger of being seen as an essentialist category. Like Zillah R. Eisenstein, however, I believe that the term is functional, even necessary, and that it is possible to conceive of it differently within different historical moments. In the present essay, I am not arguing that before the rise of commercial culture patriarchy did not exist, but rather that with the rise of commercial culture the nature of patriarchy changes in definable ways. See *The Radical Future of Liberal Feminism* (Boston: Northeastern University Press, 1986), 18–19.

56. See the first volume of *Capital:* "A use-value, or useful article, therefore, has value only because human labour in the abstract has been embodied or materialised in it. How, then, is the magnitude of this value to be measured? Plainly, by the quantity of the value-creating substance, the labour, contained in the article" (1:46).

57. A quotation in Brand's account of St. Agnes's Eve, taken from a work entitled *Poor Robin* (1733), helps to clarify the gender-specific nature of illusion and reality as they are presented in the *Eve:* "There are two remarkable days this month, and both on the getting hand, which our customers like best. There is St. Agnes's Fast, for the maids to get sweethearts, which happens the twenty-first day; and Term begins on the twenty-third day, for the lawyers to get money, but it is with a difference, and the lawyers in this, as indeed in most other cases, have the advantage. The maids, if they do undergo the mortification of fasting, expect nothing but a dream for their labour; only if they dream of the man that afterwards they are married to, it makes amends. But the lawyer is not bouy'd up with dreams, for he is awake, and will have the money, *ipso facto*, before he speaks; and if the client lose both cause and money, it will make him awake too." *Observations*, 1:36.

58. Another way of approaching the role of labor in the narrative is in more explicitly Marxian-economic terms. In the chapter on "Primitve Accumulation" in the first volume of *Capital,* Marx says that for capital to exist "two very different kinds of commodity-possessors must come face to face and into contact; on the one hand, the owners of money, means of production, means of subsistence, who are eager to increase the sum of values they possess, by buying other people's labour-power; on the other hand, free labourers" (668). In the *Eve,* Porphyro is associated with the emergent commercial life connected to the East, and thus may be seen as an owner of the means of subsistence, while Madeline and other women in the narrative (even though they are associated with aristocracy) are depicted as laborers, insofar as they weave the tapestries decorating the castle. To take this approach is to see the narrative as a symbolic projection of the union of a new economic order that, in establishing itself, also establishes a new system of values. Moreover, in seeing Madeline as a representative of the aristocracy and Porphyro as a representative of the emergent commercial class, we see in their union the cooptation of one class by another, a historical phenomenon that was to become a major literary theme in the Victorian period.

59. M. A. Goldberg, *The Poetics of Romanticism: Toward a Reading of John Keats* (Yellow Springs, Ohio: The Antioch Press, 1969), 126.

60. I am drawing here on Fredric Jameson's arguments in *Marxism and Form* about the nature of bourgeois art. While Jameson is writing on Lukács, his comments bear directly on my argument about Keats, which is that the poet does not stand outside his own world to write about another world, but rather writes about it from within very specific constraints and under specific conditions. See *Marxism and Form: Twentieth-Century Dialectical Theories of Literature* (Princeton: Princeton University Press, 1971), 160–68.

Chapter 4. "As If Calamity Had But Begun": *Hyperion*

1. Hazlitt, *Works*. 5:58.
2. Muir, "The Meaning of *Hyperion*," 106; Barnard, *John Keats*, 58, 59.
3. Ward, *John Keats*, 219; Marilyn Butler, *Romantics, Rebels and Reactionaries: English Literature and its Background* (Oxford: Oxford University Press, 1981), 151.
4. William Godwin, *The Pantheon: Or, Ancient History of the Gods of Greece and Rome* (1814; reprint, New York: Garland Publishing, Inc., 1984), v–vi.
5. Ian Jack discusses Godwin's intention of correcting the deficiencies in Tooke, but he does not raise the question of whether the debate itself over interpretation of classical mythology may have influenced Keats's thinking. See *Keats and the Mirror of Art* (Oxford: Oxford University Press, 1967), 282–83. In addition to Jack, Aileen Ward has noted the probable influence on Keats of Godwin's work. *John Keats*, 429.
6. For a discussion of "the revolutionary interpretation of classicism" on the continent during the romantic period, see, for instance, Howard Mumford Jones, *Revolution and Romanticism* (Cambridge: The Belknap Press of Harvard University Press, 1974), 342–49.
7. For a discussion of the political significance of classical mythology for Shelley, see Stuart Curran's "The Political Prometheus," *Studies in Romanticism* 25 (1986): 429–55.
8. Percy Bysshe Shelley, *A Philosophical View of Reform*, in *Shelley's Prose, or the Trumpet of a Prophecy*, ed. David Lee Clark (Albuquerque: The University of New Mexico Press, 1954), 237.
9. See, for instance, Byron's "Ode" on Napoleon.
10. See Sperry's excellent comments on the role of Oceanus in the narrative. Recognizing that Oceanus is not likely to be simply a spokesman for Keats, Sperry remarks: "Yet to accept his [Oceanus's] speech as the point of the poem is to ignore the dramatic context in which it is delivered. For all his wisdom he has not been able to preserve his godhead or to escape a scalding in the sea, while his plea for calm of mind arises from a stoic resignation that does not approach the ideal of sublimity Keats was intent on expressing in the character of Apollo, as the ending of the fragment makes clear. Thus Oceanus's impassiveness is juxtaposed against both the overemotional but instinctive insight of Clymene and the mighty but self-destructive power of Enceladus." *Keats the Poet*, 185–86. While I do not agree with Sperry's comments on Apollo, I believe that his description of the dramatic context within which Oceanus must be understood is excellent.
Note also Bostetter's comment that during the months Keats was writing the poem he came to believe that "the evolutionary creed of Oceanus was too simple, too naive for the Keats of the journal letter [*LJK* 2 : 101]." *Romantic Ventriloquists*, 154.
11. Sharp, *Keats, Skepticism, and the Religion of Beauty*, 138.
12. Jones, *Adam's Dream*, 179, 180. It should be noted that Jones goes on to speak of "Apollo-Keats's deification" (181), identifying the poet's individual desires with the character that he draws. In this sense Jones is following Sperry, who states that "*Hyperion* is something more than the deliberate elabortion of a set of themes through adaptation of epic legend, as every intelligent reader has more or less sensed. It is also a poem of considerable self-involvement. It represents Keats's attempt to realize the central action of his poem, the transition between two orders of deity, on the level of his own emotional and psychological life and in terms of the symbolic value each god had steadily assumed for him" (188).

I agree with Jones and Sperry about Keats's intense personal involvement in the ideas set down in *Hyperion*, but it is important to investigate why this is so, to explore the historical and ideological contexts that energize Keats's imagination and shape it in this way. To do this is to acknowledge the importance of intention and at the same time to situate it within a social rather than a purely psychological framework.

13. Walter Benjamin, *Illuminations*, ed. Hannah Arendt, trans. Harry Zohn (New York: Schocken Books, 1969), 256.

14. See, for instance, Jones's comment that "*Hyperion* is an epic on the theme of consciousness." *Adam's Dream*, 179.

15. In his excellent discussion of *Hyperion*, Kenneth Muir distinguishes Apollo from the Titans in terms of identity, and uses this distinction to draw parallels between Keats's ideas set down in his letters (especially his notion of "Negative Capability") and the ideas set down in the poem. As Muir puts it: ". . .it is noteworthy that Saturn and the other Gods of the old dispensation possess identities. Saturn speaks of his 'strong identity,' his 'real self'; but Apollo has no identity. He possesses to a supreme degree the negative capability that Keats had laid down as the prime essential of a poet. In other words, the old gods are men of power, the new gods are men of achievement." See "The Meaning of *Hyperion*," 108. While I do not wish to quarrel with Muir's main thesis—his essay, in my opinion, is one of the best on the poem—I do wish to suggest that identity is a vexed issue in this poem, and that an explanation of Apollo in terms of negative capability runs the risk of obscuring the kind of identity that he possesses. One brief feature of the narrative will illustrate the point I wish to make: in Apollo's comments to Mnemosyne (which are presented in 48 lines), the young god uses the word "I" eighteen times, a fact that suggests that he is not entirely without identity.

16. The tribulations experienced by Apollo are similar to those that Keats attributes to himself two years earlier in *God of the golden bow*, a poem that exalts Apollo as a symbol of creativity and perfect harmony, while at the same time describing the hardship of one who would become a poet. In that poem, while he does not speak directly in terms of the pain associated with attempting to become a poet, Keats emphasizes the anxiety, describing himself as a "blank idiot" (8), a "worm" (11), a "germ" (23), and as a "madman" (32) who would "put on thy [Apollo's] wreath" (8), while Apollo himself is surrounded by "glory" (9), confident and unchallenged in his authority over the heavens and in his command of the mysteries that the poet would fathom.

17. Again, Bostetter is very good in explaining the difficulties Keats faced in the composition of the poem, although his explanation tends to be psychological rather than historical. "*Hyperion*," he says, "was an epic about gods, but very plainly its philosophy was for men. And the history of neither gods nor men supported so optimistic a faith [as that presented in Oceanus' speech]. . . . Furthermore, *Hyperion* failed to take into account the limitations of nature and human life, of which Keats had now become acutely aware. Above the gods, as above men, was 'a heaven with its stars,' and the beauty of the gods was subject to decay and death. There was a point beyond which beauty could not progress, and this point was constant and eternal, known to every generation." *Romantic Ventriloquists*, 154.

Chapter 5. "Coming to the Sacrifice": *Ode on a Grecian Urn*

1. Tilottama Rajan, *Dark Interpreter: The Discourse of Romanticism* (Ithaca: Cornell University Press, 1980), 133.
2. Rajan, *Dark Interpreter*, 133, 135.
3. Rajan, *Dark Interpreter*, 135.
4. I am not suggesting that questions of textuality (or aesthetics) are unimportant, but

rather that textual and aesthetic matters never escape the matrices of history. The discriminations between surface and depth that Rajan makes—between the living figures on the urn and the ashes of the dead within it—and between poetic and sculptural forms of art are, as I have noted, in fact discriminations within a single historical reality; the poem is a symbolic formulation of this reality, a means of entering into and categorizing at least portions of it. Although the poem would suppress history (for instance, by withholding all comments about the function of the urn), it succeeds only in displacing and presenting it in other terms, necessarily inscribing history—elliptically and evasively—in the very figures and images that would supplant it. On the historical dimensions of subjectivity, see Eli Zaretsky, *Capitalism, the Family, & Personal Life*.

5. For an instance of the critical acceptance of this patriarchal vision, see Sperry's *Keats the Poet*. Sperry notes that "the sexual metaphor [presented at the beginning of the poem] is central to the wit and logic of the poem, for it suggests that vital penetration of imagination necessary to bring any object of regard into the fullness of aesthetic apprehension. In this sense the ode is the expression of Keats's love for the urn" (269). What is not said here is that this love involves a transformation and redefinition of the urn to meet the poet's particular needs and desires.

6. Much romantic criticism has tended to accept this nondialectical formulation of history, with direct consequences for interpretations of the *Urn*. Note, for instance, Earl R. Wasserman's comment that "the poet is no more justified than the urn would be in concluding that the sum of necessary earthly wisdom is the identity of beauty and truth. Certainly when he returned to the dimensional world in stanza four he found the two to be antithetical, not identical." *The Finer Tone: Keats's Major Poems* (1953; reprint, Baltimore: The Johns Hopkins University Press, 1967), 59. Also note Helen Vendler's remark that "in the *Urn* the artist is long dead, and only the artifact and its audience remain, but in this art corresponding to the sense of sight, Truth as well as Beauty has become constitutive of creative expression, and the mind is permitted its allegorizing, interrogatory, and propositional functions." *The Odes of John Keats* (Cambridge: The Belknap Press of Harvard University Press, 1983), 151. In addition, see Sperry's comment in *Keats the Poet* that "in 'Grecian Urn' Keats begins . . . from the world of myth, or as much of it as any work of art can capture, and seeks to elucidate its mystery within the terms of human life and history, to make it speak to the impatient needs and questions of his human situation" (267–68). Finally, note James Land Jones's comment in *Adam's Dream* that "empathizing in fellowship with the urn, Keats reaches a point of self-surrender that is too self-destroying and . . . is forced to withdraw to a middle distance from which the urn is seen not as a possible reality on earth—Keats does not confuse art and reality—but as a paradigm and artifice of eternity" (79).

The fullest and most compelling study of the critical tendency to accept this romantic formulation is McGann's *Romantic Ideology*. Also, for an excellent discussion of Keats's *Ode to Autumn* that draws on many of the same principles I am adopting, see McGann's "Keats and the Historical Method in Literary Criticism." Finally, for a general discussion of dialectics and dualism that is relevant to the argument here, see Juliet Mitchell, *Woman's Estate* (1971; reprint, New York: Vintage, 1973), especially 87–96.

7. That is, I am concerned with the role patriarchal morality plays in the imaginative, or poetic, reconciliation of real social contradiction. I leave unexamined the question of why it is women who are oppressed in Keats's vision, seeking rather to document the fact of oppression. A through study of the objective conditions of women in the romantic period would be necessary to elaborate the precise material grounds of Keats's portrayal of women.

Two essays on the *Urn* have been particularly influential on my thinking about this topic, although their emphasis is quite different from my own: Philip Fisher's "A Museum with

One Work Inside: Keats and the Finality of Art," *Keats-Shelley Journal* 33 (1984): 85–102, and Stuart Peterfreund's "The Truth about 'Beauty' and 'Truth': Keats's 'Ode on a Grecian Urn,' Milton, Shakespeare, and the Uses of Paradox," *Keats-Shelley Journal* 35 (1986): 62–82. Fisher's essay is particularly useful in its emphasis on the past and on the way history produces art on "an emergency basis" (87), and Peterfreund's in its emphasis on Keats's handling of the feminine.

8. Again, as I remarked in note 55 of chapter 3, I am aware that "patriarchy" is a controversial and perhaps unsatisfactory term for the sort of analysis I am offering, in that it runs the risk of being established as a universal rather than historical category. I use it simply as a shorthand for the stratification along gender lines that can be found in *Urn*. For a discussion of the debates surrounding this term, see Annette Kuhn and AnnMarie Wolpe, eds., *Feminism and Materialism: Women and Modes of Production* (London: Routledge and Kegan Paul, 1978), 11–67; Eisenstein, *The Radical Future of Liberal Feminism*, 14–26; and Ellen Carol DuBuois, et al., *Feminist Scholarship: Kindling in the Groves of Academe* (Urbana: University of Illinois Press, 1985), 145–46.

9. The relevant portion of the letter reads as follows: "The more we know the more inadequacy we discover in the world to satisfy us. . . . This same inadequacy is discovered (forgive me little George you know I don't mean to put you in the mess) in Women with few exceptions—the Dress Maker, the blue Stocking and the most charming sentimentalist differ but in a Slight degree, and are equally smokeable—But I'll go no further—I may be speaking sacrilegiously—and on my word I have thought so little that I have not one opinion upon any thing except in matters of taste—I never can feel certain of any truth but from a clear perception of its Beauty" (*LJK* 2:18–19).

10. It is instructive to note one of the more traditional explanations of these lines. David Perkins says that "the priest, for example, is 'mysterious' not only because his religion is a mystery, but also because the poet cannot be certain of his identity or of anything about him. Similarly, the altar is 'green' or vital; but the flanks of the heifer are 'silken,' and the adjective perfectly reflects the ambiguity of the poem. 'Silken' may picture the sheen of the living animal, or it may describe the pallor of the marble figure. It is precisely this sort of ambiguity that permits the poet to speculate about the little town." *The Quest for Permanence: The Symbolism of Wordsworth, Shelley, and Keats* (Cambridge: Harvard University Press, 1959), 239. The striking feature of this interpretation is that it approaches the lines entirely from within the framework of what Perkins assumes Keats's intention to be, and thus it never questions the stated connections between religion and violence or the significance of gender in presenting this connection.

11. Barrett, *Women's Oppression Today*, 83. Barrett is here striking a blow against those French feminists who present the body as the site of difference, and who argue that women must assert the liberating power of this difference. As Ann Rosalind Jones succinctly poses the key question that feminism must answer: "Does female sexuality exist prior to or in spite of social experience?" "Writing the Body: Toward an Understanding of *l'ecriture Feminine*," in *Feminist Criticism and Social Change: Sex, Class and Race in Literature and Culture*, ed. Judith Newton and Deborah Rosenfelt (New York: Methuen, 1985), 91. Barrett's position, and the position I am attempting to argue in this essay, is that it does not. To use the catch phrase of materialist feminism: gender is not born but produced.

12. Rosemary Radford Ruether, *New Woman New Earth: Sexist Ideologies & Human Liberation* (New York: The Seabury Press, 1975), 5.

13. Ruether, *New Woman New Earth*, 7. Ruether does not offer specific dates to mark the historical developments she discusses, but we can assume that by urban revolution she refers to the rise of the classical societies of antiquity, and that by industrial revolution she refers to the social changes of the seventeenth through the nineteenth centuries in Western Europe.

It should also be noted that Ruether's account refuses to accept the notion of a primitive matriarchal culture (which many feminists take as the necessary starting point in investigating patriarchal culture), for, in her view, such a notion uses myth as the basis for analysis, and thus is ahistorical (5–6). She begins, rather, with a consideration of a historically definable "village culture" (6) and traces the historical developments from this sociocultural arrangement to later ones.

14. Ruether, *New Woman New Earth*, 8.
15. Ruether, *New Woman New Earth*, 10, 195.
16. Ruether, *New Woman New Earth*, 19. Of this stage, Josephine Donovan remarks that "much of the history of Christian theology may be located . . . [here]. A transcendent, immortal male deity was projected into the heavens far from the corrupt feminine world of nature; but the transcendent deity remained master of the subservient world." *Feminist Theory: The Intellectual Traditions of American Feminism* (New York: Ungar, 1985), 133.
17. Ruether, *New Woman New Earth*, 19.
18. Ruether, *New Woman New Earth*, 20–21. It is this phase that gave rise to the Victorian cult of True Womanhood. As Ruether notes, "The Victorian ideal of Pure Womanhood was essentially a class ideal, forged not only as a bulwark against the industrial world, but also against the revolt of the masses. Its ideal of feminine purity, untainted by sexual feeling, found its compensation in the proliferation of houses of prostitution. Its bourgeois ideal of the frail, lily-white Lady of leisured society had as its unspeakable underpinnings the sweatshops where working-class women labored long hours for slave wages" (21).
19. Ruether, *New Woman New Earth*, 23.
20. For a helpful discussion of the exclusion of women from historical investigation and historical thinking, see Sheila Rowbotham's introduction to *Hidden from History: Rediscovering Women in History from the 17th Century to the Present* (1973; reprint, New York: Vintage Books, 1976), xvi–xxii.
21. Ruether, *New Woman New Earth*, 195–96.
22. It is worth noting the definitions of this term included in the *OED*, if only to provide a defense against those critics who would see the poem in purely innocent terms as a depiction of pastoral bliss. The first definition given by the *OED* is "hostile, angry, spiteful"; the second is "repulsive, unpleasant, hateful"; the third is "ugly"; the fourth is "averse, disinclined, reluctant, unwilling." Only the fourth definition is listed as being current through the nineteenth century, but the others were prominent well into the Renaissance, much of whose literature Keats new virtually by heart.
23. See, for instance, Stillinger's comments in *The Hoodwinking of Madeline and Other Essays*, 108.
24. For an excellent though fairly conventional discussion of the religious dimension of the *Urn*, see David Kerner, "The Problem of Evil in the 'Ode on a Grecian Urn'," *Texas Studies in Language and Literature* 28 (1986): 227–49.
25. Tellingly, however, even as these lines are spoken—either by the urn or by the poet—limitations are placed upon knowledge ("that is all ye *need* to know"), once again discouraging too close scrutiny of the conflicts and struggles that purchase the wisdom in these concluding lines. The urn is unravished, it represents purity, but it is also limiting. With respect to the punctuation of these final lines, the textual difficulties that for years have occupied critics are not thematic difficulties within the frame of reference that I am trying to establish. That is, whether it is the urn or the poet who speaks these lines, the value system is masculine, falling fully within the parameters of patriarchal belief. Under patriarchy, women no less than men express masculine values (this is what Josephine Donovan, in *Feminist Theory*, calls the "internalization of Otherness" [136]), just as in a bourgeois culture both the middle and working classes express the values of the ruling elite. Note, on this topic, Marx's famous comment that "the ruling ideas of every age are

the ideas of the ruling class." For an excellent discussion of these final lines of the poem, see Stillinger's essay in *Hoodwinking*, 167–73.

26. Thomas Szasz, *The Manufacture of Madness* (New York: Delta, 1970), 287.

27. Simone de Beauvoir, *The Second Sex*, xxxiii–xxxiv.

28. For a typical example of this view, see Wasserman's comment in *Finer Tone* that "the great end of poetry, Keats wrote, is 'that it should be a friend / To sooth the cares, and lift the thoughts of man,' for art (unlike man, who cannot return to tell us of his postmortal existence) allows a glimpse into that region which shows the full meaning of those experiences which now produce only mortal suffering, divulges the end for which they are destined, and so eases the burden of the mystery" (61).

29. Note, for instance, S. R. Swaminathan's comment that the reference to the "ditties of no tone" in the poem "is obviously a finer music heard only by the soul." *The Still Image in Keats's Poetry* (Salzburg, Austria: Institut für Anglistik und Amerikanistik, Universität Salzburg, 1981), 329.

30. I do not here intend to offer a feminist critique of Keats's *Nightingale* poem, but I do mean to suggest that the gender issue is vital in this poem as well, as the myth of Procne, Philomela, and Tereus suggests.

31. My view here is similar to, though not identical with, Walter Evert's discussion of the *Urn*. Note especially his comment that "the urn is at once a self-contained, serenely still and integrated entity and the messenger of a vigorous, noisy, impassioned existence somewhere else in space and time." See *Aesthetic and Myth*, 315.

32. For a very different interpretation of these opening lines, see Wasserman's comment in *Finer Tone* that "by enduring long, it [the urn] has not only caused them [all things mutable] to become secondary factors in its existence (an unravished *bride*, and a *foster*-child), but has become related to their dimensional negatives: quietness, silence, slow time" (16–17). Such a view becomes plausible only when gender itself is denied its historicity.

33. Rajan, *Dark Interpreter*, 133.

34. Rajan, *Dark Interpreter*, 136.

35. Georg Lukács, *Realism in Our Time: Literature and the Class Struggle* (1964; reprint, New York: Harper & Row, Publishers, 1971), 21. Lukács is speaking of Heidegger, but the phrase applies equally to Keats.

36. Caudwell, *Illusion and Reality*, 108. Caudwell's full indictment of Keats runs as follows: "Keats's . . . knowledge of bourgeois reality . . . led him to a position which was to set the keynote for further bourgeois poetry: 'revolution' as a flight *from* reality. Keats is the bannerbearer of the Romantic Revival. The poet now escapes upon the 'rapid wings of poesy' to a world of romance, beauty and sensuous life separate from the poor, harsh, real world of everyday life, which it sweetens and by its own loveliness silently condemns" (108).

Note also G. V. Plekhanov's general comment in *Art and Social Life* about romanticism: "[T]he romanticists really were at odds with their bourgeois social environment. True, there was nothing dangerous in this to the bourgeois social relationships. The romanticist circles consisted of young bourgeois who had no objection to these relationships, but were revolted by the sordidness, the tedium and the vulgarity of bourgeois existence. The new art with which they were so strongly infatuated was for them a refuge from this sordidness, tedium and vulgarity" (14).

While these comments describe an important dimension of romantic literature, it does not follow that the literature is politically or aesthetically unimportant. In fact, the very evasiveness that defines so much of romantic poetry constitutes a critique of the conditions under which it was produced. For an excellent discussion of romanticism from this direction, see Robert Sayre and Michael Lowy, "Figures of Romantic Anti-Capitalism," noted in the preface to this study.

37. Plekhanov, *Art and Social Life*, 30.
38. Thorpe, *John Keats: Complete Poems*, 78.
39. Benjamin R. Haydon, *The Diary of Benjamin Robert Haydon*, ed. Williard B. Pope (Cambridge: Harvard University Press, 1960), 1:434–35.
40. Hazlitt, *Works*, 4:79.
41. Marchand states in a note to this letter that "Hobhouse took a more favourable view of Elgin's work than did Byron, contending that preservation of the Greek marbles in London would benefit an infinitely greater number of rising architects and sculptors. . . . Byron's reply to this in his first letter on Bowles was: 'I opposed, and will ever oppose, the robbery of ruins from Athens, to instruct the English in sculpture (who are as capable of sculpture as the Egyptians are of skating)'" (*BLJ* 2:66).
42. See Perkins, *Quest for Permanence*, 238–39.
43. See Rajan, *Dark Interpreter*, 133–36.
44. While I have not been very specific about these actual human struggles and atrocities, they are not difficult to find. The most cursory glance at the *Examiner* during 1817–19 on the fear of national banktuptcy, or at the writings of Cobbett on the plight of the working people, illustrate these matters vividly. Note too the uncertainty and general despair pervading Europe and England after the defeat of Napoleon, exemplified clearly in Byron's remark that "every hope of a republic is over, and we must go on under the old system. But I am sick at heart of politics and slaughters; and the luck which Providence is pleased to lavish on Lord [Castlereagh] is only a proof of the little value the gods set upon prosperity" (*BLJ* 4:302).
45. Phyllis Chessler, *Women and Madness* (New York: Avon Books, 1972), 79.
46. In an essay entitled "Resisting Amnesia: History and Personal Life," Adrienne Rich stresses the importance of understanding women's issues in historical terms. Warning that "history is not something we can take or leave" (139), she urges feminists to "recover history, or herstory" (141), which means resisting the pressure and temptation to "assimilate"—i.e., constructing an ideal of Americanization and equating this with virtue" (141)—and to think that we can be "twice born" (141): "The Christian fundamentalist model of the twice-born is of a soul once drenched in sin—in negativity—which through some charismatic encounter comes to see the truth, reject its former 'path,' confess its unworthiness, accept redemption, leave sin and shame behind, and take up a new 'path' of innocence, cleansed by surrender to a higher being" (143). What must be resisted, in short, is amnesia: "Historical amnesia *is* starvation of the imagination: nostalgia is the imagination's sugar rush, leaving depression and emptiness in its wake. Breaking silences, telling our tales, is not enough. We can value that process—and the courage it may require—without believing that it is an end in itself. Historical responsibility has, after all, to do with action" (145). See Adrienne Rich, "Resisting Amnesia: History and Personal Life," in *Blood, Bread, and Poetry: Selected Prose 1979–1985* (New York: W. W. Norton & Company, 1986), 136–55.

Chapter 6. "The Great Basement of All Power": *Otho the Great*

1. Another possible reason that the play has never been taken seriously is that Brown and Keats never succeeded in getting it staged. About the time the play was completed, Kean, whom Keats felt was the only actor suitable for the tragedy, sailed for America, and thus neither Brown nor Keats seriously worked to have it produced. For typical critical assessments of the play, note John Middleton Murry's comment that it was "mere hack work," or William Walsh's description of it as an "undramatic drama." See John Middleton Murry, *Keats and Shakespeare: A Study of Keats's Poetic Life from 1816 to 1820* (London: Oxford University Press, 1925), 155, and William Walsh, *Introduction to Keats* (London:

Methuen, 1981), 115. More favorable assessments are offered by Claude Lee Finney in *The Evolution of Keats's Poetry,* 2:649–67, and Harry R. Beaudry in *The English Theatre and John Keats* (Salzburg: University of Salzburg, 1973), 178–98, but even these critics emphasize the serious deficiencies of the play.

2. Charles Armitage Brown, *The Life of John Keats.* This provides the standard compositional history of the play, and it is included in Hyder Edward Rollins, ed., *The Keats Circle* (2:52–97). The above passage is taken from 2:66.

3. Robert Gittings, *John Keats* (London: Heinemann, 1968), 332.

4. Note, for instance, Brown's comment in the *Life,* respecting the *Ode to a Nightingale* and other short poems, that Keats "cared so little for them himself, when once, as it appeared to me, his imagination was released from their influence, that it required a friend at hand to preserve them" (*KC* 2:65–66).

5. I should note that the Voltaire edition mentioned here was not widely respected in Keats's day. As Leigh Hunt states: "There is . . . a verison [sic], purporting to be that of [Voltaire's] whole works, by Smollet, Thomas Franklin, and others, which is understood to have been what is called a bookseller's job. . . . I believe it was so dull and bad, that readers instinctively recoiled from it as an incredible representation of any thing lively." See Leigh Hunt, *The Autobiography of Leigh Hunt, with Reminiscences of Friends and Contemporaries* (1850; reprint, New York: AMS Press, 1965), 171.

6. See William Fordyce Mavor, *Universal History, Ancient and Modern: From the Earliest Records of Time, to the General Peace of 1801* (London: R. Phillips, 1802–4), 17:23, and Keats's *Otho,* 2.1.123–24.

7. Edward Gibbon, *The History of the Decline and Fall of the Roman Empire* (1776–88; reprint, New York: Haprer & Brothers, 1879), 5:55.

8. Voltaire, *Works,* 13:220.

9. Mavor, *Universal History,* 17:21.

10. Mavor, *Universal History,* 17:22.

11. Mavor, *Universal History,* 17:23.

12. Voltaire, *Works,* 17:111.

13. Voltaire, *Works,* 17:99.

14. An anecdote by Raymond Williams about the Regency period compellingly reinforces the argument I am making here about Keats's poetic strategy. Williams writes: "The war against France ended in 1815. 'The play is over,' wrote a Government paper, 'we may now go to supper.' Cobbett replied: 'No, *you cannot yet go to supper.* You have not yet *paid for the play.* And, before you have paid for the play, you will find that there is no money left for the supper.'" See *Cobbett* (Oxford: Oxford University Press, 1983), 15–16. Keats, I believe, shared Cobbett's understanding that a society which stands by physical strength alone pays for its accomplishments with internal corrosion.

15. Keats's interest in the shaping role of circumstance during this period, as I have shown in previous chapters, is reflected in his letters. In his famous "vale of soul-making" letter, for instance, he says that "worldly elements will prey upon [man's] nature," and he speaks as well of "how man was formed by circumstances" (*LJK* 2:162–63).

16. Several books, unrelated to Keats studies, have been influential on my thinking about this subject. See Juliet Mitchell's *Women: The Longest Revolution: Essays on Feminism, Literature and Psychoanalysis* (London: Virago Press, 1984), especially 17–124, and *Woman's Estate,* especially 67–96. See also Tania Modleski, *Loving with a Vengeance: Mass-Produced Fantasies for Women* (Hamden, Conn: Archon Books, 1982).

17. For a discussion of Byron's dramas along these same lines, see Daniel P. Watkins, "Violence, Class Consciousness, and Ideology in Byron's History Plays"; "The Ideological Dimensions of Byron's *The Deformed Transformed,*" *Criticism* 25 (1983): 27–39; "Politics and Religion in Byron's *Heaven and Earth,*" *The Byron Journal* 11 (1983): 30–39; and "Byron and the Poetics of Revolution," *Keats-Shelley Journal* 34 (1985): 95–130.

Chapter 7. "This Mighty Cost and Blaze of Wealth": *Lamia*

1. See also *LJK* 2:124, 131, 154, 177, 178, and 179.
2. For a discussion of the poem in these terms see, for instance, Bates's remark in *John Keats* that "the simple passion of two immortals—even if it be only an immortal dream—is a prelude and contrast to the fatal passion of the mortal Lycius and the half-human, half-demonic Lamia" (157). See also the discussions by Wasserman in *Finer Tone*, 158; E. T. Norris, "Hermes and the Nymph in *Lamia*," *ELH* 2 (1935): 322–26; and Evert, *Aesthetic and Myth*, 283.
3. Evert, *Aesthetic and Myth*, 284.
4. The evidence that Evert adduces to support this claim, however, is somewhat suspect. Speaking of the Lamia/Lycius affair, Evert notes: "Lamia's palace is a perfect poem, and Lycius' lending of his spirit to it is without fault, in itself. It is when he attempts to remove himself from the 'real' world altogether, to live eternally, as a mortal, the life of a god, that he seals his own doom." *Aesthetic and Myth*, 284. The fact is, of course, that Lycius's problems begin not with his removal from the world but rather with his attempt to introduce Lamia's beauty and wealth to the world.
5. Sperry comes close to formulating a historical perspective on the narrative when he proclaims, in *Keats the Poet*, that the opening lines are preoccupied with "the usurpation of mythology of history" (295), but it would be more accurate (I believe) to insist that the entire poem is preoccupied with the way mythology (and poetry) is historically mediated. That is, history does not usurp mythology; rather, mythology is a historical product. This point is articulated powerfully in the poem and, at least on occasion, is asserted in Keats's letters as well, for instance in the "vale of soul-making" letter.
6. Note, for instance, Charles Cowden Clarke's comment on Keats's early reading: "The books . . . that were his constantly recurrent sources of attraction were Tooke's 'Pantheon,' Lempriere's 'Classical Dictionary,' which he appeared to *learn*, and Spence's 'Polymetia.' This was the store whence he acquired his intimacy with the Greek mythology." Quoted in Bate, *John Keats*, 25, 26.
7. Andrew Tooke, *The Pantheon* (1713; reprint, New York: Garland Publishing, 1976), 63.
8. Tooke, *Pantheon*, 62, 65–66.
9. These points are taken from George Grote, *A History of Greece: From the Earliest Period to the Close of the Generations Contemporary with Alexander the Great* (London: John Murray, 1888), 1:55.
10. Philostratus the Elder, *Life and Times of Apollonius of Tyana*, trans. Charles P. Eels (1923; reprint, New York: AMS Press, 1967), 5:15.
11. Philostratus, *Life and Times*, 8:7.
12. Tooke, *Pantheon*, 306.
13. Brand, *Observations*, 3:476.
14. It is worth noting—although it is uncertain whether Keats could have known this—that at the height of Cretan civilization the Snake Goddess was very prominent. In their excellent *Hellenic History*, for instance, Botsford and Robinson note that "in the palace of Monis was discovered a beautiful faience Snake Goddess showing the priestess with snakes in her hands and surrounded by models of garments, painted sea-shells, doves, a marble cross (in its origin a star), a lustral basin, and faience plaques of a goat and cow with their young. It has been supposed that the snake represented the soul of the deceased and that the goddess was thus the ruler of the lower world, but a recent suggestion makes the snake the protector of the household, something that brings good luck." See George Willis Botsford and Charles Alexander Robinson, Jr., *Hellenic History* (New York: Macmillan, 1946), 17. While it would be mere speculation to suggest that Keats knew of the prominence of the role of the Snake Goddess in Crete, the detail itself is interesting as a reminder

of the way the various details in the narrative intersect within a verifiable historical framework.

15. William Mitford, *The History of Greece* (London: T. Cadell and W. Davies, 1814), 1:279).
16. Botsford and Robinson, *Hellenic History*, 17.
17. Mitford, *History of Greece*, 1:284.
18. Bottsford and Robinson, *Hellenic History*, 51, 314. It is important to remember that Corinth was very much a part of the romantic imagination, a fact that is illustrated not only by Byron's *Siege of Corinth* but also by the numerous histories of the period (see Mavor and Mitford, e.g.) that feature Corinth prominently.
19. Mitford, *History of Greece*, 1:286.
20. See Botsford and Robinson, *Hellenic History*, 51–52.
21. Thorpe, *John Keats: Complete Poems*, xliii, xliv.
22. Tooke, *Pantheon*, 22.
23. See, for instance, Bernice Slote, *Keats and the Dramatic Principle* (Lincoln: University of Nebraska Press, 1958), which notes in conclusion that "following the brief introduction, Lamia appears as the baneful serpent in disguise, Lycius's guileful seductress. In Part Two, however, Keats borrows a standard device of the Elizabethan history play, and tilts the balance of sympathy in her favor when she comes to appear persecuted and pathetic" (308). Note also Dickstein's interesting comment that through the course of the narrative the change in Lamia's character is one of "explicit humanization." *Keats and His Poetry*, 242.
24. Philostratus, *Life and Times*, 5:15, 8:7, 1:35.
25. This description is consistent with Tooke and Philostratus, but it is interesting that this is the first descriptive point that Keats makes about the god of many roles.
26. Donald Reiman, "Keats and the Humanistic Paradox: Mythological History in *Lamia*," *Studies in English Literature* 11 (1971): 668.

Chapter 8. "Twing'd with Avarice": *The Fall of Hyperion*

1. See K. K. Ruthven, "Keats and *Dea Moneta*," *Studies in Romanticism* 15 (1976): 445–59. I should stress here, as I have in previous chapters, that I am not arguing a case for authorial intention, insisting that Keats consciously set about finding a poetic voice for his "real" concern with economics. Rather, I am arguing that economic reality provides one of the determining conditions for his poetry, and that Ruthven's research into the sources for the poem provides us with a useful starting point for critically assessing the poetic consequences of these conditions.
2. Catherine Belsey, *Critical Practice* (London: Methuen, 1980), 122. On this subject, see also Lowy and Sayre, "Figures of Romantic Anti-Capitalism."
3. See, for instance, Raymond Williams's discussion in *Culture and Society* of William Cobbett's political vision, which vehemently attacked the injustices inflicted by the manufacturing class on the laboring poor, while at the same time nostalgically looking back to a preindustrial world where the poor supposedly possessed integrity.
4. For a discussion of economic theory during the romantic period and of the absence of a real romantic theory of economics, see Joseph A. Schumpeter, *History of Economic Analysis*, ed. Elizabeth Boody Schumpeter (New York: Oxford University Press, 1954), especially pages 418–21.
5. Adam Smith, *An Inquiry into the Nature and Causes of The Wealth of Nations*, ed. Edwin Cannan (1776; reprint, New York: The Modern Library, 1965), 14. It is worth noting that the fundamental assumption here about the individual's relation to society is directly in line

with social contract theories of the period. On this topic, see C. B. McPherson, *The Theory of Possessive Individualism: Hobbes to Locke* (Oxford: The Clarendon Press, 1962).

6. Robert L. Heilbroner, *The Worldly Philosophers: The Lives, Times, and Ideas of the Great Economic Thinkers*, 4th ed. (New York: Simon and Schuster, 1953), 53–54.

7. Smith, *Wealth of Nations*, 16.

8. Belsey, *Critical Practice*, 122.

9. David Ricardo, *The Works and Correspondence of David Ricardo*, ed. P. Sraffa (Cambridge: Cambridge University Press, 1951–55), 1:5.

10. I am not suggesting here a specific causal influence or that Keats would have read Ricardo directly, but rather that Ricardo participated in a debate that Keats, in reading the dailies and weeklies of the age—especially the *Examiner*—would have been aware of.

11. Ricardo, *Works*, 3:301–2.

12. See Thomas Robert Malthus, "Remarks on Mr. Ricardo's Theory of Profits," in *Principles of Political Economy Considered with a View of Their Practical Application*, 2d. ed. (New York: Augustus M. Kelley, 1951), 291–98, and Ricardo's "Essay on Profits," in *Works*, 1:10–41.

13. For a discussion of the specifics of this issue (which is beyond the scope of this essay), see Spencer J. Pack, *Reconstructing Marxist Economics: Marx Based upon a Sraffian Commodity Theory of Value* (New York: Praeger, 1985), especially pages 13–14. See also Robert Heilbroner, *The Nature and Logic of Capitalism*.

14. See, for instance, Shelley's *Mask of Anarchy*, which condemns the identification of working people with the machines they operate:

> What is Freedom?—ye can tell
> That which slavery is, too well—
> For its very name has grown
> To an echo of your own.
>
> 'Tis to work and have such pay
> As just keeps life from day to day
> In your limbs, as in a cell
> For the tyrants' use to dwell,
>
> So that ye for them are made
> Loom, and plough, and sword, and spade,
> With or without your own will bent
> To their defence and nourishment. (156–67)

15. Zaretsky, *Capitalism, the Family, & Personal Life*, 56–57.

16. Carol Gould, *Marx's Social Ontology: Individuality and Community in Marx's Theory of Social Reality* (Cambridge: The MIT Press, 1981), 47.

17. See Tooke, *Pantheon*, 107–08.

18. Robert Burton, *The Anatomy of Melancholy* (1621; reprint, London: Dent, 1964; New York: Dutton, 1964), 1:65.

19. *Examiner*, 23 May 1819, 323.

20. Ruthven, "Keats and *Dea Moneta*," 449.

21. This is exactly the view that eventually allowed poetry into the utilitarian social scheme. As Mill describes it in his *Autobiography*, poetry provides a sort of escape valve from the real business of life, namely economic competition. On this subject see Raymond Williams, *Culture and Society*.

Further, it is worth mentioning that in this context the famous lines of Moneta about poets and dreamers—"The one pours out a balm upon the World, / The other vexes it"

(201–2)—are not at all self-evident. In fact, it is at least arguable that the lines suggest the ethical superiority of the dreamer, who would vex or change the world; who would, in other words, challenge the authority and ideology of Moneta.

22. Like Tilottama Rajan, in *Dark Interpreter,* I am assuming here of course that the *Fall* is thematically complete, even though it is formally incomplete.

23. D. G. James, *The Romantic Comedy: An Essay on English Romanticism* (1948; reprint, London: Oxford University Press, 1963), 169.

24. On a biographical note, Miriam Allott states that during this period Keats was "growing away from unreflecting delight in external nature into a wise understanding of the harsher realities of existence and the annihilation of self-regarding impulses through empathic identification with others." See *John Keats,* 6. The *Fall* demonstrates this point perfectly, not only in its development from a world of natural delight toward a world of terrible struggle, but also in its portrayal of the narrator's developing intellectual awareness that is accompanied by sympathy for and commitment to the suffering.

25. Evert, *Aesthetic and Myth,* 292, note 2.

26. See, for instance, Bate's *John Keats,* 262–305.

Chapter 9. "All Things Turn'd Topsy-turvy": *Jealousies* and *Gripus*

1. Keats elsewhere shows his awareness of industrialization and the efforts of workers to secure their rights within an exploitative labor situation. In a letter to George and Georgiana, for instance, he describes his financial situation in these terms: "As for Punmaking I wish it was as good a trade as pin-making—there is very little business of that sort going on now. We struck for wages like the manchester wevers [sic]—but to no purpose—so we are all out of employ" (*LJK* 2:214).

2. One possibility, as he wrote to Brown, was to write "on the liberal side of the question" (*LJK* 2:176) for the journals: "I shall apply to Hazlitt, who knows the market as well as any one, for something to bring me in a few pounds as soon as possible. I shall not suffer my pride to hinder me. The whisper may go round; I shall not hear it. If I can get an article in the 'Edinburg', I will" (*LJK* 2:177).

3. Compare Shelley's more systematic and extensive effort to articulate the nature and contours of historical progress. See especially *A Philosophical View of Reform.*

4. Robert Gittings, *The Mask of Keats: A Study of Problems* (Cambridge: Harvard University Press, 1956), 115–43.

Chapter 10. "The Truth of the Imagination": Conclusion

1. For an excellent, brief investigation of the historical development of bourgeois subjectivity during this period, again see Zaretsky, *Capitalism, the Family, & Personal Life.*

2. A fine brief account of the British response to the French Revolution can be found in the introduction to Harold Bloom, *Visionary Company: A Reading of English Romantic Poetry* (1961; reprint, Garden City, N.Y.: Anchor-Doubleday, 1963). See also M. H. Abrams, "English Romanticism: The Spirit of the Age," in *Romanticism Reconsidered,* ed. Northrop Frye (New York: Columbia University Press, 1963), 26–72.

3. Kinnaird, *William Hazlitt,* 83.

4. Two excellent discussions of these historical matters are George Rudé, *Revolutionary Europe: 1783–1815,* and Eric J. Hobsbawm, *The Age of Revolution: 1789–1848.*

Works Cited

Abrams, M. H. "English Romanticism: The Spirit of the Age." In *Romanticism Reconsidered*, edited by Northrop Frye, 26–72. New York: Columbia University Press, 1963.

———. *Natural Supernaturalism: Tradition and Revolution in Romantic Literature.* New York: W. W. Norton & Company, 1971.

Barnard, John. *John Keats.* Cambridge: Cambridge University Press, 1987.

Barrett, Michele. *Women's Oppression Today: Problems in Marxist Feminist Analysis.* London: Verso, 1980.

Bate, Walter Jackson. *John Keats.* Cambridge: Harvard University Press, Belknap Press, 1963.

Beach, Joseph Warren. "Keats's Realms of God." *PMLA* 49 (1934): 246–57.

Beaudry, Harry R. *The English Theatre and John Keats.* Salzburg, Austria: Institut Für Anglistik und Amerikanistik, Universität Salzburg, 1973.

Belsey, Catherine. *Critical Practice.* London: Methuen, 1980.

———. "The Romantic Construction of the Unconscious." In *Literature, Politics and Theory: Papers from the Essex Conference 1976–84*, edited by Francis Barker et al., 57–76. London: Methuen, 1986.

Benjamin, Walter. *Illuminations.* Edited by Hannah Arendt. Translated by Harry Zohn. New York: Schocken Books, 1969.

Bewell, Alan. "The Political Implication of Keats's Classicist Aesthetics." *Studies in Romanticism* 25 (1986): 220–29.

Bloom, Harold. "The Internalization of Quest-Romance." In *Romanticism and Consciousness: Essays in Criticism*, edited by Harold Bloom, 3–23. New York: W. W. Norton, 1970.

———. *The Visionary Company: A Reading of English Romantic Poetry.* 1961. Reprint. Garden City, New York: Anchor-Doubleday, 1963.

Bostetter, Edward E. *The Romantic Ventriloquists: Wordsworth, Coleridge, Keats, Shelley, Byron.* Seattle: University of Washington Press, 1963.

Botsford, George Willis, and Charles Alexander Robinson, Jr. *Hellenic History.* New York: Macmillan, 1946.

Brand, John. *Observations on the Popular Antiquities of Great Britain: Chiefly Illustrating the Origin of Our Vulgar and Provincial Customs, Ceremonies, and Superstitions.* Published 1813 in 2 vols. Revised 1841 and 1848 in 3 vols. Reprint. New York: AMS Press, 1970.

Burton, Robert. *The Anatomy of Melancholy.* 1621. Reprint. 3 vols. London: Dent, 1964; New York: Dutton, 1964.

Butler, Marilyn. *Romantics, Rebels and Reactionaries: English Literature and Its Background.* Oxford: Oxford University Press, 1981.

Byron, George Gordon, Lord. *Byron's Letters and Journals.* Edited by Leslie A. Marchand. 12 vols. Cambridge: Harvard University Press, Belknap Press, 1973–82.

Caudwell, Christopher. *Illusion and Reality: A Study of the Sources of Poetry.* 1937. Reprint. New York: International Publishers, 1973.

Chessler, Phyllis. *Women and Madness.* New York: Avon Books, 1972.

Compact Edition of the Oxford English Dictionary: Complete Text Reproduced Micrographically. Oxford: Oxford University Press, 1971.

Clarke, Charles C., and Mary Cowden Clarke. *Recollections of Writers.* London, 1878.

Curran, Stuart. "The Political Prometheus." *Studies in Romanticism* 25 (1986): 429–55.

de Beauvoir, Simone, *The Second Sex.* Translated and edited by H. M. Parshley. 1952. Reprint. New York: Vintage, 1974.

Dickstein, Morris. *Keats and His Poetry: A Study in Development.* Chicago: University of Chicago Press, 1971.

Donovan, Josephine. *Feminist Theory: The Intellectual Traditions of American Feminism.* New York: Ungar, 1985.

DuBois, Ellen Carol, et al. *Feminist Scholarship: Kindling in the Groves of Academe.* Urbana: University of Illinois Press, 1985.

Eggers, J. Philip. "Memory in Mankind: Keats's Historical Imagination." *PMLA* 86 (1971): 990–98.

Eisenstein, Zillah R. *The Radical Future of Liberal Feminism.* Boston: Northeastern University Press, 1986.

Engels, Frederick. *The Origin of the Family, Private Property and the State.* 1942. Reprint. New York: International Publishers, 1975.

Evans, B. I. "Keats's Approach to the Chapman Sonnet." *Essays and Studies by Members of the English Association* 16 (1931): 26–52.

Evert, Walter. *Aesthetic and Myth in the Poetry of Keats.* Princeton: Princeton University Press, 1965.

Fekete, John. *The Critical Twilight.* London: Routledge, Kegan Paul, 1976.

Finley, M. I. "Utopianism Ancient and Modern." In *The Critical Twilight: Essays in Honor of Herbert Marcuse,* edited by Kurt H. Wolff and Barrington Moore, Jr., 3–20. Boston: Beacon Press, 1968.

Finney, Claude Lee. *The Evolution of Keats's Poetry.* 2 vols. 1936. Reprint. New York: Russell & Russell, 1963.

Fisher, Philip. "A Museum with One Work Inside: Keats and the Finality of Art." *Keats-Shelley Journal* 33 (1984): 85–102.

Frye, Northrop. *A Study of English Romanticism.* New York: Random House, 1968.

Garrett, William. "The Glaucus Episode: An Interpretation of Book III of *Endymion.*" *Keats-Shelley Journal* 27 (1978): 23–34.

Garrod, H. W. *Keats*. 2d. ed. 1926. Reprint. Oxford: The Clarendon Press, 1962.

Gerber, Jane S. *Jewish Society in Fez, 1450–1700: Studies in Communal and Economic Life*. London: Brill, 1980.

Gibbon, Edward. *The History of the Decline and Fall of the Roman Empire*. 1776–88. Reprint. Vol. 4. New York: Harper & Brothers, 1879.

Gittings, Robert. *John Keats*. London: Heinemann, 1968.

———. *The Mask of Keats: A Study of Problems*. Cambridge: Harvard University Press, 1956.

Godfrey, Clarice. "Endymion." In *John Keats: A Reassessment*, edited by Kenneth Muir. 20–39. Liverpool: Liverpool University Press, 1969.

Godwin, William. *The Pantheon, or Ancient History of the Gods of Greece and Rome*. 1814. Reprint. New York: Garland Publishing, 1984.

Goldberg, M. A. *The Poetics of Romanticism: Toward a Reading of John Keats*. Yellow Springs, Ohio: The Antioch Press, 1969.

Gould, Carol. *Marx's Social Ontology: Individuality and Community in Marx's Theory of Social Reality*. Cambridge: MIT Press, 1981.

Grote, George. *A History of Greece: from the Earliest Period to the Close of the Generations Contemporary with Alexander the Great*. London: John Murray, 1888.

Haydon, Benjamin R. *The Diary of Benjamin Robert Haydon*. Edited by Willard B. Pope. Cambridge: Harvard University Press, 1960.

Hazlitt, William. *The Complete Works of William Hazlitt*. Edited by P. P. Howe. London: J. M. Dent and Sons, 1930.

Heilbroner, Robert L. *The Nature and Logic of Capitalism*. New York and London: W. W. Norton & Company, 1985.

———. *The Worldly Philosophers: The Lives, Times, and Ideas of the Great Economic Thinkers*. 4th ed. New York: Simon and Schuster, 1953.

Hitti, Philip K. *Lebanon in History: From the Earliest Times to the Present*. London: MacMillan & Co., 1957.

Hobsbawm, Eric J. *The Age of Revolution: 1789–1848*. New York: New American Library, 1962.

Homans, Margaret. *Women Writers and Poetic Identity: Dorothy Wordsworth, Emily Bronte, and Emily Dickinson*. Princeton: Princeton University Press, 1980.

Hunt, Leigh. *The Autobiography of Leigh Hunt, with Reminiscences of Friends and Contemporaries*. 1850. Reprint. New York: AMS Press, 1965.

Jack, Ian. *Keats and the Mirror of Art*. Oxford: Oxford University Press, 1967.

Jacoby, Russell. *Social Amnesia: A Critique of Conformist Psychology from Adler to Laing*. Boston: Beacon Press, 1975.

James, D. G. *The Romantic Comedy: An Essay on English Romanticism*. 1948. Reprint. London: Oxford University Press, 1963.

Jameson, Fredric. *Marxism and Form: Twentieth-Century Dialectical Theories of Literature*. Princeton: Princeton University Press, 1971.

———. "Religion and Ideology: A Political Reading of *Paradise Lost*." In *Literature, Politics and Theory: Papers from the Essex Conference 1976–84*, edited by Francis Barker et al., 35–56. London: Methuen, 1986.

———. *The Political Unconscious: Narrative as a Socially Symbolic Act.* Ithaca: Cornell University Press, 1983.

Jones, Ann Rosalind. "Writing the Body: Toward an Understanding of *l'ecriture Feminine.*" In *Feminist Criticism and Social Change: Sex, Class and Race in Literature and Culture,* edited by Judith Newton and Deborah Rosenfelt. 86–101. New York: Methuen, 1985.

Jones, Howard Mumford. *Revolution and Romanticism.* Cambridge: Harvard University Press, Belknap Press, 1974.

Jones, James Land. *Adam's Dream: Mythic Consciousness in Keats and Yeats.* Athens: University of Georgia Press, 1975.

Keats, John. *The Letters of John Keats.* Edited by Hyder Edward Rollins. 2 vols. Cambridge: Harvard University Press, 1958.

———. *John Keats: Complete Poems and Selected Letters.* Edited by Clarence DeWitt Thorpe. New York: Odyssey Press, 1935.

———. *The Poems of John Keats.* Edited by Jack Stillinger. Cambridge: Harvard University Press, Belknap Press, 1978.

———. *The Poems of John Keats.* Edited by Miriam Allott. London: Longman, 1970.

Kerner, David. "The Problem of Evil in the "Ode on a Grecian Urn." *Texas Studies in Language and Literature* 28 (1986): 227–49.

Kinnaird, John D. *Hazlitt: Critic of Power.* New York: Columbia University Press, 1978.

Koch, June. "Politics in Keats's Poetry." *JEGP* 70 (1972): 491–501.

Kuhn, Annette. and AnnMarie Wolpe. *Feminism and Materialism: Women and Modes of Production.* London: Routledge and Kegan Paul, 1978.

Larrain, Jorge. *A Reconstruction of Historical Materialism.* London: Allen & Unwin, 1986.

Lau, Beth. "Keats's Goddesses." *Philological Quarterly* 63 (1984): 323–41.

Le Tourneau, Roger. *Fez in the Age of the Marinidas.* Translated by Besse Alberta Clement. Norman: University of Oklahoma Press, 1961.

Lukács, Georg. *Realism in Our Time: Literature and the Class Struggle.* 1964. Reprint. New York: Harper & Row, Publishers, 1971.

———. "Realism in the Balance." In *Aesthetics and Politics.* Translation editor Ronald Taylor. 28–59. London: Verso, 1977.

McGann, Jerome J. *A Critique of Modern Textual Criticism.* Chicago: University of Chicago Press, 1983.

———. "Keats and the Historical Method in Literary Criticism." *Modern Language Notes* 94 (1979): 988–1032.

———. *The Romantic Ideology: A Critical Investigation.* Chicago: University of Chicago Press, 1983.

Macksey, Richard. "'To Autumn' and the Music of Mortality: 'Pure Rhetoric of a Language without Words.'" In *Romanticism and Language,* edited by Arden Reed, 263–308. Ithaca: Cornell University Press, 1984.

McPherson, C. B. *The Theory of Possessive Individualism: Hobbes to Locke.* Oxford: Clarendon Press, 1962.

Malthus, Thomas Robert. "Remarks on Mr. Ricardo's Theory of Profits." In *Principles of Political Economy Considered with a View to Their Practical Application*. 2d ed. New York: Augustus M. Kelley, 1951.

Marcuse, Herbert. *The Aesthetic Dimension: Toward a Critique of Marxist Aesthetics*. Boston: Beacon Press, 1978.

Marx, Karl. *Capital: A Critique of Political Economy*. Vol. 1. Moscow: Progress Publishers, 1954.

———. *Karl Marx: Economic and Philosophical Manuscripts*. Edited by Tom Bottomore. New York: McGraw-Hill, 1964.

Marx, Karl and Frederick Engels. *The German Ideology*. Moscow: Progress Publishers, 1976.

Mavor, William Fordyce. *Universal History, Ancient and Modern: from the Earliest Records of Time, to the General Peace of 1801*. Vol. 17. London: R. Phillips, 1802–4.

Mayhead, Robin. *John Keats*. Cambridge: Cambridge University Press, 1967.

Mitchell, Juliet. *Woman's Estate*. 1971. Reprint. New York: Vintage, 1973.

———. *Women: The Longest Revolution: Essays on Feminism, Literature and Psychoanalysis*. London: Virago Press, 1984.

Mitford, William. *The History of Greece*. 10 vols. London: T. Cadell and W. Davies, 1814.

Modleski, Tania. *Loving with a Vengeance: Mass-Produced Fantasies for Women*. Hamden, Conn.: Archon Books, 1982.

Muir, Kenneth. "The Meaning of *Hyperion*." In *John Keats: A Reassessment*, edited by Kenneth Muir, 103–23. Liverpool: Liverpool University Press, 1969.

Murry, John Middleton. *Keats and Shakespeare: A Study of Keats's Poetic Life from 1816 to 1820*. London: Oxford University Press, 1925.

Norris, E. T. "Hermes and the Nymph in *Lamia*." *ELH* 2 (1935): 322–26.

Pack, Spencer J. *Reconstructing Marxist Economics: Marx Based upon a Sraffian Commodity Theory of Value*. New York: Praeger, 1985.

Perkins, David. *The Quest for Permanence: The Symbolism of Wordsworth Shelley and Keats*. Cambridge: Harvard University Press, 1959.

Peterfreund, Stuart. "The Truth about 'Beauty' and 'Truth': Keats's 'Ode on a Grecian Urn,' Milton, Shakespeare, and the Uses of Paradox." *Keats-Shelley Journal* 35 (1986): 62–82.

Philostratus the Elder. *Life and Times of Apollonius of Tyana*. Translated by Charles P. Eels. 1923. Reprint. New York: AMS Press, 1967.

Plekhanov, G. V. *Art and Social Life*. Moscow: Progress Publishers, 1977.

Purchas, Samuel. *Hakluytus Posthumus, or Purchas His Pilgrimes: Contayning a History of the Worlds in Sea Voyages and Land Travells by Englishmen and Others*. 1625. Reprint. Glasgow: James MacLehose and Sons, 1906.

Rajan, Tilottama. *Dark Interpreter: The Discourse of Romanticism*. Ithaca: Cornell University Press, 1980.

Reiman, Donald. "Keats and the Humanistic Paradox: Mythological History in *Lamia*." *Studies in English Literature* 11 (1971): 659–69.

———. Review essay. *Studies in Romanticism* 20 (1981): 254–60.

Ricardo, David. *The Works and Correspondence of David Ricardo.* Edited by P. Sraffa. 10 vols. Cambridge: Cambridge University Press, 1951–55.

Rich, Adrienne. "Resisting Amnesia: History and Personal Life." In *Blood, Bread, and Poetry: Selected Prose 1979–1985*. New York: W. W. Norton & Company, 1986.

Robertson, William. *The History of America.* 3d ed. 3 vols. London: W. Strachen and T. Cadell, Edinburgh: J. Balfour, 1780.

———. *The History of the Reign of the Emperor Charles the Fifth.* 3 vols. Philadelphia: J. B. Lippincott & Co., 1876.

Rollins, Hyder Edward, ed. *The Keats Circle.* 2 vols. Cambridge: Harvard University Press, 1965.

Rowbotham, Sheila. *Hidden from History: Rediscovering Women in History from the 17th Century to the Present.* New York: Vintage Books, 1976.

Rudé, George. *Revolutionary Europe: 1783–1815.* 1964. Reprint. New York: Harper Colophon Books, 1975.

Ruether, Rosemary Radford. *New Woman New Earth: Sexist Ideologies & Human Liberation.* New York: The Seabury Press, 1975.

Ruthven, K. K. "Keats and *Dea Moneta*." *Studies in Romanticism* 15 (1976): 445–59.

Said, Edward. *Orientalism.* 1978. Reprint. New York: Vintage Books, 1979.

———. "Orientalism Reconsidered." In *Literature, Politics and Theory: Papers from the Essex Conference 1976–84*, edited by Francis Barker et al., 210–29. London: Methuen, 1986.

Sales, Roger. *English Literature in History, 1780–1830: Pastoral and Politics.* New York: St. Martin's Press, 1983.

Sayre, Robert, and Michael Lowy. "Figures of Romantic Anti-Capitalism." *New German Critique* 34 (1984): 42–92.

Schumpeter, Joseph A. *History of Economic Analysis.* Edited by Elizabeth Boody Schumpeter. New York: Oxford University Press, 1954.

Scrivener, Michael H. "*Frankenstein*'s Ghost Story: the Last Jacobin Novel." *Genre* 19 (1986): 299–318.

Sharp, Ronald A. *Keats, Skepticism, and the Religion of Beauty.* Athens: University of Georgia Press, 1979.

Shaw, George Bernard. *The Collected Works of Bernard Shaw.* Vol. 29. New York: William H. Wise, 1932.

Shelley, Percy Bysshe. *A Philosophical View of Reform.* In *Shelley's Prose, or the Trumpet of a Prophecy*, edited by David Lee Clark. Albuquerque: University of New Mexico Press, 1954.

———. *Shelley: Poetical Works.* Edited by Thomas Hutchinson. London: Oxford University Press, 1967.

Sismondi, John Charles Leonard Simonde de. *A History of the Italian Republics: Being a View of the Rise, Progress, and Fall of Italian Freedom.* 1807–18. Reprint. London: J. M. Dent & Co., 1907, New York: E. P. Dutton & Co., 1907.

Slote, Bernice. *Keats and the Dramatic Principle.* Lincoln: University of Nebraska Press, 1958.

Smith, Adam. *An Inquiry into the Nature and Causes of the Wealth of Nations.* Edited by Edwin Cannan. 1776. Reprint. New York: Modern Library, 1965.

Sperry, Stuart M. *Keats the Poet.* Princeton: Princeton University Press, 1973.

Stillinger, Jack. *The Hoodwinking of Madeline and Other Essays on Keats's Poems.* Chicago: University of Illinois Press, 1971.

Swaminathan, S. R. *The Still Image in Keats's Poetry.* Salzburg, Austria: Institut Fur Anglistik und Amerikanistik, Universitat Salzburg, 1981.

Szasz, Thomas. *The Manufacture of Madness.* New York: Delta, 1970.

Thompson, E. P. *William Morris: Romantic to Revolutionary.* 1955. Reprint. New York: Pantheon, 1976.

Thorpe, Clarence DeWitt. "Keats's Interest in Politics and World Affairs." *PMLA* 46 (1931): 1228–45.

Tooke, Andrew. *The Pantheon.* 1713. Reprint. New York: Garland Publishing, 1976.

Vendler, Helen. *The Odes of John Keats.* Cambridge: Harvard University Press, Belknap Press, 1983.

Volney, Constantin Francois. *A New Translation of Volney's Ruins.* 2 vols. 1802. Reprint. New York: Garland Publishing, 1979.

Volosinov, V. N. *Marxism and the Philosophy of Language.* Translated by Ladislav Matejka and I. R. Titunik. Cambridge: Harvard University Press, 1973.

Voltaire. *The Works of Voltaire: A Contemporary Version.* Edited by John Morley et al. 1762. Reprint. New York: E. R. DuMont, 1901.

Waldoff, Leon. *Keats and the Silent Work of the Imagination.* Urbana: University of Illinois Press, 1985.

Walsh, William. *Introduction to Keats.* London: Methuen, 1981.

Ward, Aileen. *John Keats: The Making of a Poet.* 1963. Reprint. New York: Viking, 1967.

Wasserman, Earl. *The Finer Tone: Keats's Major Poems.* 1953. Reprint. Baltimore: Johns Hopkins University Press, 1967.

Watkins, Daniel P. "A Reassessment of Keats's *Otho the Great.*" *Clio* 16 (1986): 49–66.

———. "Byron and the Poetics of Revolution." *The Keats-Shelley Journal* 34 (1985): 95–130.

———. "Personal Life and Social Authority in Keats's *Isabella.*" *Nineteenth-Century Contexts* 11 (1987): 23–49.

———. "Politics and Religion in Byron's *Heaven and Earth.*" *The Byron Journal* 11 (1983): 30–39.

———. *Social Relations in Byron's Eastern Tales.* Rutherford, New Jersey: Fairleigh Dickinson University Press, 1987.

———. "The Ideological Dimensions of Byron's *The Deformed Transformed. Criticism* 25 (1983): 27–39.

———. "Violence, Class Consciousness, and Ideology in Byron's History Plays." *ELH* 48 (1981): 799–816.

Weimann, Robert. *Structure and Society in Literary History: Studies in the History and Theory of Historical Criticism.* Baltimore: Johns Hopkins University Press, 1984.

Williams. Raymond. *Cobbett*. Oxford and New York: Oxford University Press, 1983.

———. *Culture and Society 1780–1850*. New York: Harper & Row, 1958.

———. *Marxism and Literature*. Oxford: Oxford University Press, 1977.

———. *The Sociology of Culture*. New York: Schocken Books, 1982.

Wilson, Douglas B. "Reading the Urn: Death in Keats's Arcadia." *Studies in English Literature* 25 (1985): 823–44.

Winegarten, Renée. *Writers and Revolution: The Fatal Lure of Action*. New York: New Viewpoints, 1974.

Wolfson, Susan. "Keats's *Isabella* and the 'Digressions' of 'Romance.'" *Criticism* 27 (1985): 247–61.

Woodring, Carl. *Politics in English Romantic Poetry*. Cambridge: Harvard University Press, 1970.

Zaretsky, Eli. *Capitalism, the Family, & Personal Life*. New York: Harper & Row, 1976.

Index

Allott, Miriam, 74, 77, 200n.11, 216n.24
Althusser, Louis, 196n.5
Anxiety, 12, 25, 26, 31, 32, 33, 34, 37, 44–45, 70, 71, 75, 94, 95, 105, 107, 108, 117, 119, 142, 164, 181
Aristocracy, 69, 70, 185, 186
Arnold, Matthew, 179
Authorial intention, 25, 35

Bailey, Benjamin, 107, 113, 122
Bank Restriction Act (of 1797), 159
Barnard, John, 23, 88
Barrett, Michele, 198n.39
Beach, Joseph Warren, 194–95n.11
Beauty, 9, 10, 35, 36, 38, 39, 42, 46, 47, 51, 98, 108, 113, 114, 116, 118, 180, 184, 186–87
Belsey, Catherine, 45, 157, 161, 197n.25
Benjamin, Walter: *Theses on the Philosophy of History*, 100
Bentham, Jeremy, 36
Blake, William, 165; *The Chimney Sweeper*, 41; *London*, 148; *Songs of Innocence*, 114
Bloom, Harold, 42
Bostetter, Edward E., 197n.24, 205n.10, 206n.17
Botsford, George Willis, 141, 213n.14
Bourgeois art, 83, 84
Bourgeoisie, 24, 25
Brand, John, 78, 140, 204n.57; *Observations on the Popular Antiquities*, 78, 139
Brawne, Fanny, 63, 122, 135
Brown, Charles Armitage, 121–22, 177, 212n.4
Burdett, Sir Francis, 64
Burton, Robert, 78, 137; *Anatomy of Melancholy*, 137, 138, 161–62
Butler, Marilyn, 88
Byron, George Gordon, Lord, 24, 25, 42, 57, 58, 59, 62, 63, 64, 67, 70, 85, 89, 90, 91, 93, 118, 134, 165, 179, 181, 185, 190; *Childe Harold's Pilgrimage*, 25, 37, 118; *The Curse of Minerva*, 118; *Don Juan*, 179; *Manfred*, 37, 45, 52, 165, 185; *Marino Faliero*, 121; *Sardanapalus*, 62, 121; *The Two Foscari*, 121

Capitalism, 12, 37, 47, 55–57, 58, 71, 111, 161, 185, 190
Caudwell, Christopher, 11, 36, 37, 193n.4, 210n.36
Charles V (of Spain), 29, 66, 72
Chessler, Phyllis, 119
Circumstance, 23, 58, 59, 97
Clarke, Charles Cowden, 213n.6
Class relations, 57, 58, 180, 186
Cobbett, William, 21, 55, 63, 64, 93, 157, 211n.44
Coleridge, Samuel Taylor, 50, 63, 67, 72; *Kubla Khan*, 50, 72
Commerce, 77, 142–43
Commodification of art, 10
Corn Laws (of 1815), 37, 160
Crime, 59

de Beauvoir, Simone, 49, 113
Desire, 44, 45, 46, 108, 116–17
Dickstein, Morris, 197n.20, 198n.44
Dilke, Charles, 21
Donovan, Josephine, 209n.16

East, the (Orient), 47–48, 74
Economic relations, 9, 48, 55, 58, 83, 157–61
Elgin Marbles, the, 62, 89, 90, 117–18, 191
Engels, Frederick: *Origin and History of the Family*, 109
Evans, B. Ifor, 27

225

Evert, Walter, 53, 175, 197 n.21, 210 n.31
Examiner, The, 21, 24, 37, 42, 55, 63, 85, 92, 93, 159, 162, 178, 189, 196 n.12, 201 nn. 25 and 27, 211 n.44

False consciousness, 26
Fekete, John, 10, 36, 161
Ferdinand VII (king of Spain), 24, 63, 92, 189, 201 n.27
Feudalism, 23, 24, 36, 65, 66, 67, 68, 69, 73, 75, 77, 80, 82, 83, 190
Finley, M. I., 11
Finney, Claude Lee, 199 n.2
Fisher, Peter, 207–8 n.7
Forces and relations of production, 36, 60
Franklin, Benjamin, 64
French Revolution, the, 91, 110, 189
Freud, Sigmund, 119
Friendship, 35, 38, 45, 52
Frye, Northrop, 196 n.17

Garrett, William, 45
Garrod, H. W., 22, 193
Gender relations, 46, 47, 48–51, 78–82, 111, 130–31, 148–53
Gerber, Jane S.: *Jewish Society in Fez, 1450–1700,* 73
Gibbon, Edward, 55, 123, 125; *Decline and Fall of the Roman Empire,* 123
Gifford, William, 86, 87, 93, 94, 96, 99, 102, 180
Gittings, Robert, 122, 179, 183
Godwin, William, 36, 89, 90; *The Pantheon,* 89
Goldberg, M. A., 82
Gould, Carol C., 161; *Marx's Social Ontology,* 161

Haydon, Benjamin Robert, 85, 86, 90, 102, 117–18, 194 n.1
Hazlitt, William, 21, 22, 24, 67, 75, 85, 86, 87, 88, 93, 96, 99, 118, 157, 162, 178, 180, 201 n.25; *Lectures on the English Poets,* 85–87; *The Life of Napoleon Buonaparte,* 67
Heilbroner, Robert L., 55, 56, 157; *The Nature and Logic of Capitalism,* 55
Hellenism, 90–91
Hesiod's *Theogony,* 89
Historical anxiety, 25, 37, 71, 104, 141, 142, 190, 191, 201 n.27

History, 9, 11, 12, 13, 23, 31, 38, 44, 51, 60, 65, 83, 100, 104, 105–6, 111, 112, 113, 115, 117, 121, 142, 188
Hitti, Philip, 76, 203 n.48
Hoagwood, Terence A., 196 n.14
Hobhouse, John Cam, 93, 118
Hobsbawm, Eric J., 36
Holy Alliance, the, 93
Human nature, 168–69
Hunt, Henry "Orator," 21, 93, 178
Hunt, Leigh, 21, 64, 85, 92, 162, 189, 194 n.1, 212 n.5

Ideology, 12, 31, 38, 46, 47, 48, 56, 79–80, 106, 108, 143, 158, 159
Imagination, 10, 12, 26, 27, 37, 38, 43, 47, 50, 62–63, 85, 86–87, 90, 93, 94, 99, 107, 136, 141, 164, 180
Imperialism, 31, 38, 47
Inductions (to *Endymion*), 44, 51
Industrialism, 10, 12, 23, 25, 37

Jacoby, Russell, 43
Jameson, Fredric, 25, 40, 83, 84, 196 n.16, 197 nn. 17 and 18, 198 n.39, 204 n.60; *Marxism and Form,* 83
Jones, Ann Rosalind, 208 n.11
Jones, Isabella, 78
Jones, James Land, 98, 207 n.6
Jonson, Ben, 78

Keats, George, 21, 22, 63, 86, 93, 177, 200 n.14, 216 n.1
Keats, Georgiana, 21, 63, 86, 93, 200 n.14, 216 n.1
Keats, John: works, *Calidore,* 33; *Endymion,* 35–53, 86, 102, 105, 154, 182; *Epistle to John Hamilton Reynolds,* 59; *The Eve of St. Agnes,* 16, 63–84, 107, 121, 184; *The Fall of Hyperion,* 55, 107, 155, 179, 180, 184, 187, 188; *Hyperion,* 12, 31, 64, 85–103, 104, 121, 140, 159, 162, 175, 180, 181, 182; *Isabella,* 12, 31, 55–63, 85, 161, 172, 189; *I stood tip-toe upon a little hill,* 33; *King Stephen,* 103, 121; *La Belle Dame Sans Merci,* 107, 180, 182; *Lamia,* 12, 31, 55, 107, 135–55, 168; *Ode on a Grecian Urn,* 81, 104–20, 121, 149, 184, 189; *Ode on Melancholy,* 168; *Ode to Psyche,* 104, 182; *On First Looking into Chapman's Homer,* 12, 23, 26–31; *Otho the Great,* 12, 22, 31, 103,

121–34, 135, 175, 188; *Robin Hood*, 12; *Sleep and Poetry*, 31–33, 85, 162, 188; *To Hope*, 33; *To My Brother George*, 21
Keats, Tom, 21, 63, 64, 85
Kinnaird, John D., 189, 194 n.6
Knowledge, 153

Labor, 59, 60, 80–81
Larrain, Jorge, 196 n.5
Lempriere's *Classical Dictionary*, 89, 137
Lewis, David, 64, 85
Lowes, John Livingston, 27
Lowy, Michael, 11
Lukács, Georg, 117, 193 n.3

McGann, Jerome J., 31, 52, 195 n.4
Macksey, Richard, 198–99 n.45
Madness, 132–33
Malthus, Thomas Robert, 160, 161
Marchand, Leslie A., 211 n.41
Market economy, 146, 157, 158, 159, 180
Marx, Karl, 54, 80, 169, 197 n.27, 203 n.49; *Capital*, 204 nn. 56 and 58
Marxist criticism, 10–11
Mavor, William Fordyce, 71, 123, 124, 125, 130, 140; *Universal History, Ancient and Modern*, 123
Milton, John, 64, 86, 87, 88, 89
Mitford, William, 141; *History of Greece*, 141
Money, 57, 156, 159, 160, 161–62, 166–67, 172, 185
Moore, Sir Thomas, 67
Muir, Kenneth, 23, 88, 206 n.15
Murry, John Middleton, 211 n.1
Myth, 38, 89, 90, 104, 110, 139–40, 154–55, 191

Napoleon (emperor of the French), 23, 24, 25, 37, 63, 64, 92, 93, 102, 158, 159, 181, 189, 190, 201 n.27
Napoleonic Wars, 24, 163, 190
Nature, 10, 40
Nostalgia, 36, 38, 171, 201 n.25

Owen, Robert, 36

Paine, Thomas, 178
Past and present, 65–67, 70, 144
Patriarchy (and patriarchal morality), 106, 107–17, 118–20, 131, 151
Perkins, David, 208 n.10

Personal life, 56–57, 62
Peterfreund, Stuart, 207–8 n.7
Peterloo Massacre, 155, 178
Philostratus, 138, 153; *Life and Times of Apollonius of Tyana*, 138
Plehkanov, G. V., 117, 210 n.36
Political unconscious, the, 25, 102, 165
Politics, 9, 21, 22, 23, 25, 37, 47, 51, 54, 55, 64, 65, 178
Power, 91–92, 98–99, 100, 101, 102, 125–27
Purchas, Samuel, 72, 73, 74, 202 n.40; *Purchas His Pilgrimes*, 72

Rajan, Tilottama, 105, 106, 111, 113, 206–7 n.4
Regency England, 52, 177, 178, 180, 183, 212 n.14
Reiman, Donald, 154, 199 n.7
Religion, 40, 68–69, 77, 129–30
Reynolds, John Hamilton, 21, 135
Ricardo, David, 36, 159, 160, 161, 162
Rich, Adrienne, 211 n.46
Robertson, William, 27, 28, 29, 30, 31, 65, 66, 71, 72, 74, 75, 178, 200 nn. 17 and 21, 201 n.32, 202 n.36; *History of America*, 27; *The History of the Reign of Charles the Fifth*, 66
Robinson, Charles Alexander, Jr., 141, 213 n.14
Rousseau, Jean-Jacques, 55
Ruether, Rosemary Radford, 108, 109, 110, 111, 112, 113, 115, 208–9 n.13, 209 n.18
Ruthven, K. K., 156, 161

Said, Edward, 47, 203 n.47
Sayre, Robert, 11
Scott, Sir Walter, 67
Shakespeare, William, 89
Sharp, Ronald, 98, 203 n.52
Shaw, George Bernard, 54
Shelley, Mary: *Frankenstein*, 37
Shelley, Percy Bysshe, 25, 89, 91, 92; *Alastor*, 37; *Hymn to Intellectual Beauty*, 37, 39; *Mask of Anarchy*, 215 n.14; *Ode to the West Wind*, 155; *Philosophical View of Reform*, 92; *Prometheus Unbound*, 91
Sidney, Algernon, 64
Silence, 81–82, 114–16
Sleep, 33, 50
Slote, Bernice, 148, 214 n.23

Smith, Adam, 157, 158, 159, 160, 161, 170; *Wealth of Nations,* 157
Snook, John, 64
Social history, 34
Social relations, 24, 40, 62, 67, 80, 119, 156
Society, 9, 12, 22, 23, 44
Spenser, Edmund, 191
Sperry, Stuart, 35, 63, 71, 142, 205 nn. 10 and 12, 207 nn. 5 and 6, 213 n.5
Spirituality, 60–61
Stillinger, Jack, 78, 184
Subjectivity, 11, 25, 38, 42, 43, 44, 52, 53
Swaminathan, S. R., 210 n.29, 213 n.4

Taylor, John, 54
Tennyson, Alfred, Lord, 28, 179
Thompson, E. P., 10, 36, 196 n.5
Thorpe, Clarence DeWitt, 23, 50, 117, 146, 198 n.45
Tooke, Andrew: *The Pantheon,* 89, 90, 137, 138, 139, 147, 161

Urbanization, 182–83
Utopianism, 11, 39, 43, 58, 104

Vendler, Helen, 207 n.6

Violence, 59, 65, 68, 104, 108, 118, 124, 129, 131–32
Volney, Constantin Francois, 202–3 n.43; *Volney's Ruins,* 77
Voltaire, 55, 71, 72, 73, 123, 124, 125, 130; *Ancient and Modern History,* 72, 123; *Annals of the Empire,* 124

Walsh, William, 211 n.1
Ward, Aileen, 88
Washington, George, 64
Wasserman, Earl R., 207 n.6, 210 nn. 28 and 32
Waterloo, 23, 24, 37, 42, 52, 63, 64, 91, 189, 190
Wealth, 142–44, 153
Weimann, Robert, 52, 196 n.5
Williams, Raymond, 36, 60, 212 n.14
Wolfson, Susan, 55, 199 n.2
Woodhouse, Richard, 54, 78
Woodring, Carl, 23
Wordsworth, Dorothy, 50
Wordsworth, William, 10, 50; *The Excursion,* 37; *The Prelude,* 45; *Tintern Abbey,* 50

Zaretsky, Eli, 57, 161